BF
723
.S43
S36
1993

Separate social
worlds of siblings.

$49.95

DATE			

SEPARATE SOCIAL WORLDS OF SIBLINGS
The Impact of Nonshared Environment on Development

SEPARATE SOCIAL WORLDS OF SIBLINGS
The Impact of Nonshared Environment on Development

Edited by

E. Mavis Hetherington
University of Virginia

David Reiss
George Washington University Medical Center

Robert Plomin
The Pennsylvania State University

LEA LAWRENCE ERLBAUM ASSOCIATES, PUBLISHERS
1994 Hillsdale, New Jersey   Hove and London

Lawrence Erlbaum Associates, Inc., Publishers
365 Broadway
Hillsdale, New Jersey 07642

Library of Congress Cataloging-in-Publication Data

Separate social worlds of siblings : the impact of nonshared
  environment on development / edited by E. Mavis Hetherington, David
  Reiss, Robert Plomin.
    p.   cm.
    Includes bibliographical references and index.
    ISBN 0-8058-1311-X
    1. Brothers and sisters. 2. Individual differences.
3. Environmental psychology. 4. Nature and nurture.
I. Hetherington, E. Mavis (Eileen Mavis), 1926–   . II. Reiss,
David, 1937–   . III. Plomin, Robert, 1948–   .
BF723.S43S36   1994
155.44'3 – dc20   92-36907
                                                CIP

Books published by Lawrence Erlbaum Associates are printed on acid-free
paper, and their bindings are chosen for strength and durability.

Printed in the United States of America
10 9 8 7 6 5 4 3 2 1

Contents

Preface

One of the most notable findings in contemporary behavior genetics is that children growing up in the same family are not very similar. Sibling correlations for cognitive measures are about .40, for personality measures about .20, and concordance rates for psychopathology are often less than 10%. These findings suggest that in order to understand individual differences between siblings it is necessary to examine not only the shared experiences but also the differences in experiences of children growing up in the same family. In the past decade, a small group of investigators has begun to examine the contributions of genetics, shared environment, and nonshared environment to development. As with many new research endeavors, this has proven to be a difficult task with much controversy and disagreement about the most appropriate models and methods of analysis to be used and the interpretation of findings. We hope that, on reading the chapters in this volume, the reader will agree that it has also been a fruitful endeavor. The chapters in this book were written by some of the foremost scholars working in the area of nonshared environment and present their perspectives, concerns, strategies, and research findings with regard to the impact of nonshared environment on individual differences in the development of siblings. It is expected that this volume will have heuristic value in stimulating researchers to think in new ways about the interactions between heredity, shared environment, and nonshared environment and the challenges in identifying their contributions to sibling differences.

The first chapter in the book, by Robert Plomin, Heather Chipuer, and Jenae Neiderhiser, presents a thoughtful review of the genetic evidence for the importance of nonshared environment. The second chapter, by Michael Rovine, discusses the use of sibling discrepancy scores in estimating nonshared environment. It will be seen in the subsequent research chapters that different investigators may use different methods of assessing nonshared environment and its effects. The following chapters describe models or research findings dealing with the association between different types of nonshared environment and various developmental outcomes, with children ranging in age from preschool to adolescence. Reiss and his colleagues describe conceptual issues and preliminary findings from a longitudinal study of the effects of nonshared environment on depression, conduct disorders, and competence in adolescence. The chapter by Judy Dunn and Shirley McGuire uses data from the Cambridge study on the impact of the birth of a sibling and from the Colorado Adoption Project to describe differences in young siblings' behavior problems associated with differential experiences with parents, siblings, peers, and teachers as well as differences in life events. Gene Brody and Zolinda Stoneman examine the interaction between child temperament and differential parental treatment on children's adjustment and on sibling conflict. The chapter by Maria Tejerina-Allen, Barry Wagner, and Patricia Cohen uses data from the longitudinal Children in the Community study to explore what shared and nonshared aspects of parental behavior were related to differences in the depression, suicidal behavior, and oppositional behavior of adolescent sibling pairs. David Rowe, Jeanne Woulbroun, and Bill Gulley examine the influence of adolescent friendship cliques and close friends with a special attention to issues of selection versus influence in studies of the relationship between peers and adjustment. Craig Ewart presents a model for investigating nonshared environment and genetic origins of coronary-prone behavior and emotion. Finally, James Deal, Charles Halverson, and Karen Smith Wampler explore the use of dyadic-level intraclass correlations to conceptualize sibling similarities and differences and then examine cognitive and experiential factors that may affect parents' treatment of children.

It is hoped that these chapters will raise new questions about how to examine the contributions of genetic and environmental factors to development, and that the study of sibling differences and nonshared environment will cast new light on these questions. Further, these chapters may encourage a growing trend to integrate genetic and environmental perspectives in studies of development.

The editors of this volume thank the National Institute of Mental Health and the Grant Foundation for generously supporting their work on nonshared environment.

E. Mavis Hetherington
David Reiss
Robert Plomin

1

Behavioral Genetic Evidence for the Importance of Nonshared Environment

Robert Plomin
Heather M. Chipuer
Jenae M. Neiderhiser
The Pennsylvania State University

The importance of nonshared environment was discovered by accident, popping out of behavioral genetic research on heredity like the startling perceptual shift that occurs when the background becomes the figure in figure-ground illustrations. Behavioral genetics research uses twin and adoption designs to disentangle genetic and environmental sources of familial resemblance. Resemblance among siblings had long been known to exist for many traits, and the twin and adoption methods made it possible to explore the extent to which familial resemblance occurs for reasons of shared heredity or shared family environment. The answer that emerged from research that began at the turn of the century is that heredity is an important source of familial resemblance for cognitive abilities, personality, and psychopathology. Not only could examples of significant genetic influence on behavior be found, it became clear that genetic influence is substantial and ubiquitous for most domains of behavior.

Genetic influence on behavior was news, and behavioral geneticists were kept busy documenting its importance. Little attention was paid to the environmental component of variance. After decades of environmentalism, no one needed to be told that nongenetic sources of variance are important. However, an equally revolutionary finding about the environment lay hidden there. It can be expressed as a syllogism. The first premise is that, despite the evidence for substantial genetic influence, environmental factors also play an important role in development. Heritability, an estimate of the proportion of phenotypic (observed) variance for a trait due to genetic variance, seldom exceeds .50, which means that nongenetic factors are at least as important as genetic factors in the origin of most behavioral dimensions and disorders. The second premise of the syllogism is that, for nearly all dimensions and disorders, shared family environment is not a major source of environmental influence. Family members are similar primarily for reasons of shared heredity, not shared family environment. If the environment is important but shared family environment is not, what are these environmental influences? The conclusion of the syllogism sounds glib but has profound implications for the study of environmental influences in development: Environmental influences that affect development are not shared by family members. That is, whatever they are, these environmental influences are experienced differently by members of the same family. Environmental influences of this type are called nonshared in the sense that they are not shared by family members.

This chapter reviews behavioral genetic methods and evidence that have led to the conclusion that nonshared environment is the primary source of environmental influence for major domains of behavior including cognitive abilities, personality, and psychopathology. This evidence provides the foundation for the other chapters in this volume that assume the importance of nonshared environment and broach the obvious question raised by this finding: What are the nonshared environmental influences that make children growing up in the same family so different?

METHODS TO ESTIMATE
NONSHARED ENVIRONMENTAL INFLUENCE

Behavioral genetics consists of methods from quantitative genetics (Falconer, 1989) that decompose phenotypic variation in a population into genetic and environmental components of variance. In this section, we provide a brief overview of these methods as they relate to nonshared environment; for greater detail about these issues, textbooks on behavioral genetics (quantitative genetics as applied to behavioral phenomena) are available (Plomin, 1990; Plomin, DeFries, & McClearn, 1990).

Quantitative Genetic Methods

Quantitative genetic methods are quasi-experimental designs that control genetic relatedness while studying environmental influence and that control environmental relatedness while studying the effects of genetic relatedness. They can be viewed as simple natural experiments. For example, identical twins are twice as similar genetically as fraternal twins. Shared environmental influences are roughly similar for the two types of twins: Both identical and fraternal twins are born from the same womb, they are the same age and gender (when same-gender fraternal twins are studied), and they grow up in the same family. If heredity is important for a particular trait, identical twins must be more similar than fraternal twins because of the twofold greater genetical similarity of identical twins. Twin resemblance not explained by heredity is attributed to shared rearing environment, as discussed later. The extent to which identical twins differ within pairs indexes nonshared environmental factors because identical twins differ only for reasons of nonshared environmental factors in that they are identical genetically.

Another quantitative genetic design provides a direct test of shared rearing environment: the correlation for genetically unrelated children adopted into the same adoptive homes, whom we refer to as *adoptive siblings*. If shared rearing environment is important, adoptive siblings must resemble each other. Adoption designs can also estimate genetic influence from resemblance between genetically related individuals adopted apart (such as siblings adopted apart) and from comparisons between genetically related relatives versus adoptive relatives (such as nonadoptive siblings versus adoptive siblings).

Throughout this chapter, we focus on sibling and twin designs rather than parent–offspring comparisons. Although parent–offspring designs contribute importantly to estimates of quantitative genetic parameters, sibling designs are more appropriate for developmental analyses of family environment because siblings are contemporaneous in age and they are reared in the same family. In addition, a trend in quantitative genetic research is to combine designs to triangulate on estimates of genetic and environmental influence. For example, rather than conducting a twin study or a sibling study, the trend is toward studying both twins and nontwin siblings. This is an important feature of an ongoing study of nonshared environment described by Reiss et al. (chapter 3, this volume), which includes identical and fraternal twins, full siblings, half siblings, and ''blended'' siblings who are genetically unrelated.

As in any experiment, and especially in quasi-experimental designs, possible confounding factors must be considered. For the twin method, a possible confound is the so-called equal environments assumption mentioned earlier—that is, the assumption that the two types of twins share environmental influences to a similar extent. If identical twins were treated more alike by their parents than fraternal twins, greater resemblance of identical twins might be due to their greater similarity of treatment rather than to their greater hereditary similarity. However, research on the equal environments assumption suggests that it is a reasonable assumption (Plomin et al., 1990). Although identical twins are treated slightly more alike than fraternal twins; such as being dressed similarly and spending more time together, these experiences do not contribute importantly to their behavioral resemblance. Observational data also suggest that to the extent that parents treat identical twins more alike than fraternal twins, parents are responding to differences in their children's behavior (Lytton, 1977). For the adoption design, a possible confound is selective placement. That is, adopted children may be placed with adoptive parents who are similar to their birth parents. If selective placement occurred, resemblance between adoptive siblings could thus be indirectly due to genetic factors. However, if, as is the case, adoptive sibling resemblance is negligible, selective placement is not an issue.

It should be noted that quantitative genetics focuses on variance—environmental and genetic factors that make a difference in the phenotype—not to constants. Environmental factors such as nutrients, light, and oxygen are not assessed by quantitative genetic methods insofar as these factors are experienced uniformly by individuals. In the same vein, the vast majority of DNA is identical for all humans and thus cannot make individuals different from one another. Because these DNA effects are constants for members of our species, they are not detected by quantitative genetic methods. Quantitative genetics only addresses phenotypic differences among individuals in a population; its goal is to ascribe phenotypic differences to genetic and environmental sources of variance.

Three other preliminary points need to be made. First, the term *environment*, as used in behavioral genetic analyses, is essentially a residual term that refers to all phenotypic variance that cannot be ascribed to heritable effects. Its label is more properly *nongenetic*, and the concept is much broader than the usual way behavioral scientists think about the environment. In addition to psychosocial environmental influences, it includes accidents and illnesses, prenatal influences, and even DNA changes that are not transmitted hereditarily.

Second, a frequently asked question is why family correlations are not squared to estimate variance explained. The answer is that a correlation is squared only when one wishes to predict one variable from the other. A correlation is not squared when the goal is to estimate the proportion of variance that covaries because a correlation is literally the ratio of covariance to variance. For example, if we wanted to predict scores of one member of pairs of adoptive siblings from scores of the other member of the pair, we would square their correlation. However, our goal is to estimate the proportion of variance that covaries for adoptive siblings and this is the correlation itself, not the square of the correlation. The phenotypic covariance between adoptive siblings that forms the numerator of the correlation for adoptive siblings can only be due to shared environmental factors because they do not resemble each other genetically. Thus, the correlation for adoptive siblings, not the correlation squared, estimates the proportion of phenotypic variance due to shared environmental variance.

Finally, it should be noted that the quantitative genetic model is considerably more complex than we have described it. For example, the model distinguishes additive and nonadditive genetic variance, assortative mating, and genotype-environment correlation and interaction (see Plomin et al., 1990). For simplicity of exposition, we assume an additive genetic model without assortative mating or genotype–environment correlation and interaction. However, these factors need to be considered in a more sophisticated analysis of nonshared environment.

One facet of a more detailed behavioral genetic model is the focus of this chapter: Environmental variance can be decomposed into two components. One component involves variance shared by family members—that is, environmental influences that make family members similar—which is called *shared environmental influence*. The other represents the rest of the environmental variance that is not shared by family members. This is what we call *nonshared environment*.

Estimating Nonshared Environment

Because heritability, shared environment, and nonshared environment are expressed as proportions of phenotypic variance, they sum to 1.0. Thus, any design that can estimate heritability and shared environment can also be used to estimate nonshared environment. In this section, we briefly describe three commonly used quantitative genetic designs as they are used to estimate nonshared environment.

The twin design is known for estimating heritability by means of the comparison between the correlation for identical twins reared together (MZ for *monozygotic*) and the correlation for fraternal twins reared together (DZ for *dizygotic*). The results of twin studies can also be used to estimate shared environment (SE) and nonshared environment (NSE). SE can be estimated as the extent to which MZ resemblance exceeds heritability (h^2). This SE estimate ($r_{MZ} - h^2$) is equivalent to $2r_{DZ} - r_{MZ}$, which is more often seen in the literature. The complexity of doubling the DZ correlation and subtracting this from the MZ correlation suggests that the twin design does not provide a particularly powerful estimate of SE (Martin, Eaves, Kearsey, & Davies, 1978).

In the twin design, nonshared environment can be estimated more directly as 1.0 minus the MZ correlation. MZ twins are identical genetically and thus differences within pairs cannot be due to genetic factors; these differences are due to NSE plus error of measurement. Error of measurement needs to be considered because it, too, contributes to phenotypic variance. Error is especially important in the context of NSE because family members, including MZ twins, differ for reasons of error of measurement as well as for reasons of reliable NSE influences. One possibility is to correct familial correlations for unreliability of measurement, in which case reliable variance is analyzed rather than total variance, although it is no simple matter to determine the reliability of measurement in relation to familial correlations. If, as is usually the case, total variance is analyzed rather than variance corrected for error of measurement, it must be kept in mind that phenotypic variance not explained by heritability and shared environment includes error variance as well as reliable NSE variance.

As a second example for estimating NSE, consider an adoption design that compares genetically related relatives living together to genetically unrelated individuals adopted together. This design is especially useful in the present context because correlations for genetically unrelated individuals adopted together provide a direct estimate of SE. Using siblings as an example, h^2 can be estimated by doubling the difference between the correlation for full siblings reared together and the correlation for unrelated (adoptive) siblings reared together; the latter correlation estimates SE. NSE can be estimated as the remainder of the variance, that is, 1.0 minus h^2 and minus SE. This is equivalent to 1.0 minus twice the correlation for full siblings plus the correlation for adoptive siblings.

A third design compares genetically related relatives reared together to genetically related individuals adopted apart. h^2 is estimated directly by doubling the correlation for full siblings reared apart, SE is estimated as the difference between siblings reared together and siblings reared apart, and NSE is again the residual variance. This is equivalent to 1.0 minus the correlation for full siblings reared apart minus the correlation for full siblings reared together.

In summary, various behavioral genetic designs make it possible to estimate the importance of nonshared environment. It is the convergence of evidence from these different designs, each of which may have its own but different interpretive problems, that provides the most impressive case for the importance of nonshared environment.

EVIDENCE FOR NONSHARED ENVIRONMENT

In the remainder of this chapter, we review behavioral genetic research on personality, psychopathology, and cognitive abilities using the designs described in the previous section. A novel aspect of this review is its focus on distinguishing shared and nonshared environmental influence rather than distinguishing genetic and environmental influence, which is the theme of many other reviews of the behavioral genetic literature. The magnitude of genetic influence is relevant in showing that environmental influence is important and that familial resemblance can be explained by heredity rather than by shared environment. In order to keep the following review brief and focused on the issue of nonshared versus shared environment, we merely assert that most behavioral dimensions and disorders show moderate genetic influence (Plomin et al., 1990), and we note exceptions to this blanket assertion in the following review.

Personality

Personality as assessed by self-report questionnaires is the domain in which the importance of nonshared environment was first explicitly recognized and it remains the clearest example. In 1976, in a book that described the results of a twin study of personality involving 850 high school pairs, Loehlin and Nichols came to the following conclusion:

> Thus, a consistent—though perplexing—pattern is emerging from the data (and it is not purely idiosyncratic to our study). Environment carries substantial weight in determining personality—it appears to account for at least half the variance—but that environment is one for which twin pairs are correlated close to zero. . . . In short, in the personality domain we seem to see environmental effects that operate almost randomly with respect to the sorts of variables that psychologists (and other people) have traditionally deemed important in personality development. (p. 92)

As always, one can find earlier statements relevant to such discoveries. For example, in 1941, R. S. Woodworth noted, "The main causes of variation seem not to be those that differentiate one family from another in environment, or in heredity either. The causes, genetic and environmental, which make siblings differ seem to be more potent than those which differentiate one such family group from another" (p. 70). To our knowledge, the earliest statement about nonshared environment and its importance was made in 1921 by the inventor of path analysis, Sewell Wright, "The environmental factors are separated into two elements, tangible environment (E) and the intangible factors (D) which are not common even to litter mates, and yet appear to be responsible for much variation in early development" (p. 98).

Loehlin and Nichols reached their conclusion because MZ and DZ correlations for most of the measures they studied were about .50 and .30, respectively. As described in the previous section, NSE can be estimated as $1 - r_{MZ}$ which is .50, indicating that half of the total variance is due to NSE plus error of measurement. Self-report personality questionnaires generally show internal consistencies and test–retest correlations of about .80; using .80 as an estimate of reliability, nonshared environment represents about 40% of the variance corrected for unreliability by multiplying the estimate by the reliability of the measure (Loehlin, 1987). In contrast, shared environment for twins accounts for about 10% of the variance (i.e., $SE = 2r_{DZ} - r_{MZ}$).

These results are not peculiar to Loehlin and Nichols' study of high school twins; indeed, other studies generally show no effect at all of shared environment. Consider extraversion and neuroticism, the two "super-factors" of personality. A recent model-fitting meta-analysis of extraversion and neuroticism data from four twin studies in four countries included over 23,000 pairs of twins (Loehlin, 1989). The average MZ and DZ correlations were .51 and .18, respectively, for extraversion and .48 and .20 for neuroticism. Model-fitting analyses indicated that nonshared environment plus error accounted for about half of the variance for both traits. Heredity accounted for the rest of the variance; the shared environment parameter was slightly negative. Similar findings emerge from all behavioral genetic analyses of personality, including a 15-year series of studies on extraversion and neuroticism summarized in a recent book that concluded:

"While our analyses lead us to discount the 'shared' environment, we recognize that all the studies are consistent in assigning upwards of 50% of the total variation in personality test scores to environmental factors within the family" (Eaves, Eysenck, & Martin, 1989, p. 121).

A recent meta-analysis of over a dozen twin studies of personality since 1967 found average MZ and DZ correlations of .50 and .22, respectively (McCartney, Harris, & Bernieri, 1990), results similar to those of a review of earlier studies (Nichols, 1978). These results also suggest that nonshared environment plus error accounts for half of the variance whereas shared environmental influence is negligible (actually, slightly negative). This meta-analysis focused on the issue of age differences in twin correlations. The average correlation between twin correlations and mean age of the samples was −.30 for MZ twins and −.32 for DZ twins. In other words, twin correlations decline with age and declined equally for MZ and DZ twins. The parallel decline in correlations for MZ and DZ twins suggests that the change is not due to developmental changes in genetic influence. Rather, this finding suggests that there might be some shared environmental influence on personality in childhood that disappears by adulthood.

Twins Reared Apart Versus Twins Reared Together. The dual findings of the importance of nonshared environment and the unimportance of shared environment for self-report personality questionnaires are verified in two ongoing studies that combine the twin and adoption designs by comparing MZ and DZ twins reared together with twins reared apart. As mentioned earlier, siblings reared apart provide direct estimates of genetic influence and the comparison between siblings reared together and siblings reared apart estimates the influence of shared rearing environment. These powerful estimates of h^2 and SE facilitate estimates of NSE.

The Swedish Adoption/Twin Study of Aging (SATSA) was derived from the Swedish Twin Registry of nearly 25,000 pairs of same-gender twins and includes over 300 pairs of twins reared apart and matched twins reared together (Pedersen et al., 1991). The SATSA twins are over 60 years old on average, making SATSA the first behavioral genetic study of personality in the last half of the life course. The second study is the Minnesota Study of Twins Reared Apart (MSTRA), which in 1988 included 44 MZ and 27 DZ reared-apart twin pairs whose median age is 41 as well as twins reared together whose average age was 22 (Tellegen et al., 1988).

In SATSA, model-fitting analyses yielded nonsignificant estimates of shared rearing environment for 21 of 25 personality measures; the average SE estimate was 6%. (The four exceptions are mentioned later.) The average NSE estimate across the 25 measures is .63 with a remarkably small range from .52 to .73. In MSTRA, shared environment was nonsignificant for all but 2 of 14 measures (average SE = .07); NSE was significant for all measures and averaged .45 (Tellegen et al., 1988), which is lower in MSTRA than in SATSA because heritability estimates are higher for unknown reasons in MSTRA than in SATSA.

Given that being reared together or reared apart has little effect on twin personality resemblance, it is not surprising that both SATSA and MSTRA find that age at separation, degree of separation, and degree of contact of twins reared apart have little effect on personality (Bouchard, Lykken, McGue, Segal, & Tellegen, 1990; Pedersen, McClearn, Plomin, & Nesselroade, 1992). It has been suggested that the amount of current contact of adult identical twins correlates slightly with the twins' similarity on some personality traits (Rose & Kaprio, 1988; Rose, Koskenvuo, Kaprio, Sarna, & Langinvainio, 1988), although recent research suggests that similarity leads to increased contact, rather than the other way around (Lykken, McGue, Bouchard, & Tellegen, 1990). Even if the effect of adult contact were causal, it would not suggest that shared *rearing* environment is important, but rather that contact in adulthood is associated with increased resemblance.

Adoption Designs. Results of studies of nontwin siblings and other family relationships are compatible with the findings from twin research in that familial resemblance is low and can be explained by moderate heritability. For example, one of the largest family studies yielded an average sibling correlation of .16 for three widely used personality questionnaires (Ahern, Johnson, Wilson, McClearn, & Vandenberg, 1982). Parent–offspring correlations were of similar magnitude.

Four adoption studies of personality indicate that this modest familial resemblance is largely due to shared heredity rather than to shared family environment (Loehlin, Horn, & Willerman, 1981, 1990; Loehlin, Willerman, & Horn, 1985, 1987; Scarr, Weber, Weinberg, & Wittig, 1981; Scarr & Weinberg, 1978a). The average adoptive sibling correlation in these studies is .04 and the average correlation between adoptive parents and adopted children is .05.

Exceptions. There appears to be no serious disagreement with the conclusion that, in general, environmental influences on personality are nearly exclusively due to nonshared environment. The question has shifted to asking whether there are any personality traits that show shared environmental influence. Indeed, it might seem odd to report average results across a domain as diverse as personality. However, behavioral genetic results are surprisingly similar across the myriad traits measured by self-report questionnaires. The meta-analysis of twin studies by McCartney et al. focused on eight dimensions and found that the range of MZ correlations varied only from .44 to .51. This suggests that, for these most frequently investigated dimensions of personality, nonshared environment plus error accounts for about half of the variance of self-report questionnaires. Only one trait, masculinity–femininity, showed evidence for shared environmental influence—MZ and DZ correlations are .52 and .36, suggesting that shared environment accounts for as much as 20% of the variance for this trait. However, masculinity–femininity also yielded one of the greatest negative correlations with age for both MZ and DZ twins, suggesting that the importance of shared environmental influence for this trait declines with age (McCartney et al., 1990).

As mentioned earlier, only 4 of 25 personality measures in SATSA yielded evidence for significant shared rearing environment. These measures included agreeableness, assertiveness, hostility, and a luck scale from a locus of control measure (Pedersen et al., 1991). The variance explained by shared rearing environment for these four measures ranged from .19 to .31. Interestingly, heritability estimates were low (from .02 to .20) for these traits that showed effects of shared environment. Nonetheless, nonshared environment was just as important as for other personality traits in SATSA—NSE estimates ranged from .59 to .69. In MSTRA, the two scales that yielded significant but slight SE estimates were positive emotionality and social closeness which assesses intimacy (Tellegen et al., 1988). Thus, from these two studies using the powerful design of twins reared apart versus twins reared together, 6 of 39 scales yielded evidence for significant SE. This exceeds the two significant effects expected on the basis of chance alone. These hints of possible shared environmental influence merit further attention given the general absence of evidence for SE in the realm of personality.

One might expect that vocational interests would show strong shared environmental influence, but this is not the case. The results are just the same as for personality questionnaires (as reviewed by Nichols, 1978). For example, the largest twin study included over 1,500 twin pairs and showed average MZ and DZ correlations of .50 and .25, respectively, and found that the pattern of twin correlations was similar for all major dimensions of vocational interests (Roberts & Johansson, 1974). An adoption study found little resemblance between adoptive parents and their adopted children as adults—the average correlation was .07 (Scarr & Weinberg, 1978a).

Attitudes, such as traditionalism (conservatism), appear to show influence of shared family environment. For example, a review of three English twin studies yields average MZ and DZ correlations of .67 and .52, respectively (Eaves & Young, 1981); an Australian study of nearly 3,000 twin pairs yielded MZ and DZ correlations of .63 and .46, respectively (Martin et al., 1986). MZ and DZ correlations of .65 and .50 suggest SE of .35 and NSE (plus error) of .35. However, assortative mating is extremely high for conservatism (spouse correlations are about .50), in contrast to personality traits, for which assortative mating is negligible. When assortative mating is taken into account, shared environment is nonsignificant; nonshared environment thus accounts for all of the environmental influence on this major dimension of social attitudes (Eaves et al., 1989; Martin et al., 1986). In the only adoption study of social attitudes, authoritarian attitudes yielded an average correlation of .07 between adoptive parents and their adopted children (Scarr & Weinberg, 1978a), again suggesting that shared family environment has little effect.

Beliefs, such as religiosity, showed substantial evidence of shared environmental influence in the study of high school twins by Loehlin and Nichols (1976) in that correlations were substantial for both MZ and DZ twins. However, a recent MSTRA report of religiosity in adults estimated SE as only .11 for one measure of religious interests and .00 for another; NSE was estimated as .42 and .59 for these two measures (Waller, Kojetin, Bouchard, Lykken, & Tellegen, 1990).

Measures Other than Self-Report Questionnaires.   It should be noted that all of the preceding studies of personality employed self-report questionnaires. Twin and adoption studies have also been reported using parental ratings of their children's personality. These studies also show no evidence for shared environmental influence in twin studies (Buss & Plomin, 1984) or in the Colorado Adoption Project (Plomin, DeFries, & Fulker, 1988). Although few studies have been reported in which behavior has been objectively observed—because of the much greater expense of conducting such studies—the extant studies also show little evidence of shared environmental influence. For example, ratings of infants' behavior during a test situation on the Infant Behavior Record (Bayley, 1969) shows no evidence of shared environmental influence in a twin study (Matheny, 1980) or in a Colorado Adoption Project report using a sibling adoption study (which compares FST and UST) in which the average correlation for adoptive siblings was only .03 (Braungart, Plomin, DeFries, & Fulker, 1992).

However, one observational study of school-aged twins indicates that results from such studies might differ from the typical questionnaire results. The activity of twins in elementary school was assessed for a week using pedometers (Plomin & Foch, 1980). This measure yielded very high correlations for both MZ and DZ twins, which suggests substantial effects of shared environment. A recent twin study of infant twins using pedometers also found evidence for shared environment (Saudino & Eaton, 1991). However, these findings may be somewhat an artifact in that children's activity may be more a function of joint family activities than of each child's own activity level. In the former study, twins were also videotaped hitting an inflated clownlike plastic figure, a measure that has been shown to be valid and to relate to teacher and peer ratings of aggressiveness (Plomin, Foch, & Rowe, 1981). Ratings of aggressiveness yielded correlations of about .45 for both MZ and DZ twins, suggesting substantial influence of shared environment. However, as is the case for other personality research, questionnaire studies of aggressiveness yield little evidence of shared environmental influence (Plomin, Nitz, & Rowe, 1990), which suggests the need for more observational research to assess the possible role of shared environment in such measures.

Summary. Table 1.1 depicts our view of the general pattern of correlations from family, twin, and adoption studies of self-report personality questionnaires. The correlations are not precise, weighted averages of studies; rather, they represent our impressions of the research literature. This overview indicates that the results from various designs, including parent–offspring designs as well as sibling designs, converge on the conclusion that, for personality, shared environment counts for little and that nearly all of the environmental variance is of the nonshared variety.

Psychopathology

It is more difficult to draw conclusions from behavioral genetic research on psychopathology than it is in the area of personality for three reasons. First, most research involves family studies rather than twin and adoption studies. Second, samples are generally not large and results are thus less consistent. Third, the use of dichotomous diagnoses (and concordances) rather than quantitative meas-

TABLE 1.1
Approximate Estimates of Correlations for Various Types of Relatives
and of Shared (SE) and Nonshared Environment (NSE) for
Self-Report Personality Questionnaires

Type of Relative	Correlation	SE	NSE + Error
MZT	.50	.00	.50
DZT	.25	.00	.50
MZA	.50	.00	.50
DZA	.25	.00	.50
FST	.15	.05	.75
FSA	—	—	—
HST	—	—	—
HSA	—	—	—
UST	.05	.05	.75
POT	.20	.05	.65
POA	.15	.05	.65
UPOT	.05	.05	.65

Note. MZ = identical twins; DZ = fraternal twins. FS = sibling; PO = parent–offspring. T = relatives living together; A = relatives adopted apart. HS = half-sibling (children who share only one parent). UST = unrelated "siblings" (unrelated children adopted into the same adoptive family); UPOT = unrelated "parents and offspring" (adoptive parents and their adopted children). The SE and NSE parameters and h^2 were estimated using MZ and DZ comparisons for the twin correlations, FST and UST comparisons for the sibling correlations, and POT, POA, and UPOT data for the parent–offspring correlations. We are not aware of relevant data for FSA, HST, or HSA.

ures (and correlations) makes it difficult to estimate quantitative genetic parameters of NSE and SE.

We begin by mentioning the few studies that approach behavioral problems in terms of continuous dimensions rather than dichotomous diagnoses. We then consider developmental disorders, delinquency and criminality, alcoholism, depression and affective disorders, schizophrenia, and other psychopathology. As in the previous section on personality, the spotlight is on distinguishing non-shared and shared environment rather than on hereditary influence. (See also Pogue-Geile & Rose, 1987.)

Studies of Dimensions of Behavioral Problems in Unselected (Non-clinical) Samples. It seems reasonable to expect that some disorders, especially the common behavioral problems of childhood, represent the extremes of normal dimensions of personality. It is an open and increasingly debated issue whether diagnosed disorders are in fact part of dimensional continua of symptoms (Plomin, 1991). However, genetic studies of personality have not focused on those dimensions of normal personality most likely to be relevant to disorders. For example, only a few genetic studies have considered dimensions of depression, mania, aggressiveness, attention, anxiety, or problems of gender identification and attachment. The most relevant dimensional data come from twin studies of the Minnesota Multiphasic Personality Inventory (MMPI) in unselected samples of twins. A summary of five studies of the MMPI yields twin correlations similar to those of questionnaires of normal personality: The median MZ and DZ correlations are .45 and .23, respectively (Plomin, 1991), suggesting SE of .01 and NSE (plus error) of .55.

Single, unreplicated twin studies have considered other relevant dimensional traits such as anxiety and depression (Kendler, Heath, Martin, & Eaves, 1986), childhood depression (Wierzbicki, 1987), obsessions (Clifford, Fulker, & Murray, 1981), psychosomatic complaints (Wilde, 1964), fears (Rose & Ditto, 1983), childhood behavior problems (O'Connor, Foch, Sherry, & Plomin, 1980; Stevenson & Graham, 1988), and hyperactivity (Goodman & Stevenson, 1989a, 1989b). As in the case of MMPI data, these studies generally yield results similar to those for other personality questionnaires.

A possible exception to this conclusion involves delinquent acts, a dimension that appears to show greater evidence of shared environmental influence than other personality dimensions (Plomin, Nitz, & Rowe, 1990). A quantitative measure of self-reported delinquent behavior for high school twins yielded correlations of .71 and .47 for MZ and DZ twins, respectively (Rowe, 1983). These results imply SE of .23 and NSE (plus error) of .29.

However, it has been suggested that the apparent shared environmental effect for delinquent acts may be specific to twins because twins tend to be partners in delinquent acts (Rowe, 1983, 1986). It is reasonable to hypothesize that twins are more likely to show substantial shared environmental influence than nontwin siblings because twins are exactly the same age and are thus more likely to affect each other's delinquency and are more likely to have the same peers. However, in two studies of nontwin siblings' self-reported delinquency, nontwin sibling correlations were .48 and .51, respectively, for high school students (Rowe, 1986; Rowe, Rodgers, Meseck-Bushey, & St. John, 1989). The fact that these sibling correlations are similar to the fraternal twin correlation of .47 reported by Rowe (1983) suggests that the finding of substantial shared environmental influence on delinquent behavior may not be limited to twins. One further complication is that the nontwin sibling correlation for a sample of college students for retrospective reports of delinquency during adolescence is substantially lower (r = .19) than for high school students (Rowe et al., 1989). This leaves open the possibility that siblings are less similar in self-reported delinquency than are twins, although it is also possible that high school and college samples differ in terms of shared environmental influence relevant to delinquency or that the use of retrospective reports for the college siblings obfuscated the influence of shared environment. More research is needed to determine whether delinquent acts are an exception to the rule that shared environmental influence is of negligible importance in the development of behavioral problems as assessed dimensionally.

Developmental Disorders. Genetic studies of child psychiatric disorders have recently been reviewed (Rutter et al., 1990). In addition to numerous family studies, recent twin studies have considered autism (Folstein & Rutter, 1977; Le Couteur, Bailey, Rutter, & Gottesman, 1989; Steffenburg et al., 1989), hyperactivity (Goodman & Stevenson, 1989a, 1989b), anorexia nervosa (Holland, Hall, Murray, Russell, & Crisp, 1984), Tourette's syndrome (Price, Kidd, Cohen, Pauls, & Leckman, 1985), reading disability (DeFries, Fulker, & LaBuda, 1987), and specific speech disruptions (Howie, 1981). These studies generally suggest some genetic influence; however, environmental variance is substantial and appears to be nearly exclusively of the nonshared variety. It is also noteworthy that most of these studies employed diagnostic interviews rather than questionnaires. One puzzling exception to the rule of ubiquitous NSE influence is a twin study of teacher ratings of general behavioral problems that yielded extremely high DZ concordances (.90) and correlations (.65), implying very substantial shared environmental influence (Graham & Stevenson, 1985).

As is the case in general in the area of psychopathology, there are surprisingly few adoption studies of developmental disorders that directly assess the importance of shared rearing environment by studying genetically unrelated individuals reared together. Adoption studies of hyperactivity show little resemblance among adoptive relatives, suggesting a negligible role for shared environment, although these studies have been criticized, primarily in relation to diagnosis (McMahon, 1980).

Quantitative genetic research in developmental psychopathology has just begun and much work needs to be done to answer the most basic question of the extent of genetic involvement for most areas of developmental psychopathology. For example, no twin or adoption studies with reasonable sample sizes have been reported for mental retardation, anxiety disorders, childhood depression, gender identity disorders, or the "other disorders" of Axis 1 of DSM-III. Thus, for most developmental disorders, we cannot yet estimate the extent to which familial resemblance is due to shared environment or shared heredity; however, given the relatively low rates of familial concordance, it seems safe to predict that environmental variance is substantially due to nonshared environment.

Delinquency. Six twin studies of diagnosed juvenile delinquency or conduct disorder yielded average concordances of 87% for MZ twins and 72% for DZ twins, suggesting substantial shared environmental sources of resemblance (and very little genetic influence; reviewed by Cloninger & Gottesman, 1987, and Gottesman, Carey, & Hanson, 1983). This finding of substantial shared environmental influence is in line with the results of twin studies of dimensions of delinquent acts described earlier (Rowe, 1983, 1986). However, the issue of whether this is a special twin effect has not been investigated in studies of diagnosed delinquency or conduct disorder.

Although we are aware of no adoption studies of delinquency per se, an adoption study of a more specific diagnosis, aggressive conduct disorder, found little evidence for the influence of shared environment (Jary & Stewart, 1985). That is, adopted children who received diagnoses of aggressive conduct disorder had adoptive parents with no excess of antisocial personality. Similarly, adoption studies of antisocial personality and psychopathy suggest little effect of shared rearing environment (Cadoret, 1978; Bohman, 1971, 1972). For example, no difference in psychopathology (including psychopathy) was found between the adoptive relatives of psychopathic adoptees and the adoptive relatives of control adoptees (Schulsinger, 1972).

Thus, the question of the importance of shared rearing environment for delinquency remains open.

Criminality. In contrast to twin results for delinquency, twin and adoption studies of adult criminality yield evidence for the familiar pattern of nonshared environmental influence and genetic influence, with little effect of shared rearing environment (Mednick, Moffit, & Stack, 1987). On average, MZ and DZ twin concordances are 69% and 33%, respectively, in one review (Gottesman et al., 1983) and 51% and 22% in another (McGuffin & Gottesman, 1985). For instance, the best twin study involved all male twins born on the Danish Islands from 1881 to 1910 (Christiansen, 1977). MZ and DZ concordances are 42% and 21%, respectively, for crimes against persons, and 40% and 16% for crimes against property.

Adoption studies are consistent with the finding of negligible shared environment, although they suggest less genetic influence than the twin studies, which implicates a larger role for nonshared environment. For example, the best adoption study also comes from Denmark and is based on 14,427 adoptees and their biological and adoptive parents (Mednick, Gabrielli, & Hutchings, 1984). Of adopted sons who had neither adoptive nor biological criminal parents, 14% had at least one criminal conviction. For adopted sons whose adoptive (but not biological) parents had criminal records, 15% had at least one conviction, suggesting no increase in criminal convictions when adoptive parents have criminal records. Adoptive siblings yielded a concordance of 9%, whereas concordance of nonadoptive siblings adopted apart is 20%.

Alcoholism.   Alcoholism in a first-degree relative is by far the best single predictor of alcoholism (Goedde & Agarwal, 1987). About 25% of the male relatives of alcoholics are themselves alcoholics, as compared with fewer than 5% of the males in the general population. Despite the importance of this problem behavior, firm conclusions cannot as yet be reached about the relative contributions of shared environment and heredity to this familial resemblance.

Twin studies of normal drinkers show little shared environmental influence and substantial genetic influence on quantity and frequency of drinking, although the evidence is not clear concerning heavy drinking per se (Goodwin, 1985; Murray, Clifford, & Gurling, 1983). The first twin study of alcoholism has only recently been reported (McGue, Pickens, & Svikis, 1992; Pickens et al., 1990). Twin pairs were selected in which at least one member of the pair received a DSM-III diagnosis of alcohol abuse in interviews. For diagnoses of alcohol abuse, both MZ and DZ twin concordances for alcohol abuse were 27% for 57 female pairs, suggesting some shared environmental influence and no genetic influence. For 114 male pairs, MZ and DZ concordances for alcohol abuse were 76% and 61%, suggesting substantial shared environmental influence as well as the possibility of some genetic influence. In a companion questionnaire study of a sample twice as large, similar results emerged (McGue et al., 1992). For the total sample, shared environment was substantial and genetic influence was not significant for diagnoses of alcohol abuse and/or dependence. Genetic influence appeared to be greater for males than females and for younger males (< 35 years) than for older males, but shared environmental influence was substantial for all groups. The concordances for the younger males were surprisingly high—91% for MZ and 67% for DZ. However, a critical issue concerning this apparent evidence for shared environment from these two reports was not mentioned: Over half the sample is unmarried, which leads to the hypothesis that the younger and unmarried twins are living together and thus might drink together on a regular basis. Contagion of this sort in adulthood is a type of shared environment, but one that is quite different from the shared rearing environment that is the focus of this chapter.

Contrary to the results of this first twin study of alcoholism, adoption studies suggest that heredity is important but shared environment is not. Adopted-away offspring of alcoholic biological parents are more likely to be alcoholic than control adoptees, suggesting genetic influence, and their risk for alcohol problems appears to be as great as for children reared by their alcoholic biological parents (Bohman, Cloninger, Sigvardsson, & von Knorring, 1987; Goodwin, 1979; cf. Peele, 1986). Little resemblance has been found for alcoholism among adoptive siblings, although studies using this direct test of the importance of shared rearing environment are small (Cadoret, Cain, & Grove, 1980; Cadoret & Gath, 1978; Cadoret, O'Gorman, Troughton, & Heywood, 1985).

Affective Disorders.   As is the case for nearly all psychopathology, affective disorders show familial resemblance (Vandenberg, Singer, & Pauls, 1986). The most recent study consists of 235 probands with major depressive disorder and their 826 first-degree relatives (Reich et al., 1987). Major depression was diagnosed in 13% of the male relatives and in 30% of the female relatives as compared to a base rate of about 5% in the population. Bipolar illness has a lower base rate (about 1%) and familial risk is consequently lower than for unipolar depression. In seven studies of 2,500 first-degree relatives of bipolar probands, the average risk of bipolar illness is 5.8% (Rice et al., 1987).

Family studies cannot disentangle the provenances of shared environment and shared heredity. Twin studies indicate that familial resemblance for the affective disorders is largely genetic in origin, which means that environmental influence is primarily nonshared. The average concordances in seven studies of general affective disorder involving over 400 pairs of twins are 65% for MZ and 14% for DZ (Nurnberger & Gershon, 1981). Although concordances cannot be used directly to estimate components of variance for the disorder, it is clear that nonshared environmental influence must be important because the MZ concordance is substantially less than 100%. For manic depression, a Danish twin study of manic depression yields concordances of 67% for MZ twins and 18% for DZ twins (Bertelsen, Harvald, & Hague, 1977). Four adoption studies of affective disorders have been reported, and they yield mixed results in relation to genetic influence (Loehlin, Willerman, & Horn, 1988), although one of the best studies indicates some genetic influence (Wender et al., 1986). The literature suggests that milder depressive disorders, the most common presenting problem in adult outpatient practice, show less genetic influence but no greater shared environmental influence (McGuffin & Katz, 1986).

A tentative conclusion is that shared heredity rather than shared family environment is responsible for familial resemblance for affective disorders. However, direct tests of shared environment such as adoptive sibling data or comparisons between siblings reared together and siblings reared apart have not been reported except for studies with very small samples. There is an indication from a Swedish adoption study that the rate of affective disorders is elevated in adoptive fathers of depressed adoptees as compared to adoptive fathers of normal adoptees (von Knorring, 1983). However, no such hint of shared environment was found in an adoption study of bipolar disorder (Mendlewicz & Rainer, 1977). In general, it appears that environmental variance is largely if not exclusively nonshared in origin.

Schizophrenia. A summary of the extensive behavioral genetics literature on schizophrenia is available (Gottesman & Shields, 1982). In 14 older studies involving over 18,000 first-degree relatives of schizophrenics, the risk for first-degree relatives was about 8%, eight times greater than the population base rate. Recent family studies continue to yield similar results.

Twin and adoption studies suggest that this familial resemblance is due to heredity. Five twin studies since 1966 yield weighted average probandwise concordances of 46% for MZ and 14% for DZ twins (Gottesman & Shields, 1982). The most recent twin study involved all male twins who were U.S. veterans of World War II (Kendler & Robinette, 1983). Twin concordances using ICD-8 criteria were 30.9% for 164 pairs of identical twins and 6.5% for 268 pairs of fraternal twins.

As another example of recent research, a re-analysis of the Danish Adoption Study of Schizophrenia using DSM-III criteria (Kendler & Gruenberg, 1984) confirms earlier reports that schizophrenia occurs more frequently in the biological relatives of schizophrenic adoptees than in biological relatives of control adoptees (Kety, Rosenthal, & Wender, 1978). A follow-up Danish study also yielded similar results (Kety, 1987).

These studies are well known for the evidence that they provide concerning genetic influence. However, the results also provide striking evidence for the unimportance of shared environment and for the importance of nonshared environment. First, the resemblance of first-degree relatives for schizophrenia is just as great when they are separated by adoption as it is when they live together in the same family, indicating that shared environment is unimportant. Second, in the study by Kety, adoptive relatives of schizophrenic probands show no greater risk than adoptive relatives of nonschizophrenic adoptees. Results such as these support the conclusion reached by Gottesman and Shields (1982) in their review: "the presence of schizophrenia or related illnesses in the rearing family are *ruled out* as primary environmental causes of schizophrenia" (p. 145). The risk for first-degree relatives is far less than the .50 genetic resemblance between them, suggesting that environmental influence is important. Because shared rearing environment is not important, we can conclude that environmental influences that affect schizophrenia are nonshared.

The effect of rearing by a schizophrenic parent has been investigated by comparing the risk for adoptees whose biological parents were schizophrenic but who were reared by normal adoptive parents to the risk for nonadopted children reared by their affected biological parents. Such studies indicate that there is no greater risk for schizophrenia when children are reared by their schizophrenic biological parents than when they are separated from their schizophrenic biological parent early in life (Higgins, 1966, 1976; Rosenthal et al., 1975). A more direct test of shared parental influence involves cross-fostering: studying adoptees with normal biological parents reared by adoptive parents who became schizophrenic as compared to adoptees reared by normal adoptive parents. One such cross-fostering study found no effect of shared parental influence (Wender et al., 1974), although a follow-up study did not yield results as clear-cut (Wender et al., 1977).

There are surprisingly few data available, however, that directly test the importance of shared rearing environment using adoptive siblings. Studies with small samples of adoptive siblings find no resemblance (Kallman, 1946; Karlsson, 1966; Kety, Rosenthal, Wender, Schulsinger, & Jacobsen, 1975), results compatible with the other adoption and twin data in suggesting a negligible role for shared environment. Also, explicit comparisons between siblings reared together and siblings reared apart have not been reported except in a small study (Karlsson, 1966).

MZ twins discordant for schizophrenia have been used to investigate specific sources of nonshared environment. Some evidence suggests that obstetrical problems are in part responsible for MZ discordances in schizophrenia (Lewis, Chitkara, Reveley, & Murray, 1987; McNeil & Kaij, 1978). However, in their review of genetic studies of schizophrenia, Gottesman and Shields (1982) concluded:

> Despite high hopes, the study of discordant MZ pairs has not yet led to a big payoff in the identification of crucial environmental factors in schizophrenia. The problem is simply more difficult than we can cope with: Environmental variation within twin pairs is limited to a relatively narrow range, sample sizes are small, the data needed are subject to retrospective distortions, and the culprits may be nonspecific, time-limited in their effectiveness, and idiosyncratic. (p. 120)

Recent research using magnetic resonance imaging suggests that enlarged lateral and third ventricles and small anterior hippocampi are related to schizophrenia in discordant pairs of identical twins (Suddath, Christison, Torrey, Casanova, & Weinberger, 1990). Such differences cannot be genetic in origin; the study could not rule out the possibility that the anatomical brain abnormalities may be secondary to schizophrenia.

Other Psychiatric Disorders. Attention is now turning to other psychiatric disorders. For example, family studies of anxiety disorders indicate familial resemblance for generalized anxiety disorder and for panic disorder (Crowe, Noyes, Pauls, & Slyman, 1983; Vandenberg et al., 1986). Early twin studies yielded conflicting results concerning the etiology of anxiety disorders (Marks, 1986), although a more recent study of an inpatient sample suggests genetic influence for panic disorder and agoraphobia but not for generalized anxiety disorder (Torgersen, 1983). Although the relative roles of shared heredity and shared environment cannot as yet be clearly sorted out, what is clear is that nonshared environment primarily accounts for environmental influence on anxiety disorders.

Examples of research on other disorders include family and adoption studies of somatization disorder, which involves multiple and chronic physical complaints of unknown origin (Bohman, Cloninger, von Knorring, & Sigvardsson, 1984; Cloninger, Martin, Guze, & Clayton, 1986; Guze, Cloninger, Martin, & Clayton, 1986); a family study and a twin study of Tourette's syndrome (Pauls, Cohen, Heimbuch, Detlor, & Kidd, 1981; Price et al., 1985); family studies of the association between Tourette's syndrome and obsessive-compulsive symptoms (Montgomery, Clayton, & Friedhoff, 1982; Pauls, Towbin, Lechman, Azhner, & Cohen, 1986); and an adoption study of drug abuse (Cadoret, Troughton, O'Gorman, & Heywood, 1986).

Family studies indicate that familial resemblance is low for most disorders, and the few twin and adoption studies suggest that familial resemblance is primarily hereditary. Thus, the limited extant evidence is consistent with the hypothesis that nonshared environment is of prime importance in the etiology of most domains of psychopathology.

Physical Disorders. It is noteworthy that nonshared environment is not limited to behavioral dimensions and disorders in development. A recent example concerns obesity, a disorder widely thought to be due to shared rearing environmental factors such as diet. To the contrary, a recent review reaches the following conclusions:

> Experiences that are shared among family members do not play an important role in determining individual differences in weight, fatness, and obesity . . . experiences that are not shared among family members comprise most of the environmental influence on weight and obesity. . . . The conclusion that experiences that are shared among family members count for little in determining individual differences in weight, and perhaps obesity, necessitates a drastic rethinking of many current environmental etiological theories of weight. (Grillo & Pogue-Geile, in press)

Similar findings emerge from reviews of common medical disorders and physical traits (Dunn & Plomin, 1990).

Summary. There are surprisingly few studies of adoptive siblings reared together that provide the strongest test of shared environmental influence. Nonetheless, data from other designs converge on the conclusion that environmental influence is almost exclusively nonshared for most areas of psychopathology. Delinquency is the only area to date that has consistently suggested a significant role for shared environmental influence.

Cognitive Abilities

One of the most controversial issues in a "target" article on nonshared environment in *Behavioral and Brain Sciences* (Plomin & Daniels, 1987), as seen in the 32 commentaries on the target article, was the suggestion that environmental influence for IQ scores after childhood might also be due primarily to nonshared environment.

IQ. IQ has been thought to be an exception to the rule that environmental influence is nonshared for most domains of behavioral development such as personality and psychopathology for two reasons (Plomin, 1988). First, twin data are consistent with an estimate of appreciable shared environmental influence for IQ. For example, a recent meta-analysis of 42 twin studies of IQ found average correlations of .72 and .51 for MZ and DZ twins, respectively (McCartney et al., 1990). These correlations suggest that shared environment explains 30% of the variance; only about 30% of the variance is due to nonshared environment and error. However, twin studies exaggerate shared environmental influence. Fraternal twins are more alike for IQ than are nontwin siblings. For example, a review of the world's genetic literature on IQ found a weighted average correlation of .60 for more than 5,000 pairs in 41 studies; the average nontwin sibling correlation is .47 in 69 studies involving more than 25,000 pairs of siblings (Bouchard & McGue, 1981). A recent model-fitting analysis of this summary of IQ data confirms that shared environmental estimates are significantly greater for twins than for nontwin siblings (Chipuer, Rovine, & Plomin, 1990).

Second, until the past decade, research on genetically unrelated children adopted together (adoptive siblings) produced convincing evidence for the importance of shared environment. These data provide a direct estimate of shared environment because the resemblance of pairs of genetically unrelated children adopted early in life into the same family can be due only to shared environment, not to heredity. The average weighted IQ correlation for more than 700 pairs of adoptive siblings is about .30 (Bouchard & McGue, 1981). This implies that as much as 30% of the variance of IQ scores is due to shared environment.

However, it was not noticed that these studies involved children. In 1978, the first study of older adoptee pairs (16 to 22 years) was published and it yielded a strikingly different result: The IQ correlation was −.03 (Scarr & Weinberg, 1978b). Four studies of older adoptive siblings have now yielded IQ correlations of zero on average (Plomin, 1988). The most compelling study is a 10-year longitudinal follow-up of the Texas Adoption Project (Loehlin, Horn, & Willerman, 1990). The IQ correlation for 181 pairs of genetically unrelated siblings declined from .16 at the average age of 8 years to −.01 at 18 years. A longitudinal model-fitting analysis yielded a shared environment estimate of .25 at 8 years and an estimate of −.11 at 18 years.

It is remarkable that all four studies show no resemblance for older adoptive siblings. This suggests that, although shared environmental factors account for substantial variance for IQ in childhood, their influence wanes to negligible levels during adolescence. In the long run, environmental effects on IQ are nonshared. The surprise of this finding is registered in a retrospective commentary by Scarr (1981) concerning her 1978 article with Weinberg:

> Neither Rich Weinberg nor I were prepared to discover that adolescents at the end of the child-rearing period bear so little resemblance to those with whom they have lived for so many years . . . the goal of the adolescent study was to show greater resemblance among adoptees and their parents at the end of the child-rearing period! Never did we contemplate that older adoptees would be *less* like their rearing families than the younger adoptees. (p. 525)

Model-fitting analyses of IQ generally yield heritability estimates of about .50 (Chipuer et al., 1990, Loehlin, 1989), although results of individual studies vary in the general range from .30 to .70—a recent MSTRA report for a small sample of MZ twins reared apart is at the high end of this range (Bouchard et al., 1990). If shared environment is not important after adolescence, nonshared environment plus error accounts for the rest of the IQ variance. Because the reliability of IQ tests is reasonably high, perhaps as high as .90, nonshared environment appears to be responsible for a very major portion of variance in IQ scores.

Specific Cognitive Abilities. What about specific cognitive abilities? It is reasonable to expect that shared environment might be greater for some traits that seem more susceptible to such influence such as verbal ability, in contrast, for example, to spatial ability. However, few behavioral genetic studies have focused on specific cognitive abilities and no strong conclusions can be drawn. For verbal, quantitative, and performance scores, average MZ correlations are .76,..74, and .70 (McCartney et al., 1990). If reliabilities of these tests were .80, this would suggest that nonshared environment accounts for only about 20% of the variance. Nonshared environment appears to be more important for tests of perceptual speed with MZ correlations of about .55; memory was not included in the meta-analysis but in other reviews memory also appears to show lower MZ correlations than other specific cognitive abilities (Plomin & Rende, 1991). However, the likelihood that twins share environmental influences to a greater extent than nontwin siblings for specific as well as for general cognitive abilities has not been tested.

Few adoption data are available for specific cognitive abilities. Scarr and Weinberg's (1978b) study of postadolescent adoptive siblings yielded nonsignificant correlations for four WAIS subtests, although the sibling correlation for vocabulary was greater ($r = .11$) than for the other subtests. However, another study of adolescent adoptive siblings yielded slightly negative correlations for verbal, spatial, and perceptual speed factors; test–retest reliabilities were shown to be comparable to those for IQ scores (reported by Plomin, 1986). A memory factor yielded an adoptive sibling correlation of .16, suggesting the possibility of shared environmental influence for memory, although the memory factor was less reliable than the other cognitive abilities. Finally, a report of parent–offspring resemblance from the Colorado Adoption Project when adopted and nonadopted children were 7 years old found no evidence for shared environmental influence for specific cognitive abilities (Cyphers, Fulker, Plomin, & DeFries, 1989). Model-fitting estimates of shared environment were less than 1%, results that conflict sharply with the twin estimates.

Academic Performance. Twin studies of academic performance measures in high school yield results similar to those for cognitive abilities (Plomin et al., 1990). A recent study of 146 pairs of MZ twins and 132 pairs of DZ twins from 6 to 12 years of age included measures of school achievement (reading, mathematics, and language) in addition to measures of cognitive abilities (Thompson, Detterman, & Plomin, 1991). The school achievement measures indicated substantially greater shared environmental influence than for cognitive abilities in the early school years. Because no studies have been reported for older subjects, we do not know whether, as in the case of IQ, the magnitude of shared environmental influence declines to negligible levels after childhood.

In summary, for IQ, shared environmental influence is important during childhood but fades to a negligible level of influence by adolescence when nonshared environmental influences begin to dominate. Although far fewer data are available for specific cognitive abilities, a reasonable hypothesis is that nonshared environment is also of primary importance for these cognitive abilities as well.

SUMMARY AND CONCLUSIONS

Despite the novelty and far-reaching implications of the conclusion that behaviorally relevant environmental influences are of the nonshared variety, we are aware of no major criticisms of these findings or of our interpretation of them. It is rare in a field as complex as the behavioral sciences to discover such clear and consistent evidence for a finding that radically alters the way we think about an issue as basic as the influence of the family on development. So often we have assumed that the key influences on children's development are shared: their parents' personality and childhood experiences, the quality of their parents' marriage relationships, children's educational background, the neighborhood in which they grow up, and their parents' attitude to school or to discipline. Yet to the extent that these influences are shared, they cannot account for the differences we observe in children's outcome.

The importance of this finding has been put particularly forcefully by Scarr and Grajek (1982):

> Lest the reader slip over these results, let us make explicit the implications of these findings: Upper middle-class brothers who attend the same school and whose parents take them to the same plays, sporting events, music lessons, and therapists, and use similar child rearing practices on them are little more similar in personality measures than they are to working class or farm boys, whose lives are totally different. Now, perhaps this is an exaggeration of the known facts, but not by much. Given the low correlations of biological siblings and the near zero correlations of adopted siblings, it is evident that most of the variance in personality arises in the environmental differences among siblings, *not* in the differences among families. (p. 361)

The evidence for the importance of nonshared environment can be seen most clearly for self-report personality questionnaires for which virtually all of the environmental variance is nonshared. A convincing case cannot be made for shared environmental influence for any personality traits, although there are traits such as masculinity–femininity and agreeableness for which shared environmental influence cannot be ruled out. Vocational interests yield results similar to personality measures. There is some suggestion of shared environmental effects on attitudes and beliefs, but even for these variables, the case has yet to be made.

Although it is more difficult to generalize from the diverse studies of psychopathology, shared environmental effects seem for the most part to be negligible. Because heritabilities are generally modest at most, these data point to substantial influence of nonshared environment. There are surprisingly few direct tests of the importance of shared environment using adoptive sibling resemblance. One possible exception to the rule of nonshared environmental influence is delinquency which shows high correlations and concordances for both MZ and DZ twins. However, the reasonable possibility that twins participate together in delinquent activities to a greater extent than do nontwin siblings warrants caution in concluding that shared rearing environment is important until the results of other designs—especially adoptive siblings—are reported.

Recent results for IQ scores are quite surprising. Although IQ scores have been thought to be influenced substantially by shared environmental factors, this appears to be the case only in childhood. By adolescence, nearly all environmental influence is of the nonshared variety. Thus, in the long run, nonshared environment is key for explaining individual differences in IQ scores. Although far fewer studies are available for specific cognitive abilities, the results so far appear to be similar to those for IQ scores.

Not only does the discovery of the importance of nonshared environment suggest what is wrong with our previous environmental approaches to children's development, it also points clearly to what needs to be done: We need to identify environmental factors that make two children growing up in the same family so different from one another. The message is not that family experiences are unimportant but rather that the relevant environmental influences are specific to each child, not general to an entire family (Dunn & Plomin, 1990). These findings suggest that instead of thinking about the environment on a family-by-family basis, we need to think about the environment on an individual-by-individual basis. The critical question is, why are children in the same family so different? This is the key that can unlock the secrets of environmental influence on the development of all children, not just siblings, and it is the focal question of the rest of this volume.

ACKNOWLEDGMENTS

Preparation of this chapter was supported in part by a grant from the National Science Foundation to study nonshared environment (BNS 8806589; J. Dunn, J. C. DeFries, and R. Plomin, co-investigators) and by grants from the National Institute of Mental Health (MH 43373) and the William T. Grant Foundation for the project, Nonshared Environment in Adolescent Development (D. Reiss, E. M. Hetherington, and R. Plomin, co-investigators). Support for the Colorado Adoption Project (J. C. DeFries, D. W. Fulker, and R. Plomin, co-investigators) is provided by the National Institutes of Health (HD 10333, HD 18426, MH 43899). The Swedish Adoption/Twin Study of Aging (G. E. McClearn, J. R. Nesselroade, N. Pedersen, and R. Plomin, co-investigators) is supported by the National Institute of Aging (AG 04563) and the MacArthur Foundation Research Network on Successful Aging.

REFERENCES

Ahern, F. M., Johnson, R. C., Wilson, J. R., McClearn, G. E., & Vandenberg, S. G. (1982). Family resemblances in personality. *Behavior Genetics, 12,* 261–280.

Bayley, N. (1969). *Manual for the Bayley Scales of Infant Development.* New York: Psychological Corporation.

Bertelsen, A., Harvald, B., & Hauge, M. (1977). A Danish study of manic depressive disorders. *British Journal of Psychiatry, 130,* 330–351.

Bohman, M. (1971). A comparative study of adopted children, foster children and children in their biological environment born after undesired pregnancies. *Acta Pediatric Scandinavica,* Supplement 221.

Bohman, M. (1972). The study of adopted children, their background, environment and adjustment. *Acta Pediatric Scandinavica, 61,* 90–97.

Bohman, M., Cloninger, C. R., Sigvardsson, S., & von Knorring, A.-L. (1987). The genetics of alcoholisms and related disorders. *Journal of Psychiatric Research, 21,* 447–452.

Bohman, M., Cloninger, C. R., von Knorring, A.-L., & Sigvardsson, S. (1984). An adoption study of somatoform disorders. Part 3: Cross-fostering analysis and genetic relationship to alcoholism and criminality. *Archives of General Psychiatry, 41,* 872–878.

Bouchard, T. J., Jr., Lykken, D. T., McGue, M., Segal, N. L., & Tellegen, A. (1990). Sources of human psychological differences: The Minnesota Study of Twins Reared Apart. *Science, 250,* 223–228.

Bouchard, T. J., Jr., & McGue, M. (1981). Familial studies of intelligence: A review. *Science, 212,* 1055–1059.

Braungart, J. M., Plomin, R., DeFries, J. C., & Fulker, D. W. (1992). Genetic influence on tester-rated infant temperament: Nonadoptive and adoptive siblings and twins. *Developmental Psychology.*

Buss, A. H., & Plomin, R. (1984). *Temperament: Early developing personality traits.* Hillsdale, NJ: Lawrence Erlbaum Associates.

Cadoret, R. J. (1978). Evidence for genetic inheritance of primary affective disorder in adoptees. *American Journal of Psychiatry, 133,* 463–466.

Cadoret, R. J., Cain, C. A., & Grove, W. M. (1980). Development of alcoholism in adoptees raised apart from alcoholic biologic relatives. *Archives of General Psychiatry, 37,* 561–563.

Cadoret, R. J., & Gath, A. (1978). Inheritance of alcoholism in adoptees. *British Journal of Psychiatry, 132,* 252–258.

Cadoret, R. J., O'Gorman, T. W., Troughton, E., & Heywood, M. A. (1985). Alcoholism and antisocial personality: Interrelationships, genetic, and environmental factors. *Archives of General Psychiatry, 42,* 161–167.

Cadoret, R. J., Troughton, E., O'Gorman, T. W., & Heywood, M. A. (1986). An adoption study of genetic and environmental factors in drug abuse. *Archives of General Psychiatry, 43,* 1131–1136.

Chipuer, H. M., Rovine, M., & Plomin, R. (1990). LISREL modelling: Genetic and environmental influences on IQ revisited. *Intelligence, 14,* 11–29.

Christiansen, K. O. (1977). A preliminary study of criminality among twins. In S. A. Mednick & K. O. Christiansen (Eds.), *Biosocial bases of criminal behavior* (pp. 89–108). New York: Gardner.

Clifford, C. A., Fulker, D. W., & Murray, R. M. (1981). A genetic and environmental analysis of obsessionality in normal twins. In L. Gedda, P. Parisi, & W. E. Nance (Eds.), *Twin research 3, part B: Intelligence, personality, and development.* New York: Alan R. Liss.

Cloninger, C. R., & Gottesman, I. I. (1987). Genetic and environmental factors in antisocial behavior disorders. In S. Mednick, T. Moffit, & S. Stack (Eds.), *The causes of crime* (pp. 92–109). New York: Cambridge University Press.

Cloninger, C. R., Martin, R. L., Guze, S. B., & Clayton, P. J. (1986). A prospective follow-up and family study of somatization in men and women. *American Journal of Psychiatry, 143,* 873–878.

Crowe, R. R., Noyes, R., Pauls, D. L., & Slyman, D. (1983). A family study of panic disorder. *Archives of General Psychiatry, 40,* 1065–1069.

Cyphers, L. H., Fulker, D. W., Plomin, R., & DeFries, J. C. (1989). Cognitive abilities in the early school years: No effects of shared environment between parents and offspring. *Intelligence, 13,* 369–386.

DeFries, J. C., Fulker, D. W., & LaBuda, M. C. (1987). Evidence for a genetic aetiology in reading disability in twins. *Nature, 329,* 537–539.

Dunn, J., & Plomin, R. (1990). *Separate lives: Why siblings are so different.* New York: Basic Books.

Eaves, L. J., Eysenck, H. J., & Martin, N. G. (1989). *Genes, culture and personality: An empirical approach.* New York: Academic Press.

Eaves, L. J., & Young, P. A. (1981). Genetical theory and personality differences. In R. Lynn (Ed.), *Dimensions of personality.* Oxford: Pergamon Press.

Falconer, D. S. (1989). *Introduction to quantitative genetics* (3rd ed.). New York: Wiley.

Folstein, S., & Rutter, M. (1977). Infantile autism: A genetic study of 21 twin pairs. *Journal of Child Psychology and Psychiatry, 18,* 297–332.

Goedde, H. W., & Agarwal, D. P. (Eds.). (1987). *Genetics and alcoholism.* New York: Alan R. Liss.

Goodman, R., & Stevenson, J. (1989a). A twin study of hyperactivity: I. An examination of hyperactivity scores and categories derived from Rutter teacher and parent questionnaires. *Journal of Child Psychology and Psychiatry, 30,* 671–689.

Goodman, R., & Stevenson, J. (1989b). A twin study of hyperactivity: II. The aetiological role of genes, family relationships and perinatal adversity. *Journal of Child Psychology and Psychiatry, 30*, 691-709.

Goodwin, D. W. (1979). Alcoholism and heredity. *Archives of General Psychiatry, 36*, 57-61.

Goodwin, D. W. (1985). Alcoholism and genetics. *Archives of General Psychiatry, 42*, 171-174.

Gottesman, I. I., Carey, G., & Hanson, D. R. (1983). Pearls and perils in epigenetic psychopathology. In S. B. Guze, E. J. Earls, & J. E. Barrett (Eds.), *Childhood psychopathology and development* (pp. 287-300). New York: Raven Press.

Gottesman, I. I., & Shields, J. (1982). *Schizophrenia: The epigenetic puzzle.* Cambridge: Cambridge University Press.

Graham, P., & Stevenson, J. (1985). A twin study of genetic influences on behavioral deviance. *Journal of the American Academy of Child Psychiatry, 24*, 33-41.

Grillo, C. M., & Pogue-Geile, M. F. (in press). The nature of environmental influences on weight and obesity: A behavior genetic analysis. *Psychological Bulletin.*

Guze, S. B., Cloninger, C. R., Martin, R. L., & Clayton, P. J. (1986). A follow-up and family study of Briquet's syndrome. *British Journal of Psychiatry, 149*, 17-23.

Higgins, J. (1966). Effects of child rearing by schizophrenic mothers. *Journal of Psychiatric Research, 4*, 153-167.

Higgins, J. (1976). Effects of child rearing by schizophrenic mothers: A follow-up. *Journal of Psychiatric Research, 13*, 1-9.

Holland, A. J., Hall, A., Murray, R., Russell, G. F. M., & Crisp, A. H. (1984). Anorexia nervosa: A study of 34 twin pairs and one set of triplets. *British Journal of Psychiatry, 145*, 414-419.

Howie, P. M. (1981). Intrapair similarity in frequency of disfluency in monozygotic and dizygotic twin pairs containing stutterers. *Behavior Genetics, 11*, 227-238.

Jary, M. L., & Stewart, M. A. (1985). Psychiatric disorder in the parents of adopted children with aggressive conduct disorder. *Neuropsychobiology, 13*, 7-11.

Kallman, F. J. (1946). The genetic theory of schizophrenia: An analysis of 691 schizophrenic twin index families. *American Journal of Psychiatry, 103*, 309-322.

Karlsson, J. L. (1966). *The biologic basis of schizophrenia.* Springfield, IL: Charles C. Thomas.

Kendler, K. S., & Gruenberg, A. M. (1984). An independent analysis of the Danish Adoption Study of Schizophrenia. *Archives of General Psychiatry, 41*, 555-564.

Kendler, K. S., Heath, A., Martin, N. G., & Eaves, L. J. (1986). Symptoms of anxiety and depression in a volunteer twin population. *Archives of General Psychiatry, 43*, 213-221.

Kendler, K. S., & Robinette, C. D. (1983). Schizophrenia in the National Academy of Sciences-National Research Council twin registry: A 16-year update. *American Journal of Psychiatry, 140*, 1551-1563.

Kety, S. S. (1987). The significance of genetic factors in the etiology of schizophrenia: Results from the national study of adoptees in Denmark. *Journal of Psychiatric Research, 21*, 423-429.

Kety, S. S., Rosenthal, D., & Wender, P. H. (1978). Genetic relationships with the schizophrenia spectrum: Evidence from adoption studies. In R. L. Spitzer & D. F. Klein (Eds.), *Critical issues in psychiatric diagnosis* (pp. 213-223). New York: Raven Press.

Kety, S. S., Rosenthal, D., Wender, P. H., Schulsinger, F., & Jacobsen, B. (1975). Mental illness in the biological and adoptive families of adopted individuals who have become schizophrenic: A preliminary report based on psychiatric interviews. In R. R. Fieve, D. Rosenthal, & H. Brill (Eds.), *Genetic research in psychiatry* (pp. 147-166). Baltimore: Johns Hopkins University Press.

Le Couteur, A., Bailey, A., Rutter, M., & Gottesman, I. (1989, August). *Epidemiologically-based twin study of autism.* Paper presented at the First World Congress on Psychiatric Genetics, Churchill College, Cambridge.

Lewis, S. W., Chitkara, B., Reveley, R. M., & Murray, R. M. (1987). Family history and birthweight in monozygotic twins concordant and discordant for psychosis. *Acta Geneticae Medicae et Gemellologiae, 36*, 267-273.

Loehlin, J. C. (1987). *Latent variable models: An introduction to factor, path, and structural analysis.* Hillsdale, NJ: Lawrence Erlbaum Associates.

Loehlin, J. C. (1989). Partitioning environmental and genetic contributions to behavioral development. *American Psychologist, 44,* 1285-1292.

Loehlin, J. C., Horn, J. M., & Willerman, L. (1981). Personality resemblance in adoptive families. *Behavior genetics, 11,* 309-330.

Loehlin, J. C., Horn, J. M., & Willerman, L. (1990). Heredity, environment, and personality change: Evidence from the Texas Adoption Project. *Journal of Personality, 58,* 221-243.

Loehlin, J. C., & Nichols, R. C. (1976). *Heredity, environment and personality.* Austin: University of Texas Press.

Loehlin, J. C., Willerman, L., & Horn, J. M. (1985). Personality resemblance in adoptive families when the children are late adolescents and adults. *Journal of Personality and Social Psychology, 48,* 376-392.

Loehlin, J. C., Willerman, L., & Horn, J. M. (1987). Personality resemblance in adoptive families: A 10-year follow-up. *Journal of Personality and Social Psychology, 53,* 961-969.

Loehlin, J. C., Willerman, L., & Horn, J. M. (1988). Human behavior genetics. *Annual Review of Psychology, 38,* 101-133.

Lykken, D. T., McGue, M., Bouchard, T. J., Jr., & Tellegen, A. (1990). Does contact lead to similarity or similarity to contact? *Behavior Genetics, 20,* 547-561.

Lytton, H. (1977). Do parents create or respond to differences in twins? *Developmental Psychology, 13,* 456-459.

Marks, I. M. (1986). Genetics of fear and anxiety disorders. *British Journal of Psychiatry, 149,* 406-418.

Martin, N. G., Eaves, L. J., Heath, A. C., Jardine, R., Feingold, L. M., & Eysenck, H. J. (1986). Transmission of social attitudes. *Proceedings of the National Academy of Sciences USA, 83,* 4364-4368.

Martin, N. G., Eaves, L. J., Kearsey, M. J., & Davies, P. (1978). The power of the classical twin study. *Heredity, 40,* 97-116.

Matheny, A. P., Jr. (1980). Bayley's Infant Behavior Record: Behavioral components and twin analyses. *Child Development, 51,* 1157-1167.

McCartney, K., Harris, M. J., & Bernieri, F. (1990). Growing up and growing apart: A developmental meta-analysis of twin studies. *Psychological Bulletin, 107,* 226-237.

McGue, M., Pickens, R. W., & Svikis, D. S. (1992). Sex and age effects on the inheritance of alcohol problems: A twin study. *Journal of Abnormal Psychology, 101*(1), 3-17.

McGuffin, P., & Gottesman, I. I. (1985). Genetic influences on normal and abnormal development. In M. Rutter & L. Hersov (Eds.), *Child and adolescent psychiatry: Modern approaches* (2nd ed., pp. 17-33). Oxford: Blackwell Scientific Publications.

McGuffin, P., & Katz, R. (1986). Nature, nurture and affective disorder. In J. F. W. Deakin (Ed.), *The biology of depression* (pp. 26-52). London: The Royal College of Psychiatrists/Gaskell Press.

McMahon, R. C. (1980). Genetic etiology in the hyperactive child syndrome: A critical review. *American Journal of Orthopsychiatry, 50,* 145-150.

McNeil, T., & Kaij, L. (1978). Obstetric factors in the development of schizophrenia: Complications in the births of preschizophrenics and in reproduction by schizophrenic parents. In L. C. Wynne, R. L. Cromwell, & S. Matthysse (Eds.), *The nature of schizophrenia: New approaches to research and treatment* (pp. 401-429). New York: Wiley.

Mednick, S. A., Gabrielli, W. F., Jr., & Hutchings, B. (1984). Genetic influences in criminal convictions: Evidence from an adoption cohort. *Science, 224,* 891-894.

Mednick, S. A., Moffitt, T. E., & Stack, S. (1987). *The causes of crime: New biological approaches.* New York: Cambridge University Press.

Mendlewicz, J., & Rainer, J. D. (1977). Adoption study supporting genetic transmission in manic-depressive illness. *Nature, 268,* 327-329.

Montgomery, M. A., Clayton, P. J., & Friedhoff, A. J. (1982). Psychiatric illness in Tourette's syndrome patients and first-degree relatives. In A. J. Friedhoff & T. N. Chase (Eds.), *Gilles de la Tourette Syndrome* (pp. 335-339). New York: Raven Press.

Murray, R. M., Clifford, C., & Gurling, H. M. (1983). Twin and alcoholism studies. In M. Galanter (Ed.), *Recent developments in alcoholism* (pp. 25-69). New York: Gardner Press.

Nichols, R. C. (1978). Twin studies of ability, personality, and interests. *Homo, 29,* 158-173.

Nurnberger, J. I., & Gershon, E. S. (1981). Genetics of affective disorders. In E. Friedman (Ed.), *Depression and antidepressants: Implications for courses and treatment* (pp. 23-39). New York: Raven Press.

O'Connor, M., Foch, T., Sherry, T., & Plomin, R. (1980). A twin study of specific behavioral problems of socialization as viewed by parents. *Journal of Abnormal Child Psychology, 8,* 189-199.

Pauls, D. L., Cohen, D. J., Heimbuch, R., Detlor, J., & Kidd, K. K. (1981). Familial pattern and transmission of Gilles de la Tourette's syndrome and multiple tics. *Archives of General Psychiatry, 38,* 1091-1093.

Pauls, D. L., Towbin, K. E., Leckman, J. F., Zahner, G. E. P., & Cohen, D. J. (1986). Evidence supporting a genetic relationship between Gilles de la Tourette's syndrome and obsessive compulsive disorder. *Archives of General Psychiatry, 43,* 1180-1182.

Pedersen, N. L., McClearn, G. E., Plomin, R., Nesselroade, J. R., Berg, S., & DeFaire, U. (1991). The Swedish Adoption/Twin Study of Aging: An update. *Acta Geneticae Medicae et Gemellologiae, 40,* 7-20.

Pedersen, N. L., McClearn, G. E., Plomin, R., & Nesselroade, J. R. (1992). Effects of early rearing environment on twin similarity in the last half of the life span. *British Journal of Developmental Psychology, 10,* 255-267.

Peele, S. (1986). The implications and limitations of genetic models of alcoholism and other addictions. *Journal of Studies on Alcohol, 47,* 63-73.

Pickens, R. W., Svikis, D. S., McGue, M., Lykken, D. T., Heston, L. L., & Clayton, P. J. (1990). Heterogeneity in the inheritance of alcoholism: A study of male and female twins. *Archives of General Psychiatry, 48,* 19-28.

Plomin, R. (1986). *Development, genetics, and psychology.* Hillsdale, NJ: Lawrence Erlbaum Associates.

Plomin, R. (1988). The nature and nurture of cognitive abilities. In R. Sternberg (Ed.), *Advances in the psychology of human intelligence* (Vol. 4, pp. 1-33). Hillsdale, NJ: Lawrence Erlbaum Associates.

Plomin, R. (1990). *Nature and nurture: An introduction to human behavioral genetics.* Pacific Grove, CA: Brooks/Cole.

Plomin, R. (1991). Genetic risk and psychosocial disorders: Links between the normal and abnormal. In M. Rutter & P. Casaer (Eds.), *Biological risk factors for psychosocial disorders* (pp. 101-138). New York: Cambridge University Press.

Plomin, R., & Daniels, D. (1987). Why are children in the same family so different from each other? *The Behavioral and Brain Sciences, 10,* 1-16.

Plomin, R., DeFries, J. C., & Fulker, D. W. (1988). *Nature and nurture during infancy and early childhood.* New York: Cambridge University Press.

Plomin, R., DeFries, J. C., & McClearn, G. E. (1990). *Behavioral genetics: A primer* (2nd ed.). New York: Freeman.

Plomin, R., & Foch, T. T. (1980). A twin study of objectively assessed personality in childhood. *Journal of Personality and Social Psychology, 39,* 680-688.

Plomin, R., Foch, T. T., & Rowe, D. C. (1981). Bobo clown aggression in childhood: Environment, not genes. *Journal of Research in Personality, 15,* 331-342.

Plomin, R., Nitz, K., & Rowe, D. C. (1990). Behavioral genetics and aggressive behavior in childhood. In M. Lewis & S. M. Miller (Eds.), *Handbook of developmental psychopathology* (pp. 119-133). New York: Plenum.

Plomin, R., & Rende, R. (1991). Human behavioral genetics. *Annual Review of Psychology, 42,* 161-190.

Pogue-Geile, M. F., & Rose, R. J. (1987). Psychopathology: A behavior genetic perspective. In T. Jacob (Ed.), *Family interaction and psychopathology: Theories, methods, and findings* (pp. 629–650). New York: Plenum.

Price, R. A., Kidd, K. K., Cohen, D. J., Pauls, D. L., & Leckman, J. F. (1985). A twin study of Tourette syndrome. *Archives of General Psychiatry, 43,* 815–820.

Reich, T., Van Eerdewegh, P., Rice, J., Mullaney, J., Endicott, J., & Klerman, G. L. (1987). The familial transmission of primary major depressive disorder. *Journal of Psychiatric Research, 21,* 613–624.

Rice, J. P., Reich, T., Andreasen, N. C., Endicott, J., Van Eerdewegh, M., Fishman, A., Hirschfield, R. M. A., & Klerman, G. L. (1987). The familial transmission of bipolar illness. *Archives of General Psychiatry, 41,* 441–447.

Roberts, C. A., & Johansson, C. B. (1974). The inheritance of cognitive interest styles among twins. *Journal of Vocational Behavior, 4,* 237–243.

Rose, R. J., & Ditto, W. B. (1983). A developmental-genetic analysis of common fears from early adolescence to early adulthood. *Child Development, 54,* 361–368.

Rose, R. J., & Kaprio, J. (1988). Frequency of social contact and intrapair resemblance of adult monozygotic cotwins—Or does shared experience influence personality after all? *Behavior Genetics, 18,* 309–328.

Rose, R. J., Koskenvuo, M., Kaprio, J., Sarna, S., & Langinvainio, H. (1988). Shared genes, shared experiences, and similarity of personality: Data from 14,288 adult Finnish co-twins. *Journal of Personality and Social Psychology, 54,* 161–171.

Rosenthal, D., Wender, P. H., Kety, S. S., Schulsinger, F., Welner, J., & Rieder, R. O. (1975). Parent–child relationships and psychopathological disorder in the child. *Archives of General Psychiatry, 32,* 466–476.

Rowe, D. C. (1983). Biometrical genetic models of self-reported delinquent behavior: Twin study. *Behavior Genetics, 13,* 473–489.

Rowe, D. C. (1986). Genetic and environmental components of antisocial behavior: A study of 265 twin pairs. *Criminology, 24,* 513–532.

Rowe, D. C., Rodgers, J. L., Meseck-Bushey, S., & St. John, C. (1989). Sexual behavior and nonsexual deviance: A sibling study of their relationship. *Developmental Psychology, 25,* 61–69.

Rutter, M., Macdonald, H., Le Couteur, A., Harrington, R., Bolton, P., & Bailey, A. (1990). Genetic factors in child psychiatric disorders: II. Empirical findings. *Journal of Child Psychology and Psychiatry, 31,* 39–83.

Saudino, K. J., & Eaton, W. O. (1991). Infant temperament and genetics: An objective twin study of motor activity level. *Child Development, 62,* 1167–1174.

Scarr, S. (1981). *Race, social class, and individual differences in I.Q.* Hillsdale, NJ: Lawrence Erlbaum Associates.

Scarr, S., & Grajek, S. (1982). Similarities and differences among siblings. In M. E. Lamb & B. Sutton-Smith (Eds.), *Sibling relationships: Their nature and significance across the lifespan* (pp. 357–382). Hillsdale, NJ: Lawrence Erlbaum Associates.

Scarr, S., Webber, P. I., Weinberg, R. A., & Wittig, M. A. (1981). Personality resemblance among adolescents and their parents in biologically related and adoptive families. *Journal of Personality and Social Psychology, 40,* 885–898.

Scarr, S., & Weinberg, R. A. (1978a, April). Attitudes, interests, and IQ. *Human Nature,* 29–36.

Scarr, S., & Weinberg, R. A. (1978b). The influence of "family background" on intellectual attainment. *American Sociological Review, 43,* 674–692.

Schulsinger, F. (1972). Psychopathy: Heredity and environment. *International Journal of Mental Health, 1,* 190–206.

Steffenburg, S., Gillberg, C., Hellgren, L., Andersson, L., Gillberg, I. C., Jakobsson, G., & Bohman, M. (1989). A twin study of autism in Denmark, Finland, Iceland, Norway and Sweden. *Journal of Child Psychology and Psychiatry, 30,* 405–416.

Stevenson, J., & Graham, P. (1988). Behavioral deviance in 13-year-old twins: An item analysis. *Journal of the American Academy of Child and Adolescent Psychiatry, 27,* 791–797.

Suddath, R. L., Christison, G. W., Torrey, E. F., Casanova, M. F., & Weinberger, D. R. (1990). Anatomical abnormalities in the brains of monozygotic twins discordant for schizophrenia. *The New England Journal of Medicine, 322,* 789–794.

Tellegen, A., Lykken, D. T., Bouchard, T. J., Jr., Wilcox, K., Segal, N., & Rich, S. (1988). Personality similarity in twins reared apart and together. *Journal of Personality and Social Psychology, 54,* 1031–1039.

Thompson, L. A., Detterman, D. K., & Plomin, R. (1991). Associations between cognitive abilities and scholastic achievement: Genetic overlap but environmental differences. *Psychological Science, 2,* 158–165.

Torgersen, S. (1983). Genetic factors in anxiety disorders. *Archives of General Psychiatry, 40,* 1085–1089.

Vandenberg, S. G., Singer, S. M., & Pauls, D. L. (1986). *The heredity of behavior disorders in adults and children.* New York: Plenum.

von Knorring, A.-L. (1983). *Adoption studies on psychiatric illness—epidemiological, environmental and genetic aspects* (Umea University Medical Dissertations, New Series No. 101-ISSNN0346-6612). Umea, Sweden: Umea University.

Waller, N. G., Kojetin, B. A., Bouchard, T. J., Jr., Lykken, D. T., & Tellegen, A. (1990). Genetic and environmental influences on religious interests, attitudes, and values: A study of twins reared apart and together. *Psychological Sciences, 1,* 138–142.

Wender, P. H., Kety, S. S., Rosenthal, D., Schulsinger, F., Ortmann, J., & Lunde, I. (1986). Psychiatric disorders in the biological and adoptive families of adopted individuals with affective disorders. *Archives of General Psychiatry, 43,* 923–929.

Wender, P. H., Rosenthal, D., Kety, S. S., Schulsinger, F., & Welner, J. (1974). Crossfostering: A research strategy for clarifying the role of genetic and experimental factors in the etiology of schizophrenia. *Archives of General Psychiatry, 30,* 121–128.

Wender, P. H., Rosenthal, D., Rainer, J. D., Greenhill, L., & Sarlin, M. B. (1977). Schizophrenics' adopting parents: Psychiatric status. *Archives of General Psychiatry, 34,* 777–784.

Wierzbicki, M. (1987). Similarity of monozygotic and dizygotic child twins in level and lability of subclinically depressed mood. *American Journal of Orthopsychiatry, 57,* 33–40.

Wilde, G. J. S. (1964). Inheritance of personality traits: An investigation into the hereditary determination of neurotic instability, extroversion, and other personality traits by means of a questionnaire administered to twins. *Acta Psychologica, 22,* 37–51.

Woodworth, R. S. (1941). *Heredity and environment: A critical survey of recently published material on twins and foster children.* New York: Social Science Research Council.

Wright, S. (1921). Systems of mating. I. The biometric relations between parent and offspring. *Genetics, 6,* 111–125.

2

Estimating Nonshared Environment Using Sibling Discrepancy Scores

Michael J. Rovine
The Pennsylvania State University

Behavioral genetics represents the attempt to quantify the genetic influences that affect differences in behavior among individuals (Plomin, DeFries, & McClearn, 1990). Methods have been developed to take a behavior, and through the use of appropriate quasi-experimental designs, determine what proportion of the variance of the behavior can be attributed to genetic and environmental sources (Chipuer, Rovine, & Plomin, 1990; Falconer, 1984). Regarding the contribution of environment, certain design strategies allow the partitioning of the environmental component into shared and nonshared environment (Plomin, this volume; Plomin & Daniels, 1987).

Behavioral genetics designs, however, focus on components of variance and do not consider relationships between specific environmental and behavioral measures. As these component models have shown a preponderance of nonshared environmental influence on such characteristics as cognition, personality, and psychopathology, they suggest, as the logical next step, an attempt to link specific sources of nonshared environment with these behaviors (Plomin & Daniels, 1987). Such analyses use a model to create a discrepancy score between siblings within a family for a particular measure of the environment. This score can act as a source of nonshared environment. For the purpose of this chapter, I consider any discrepancy between siblings as an indication of difference, regardless of the model being used.

One major issue raised by the use of sibling discrepancy scores is the selection of a model for estimating nonshared environment that matches the question of substantive interest. Nonshared environment refers to what two family members do not have in common. Attempts to use discrepancies as an index are assessing the construct indirectly, because they use an index of the lack of shared environment as the measure of the construct. Using a discrepancy (e.g., a difference score) as the estimate of nonshared environment casts the problem as one of determining the degree of change on some criterion as one moves from Sibling 1 to Sibling 2 within a family. Considered this way, the problem is essentially a repeated measures problem with the family as the unit of analysis, and with the sibling functioning as the level of the repeated measures factor.

The choice of models for a repeated measures problem has received considerable attention (Burr & Nesselroade, 1990; Campbell, Mutran, & Parker, 1986; Games, 1990). Four basic kinds of models have been proposed. *Regression* or *stability* models appear often in the developmental literature in the form of path models. *Difference score* or *trend* models look at mean level change across the repeated measure. The process of creating the trend score allows the additional consideration of individual differences in the trends. This very often appears in the literature as the analysis of growth. *Contingency table* or *state* models (von Eye, 1990a) can be used to consider the same questions as the regression and difference score models. These models, however, are concerned with variables that can be considered at the nominal or interval level of measurement. *Common factor* models have been used to look at patterns of change across time (Tisak & Meredith, 1990). These models have also been used to decompose individual behaviors into their genetic and environmental components (Loehlin, 1987).

When interval level scores have been collected, the regression and difference models can be used to create a discrepancy score for each pair. Although these scores are mathematically similar, they look at different facets of the lack of resemblance between siblings. For categorical level measures, the contingency table model can group sibling pairs into those that occupy the same and those that appear in different states represented by the level of categorical variable. For ordinal level variables, some rank order degree of difference can also be determined. The categorization leads to the determination of whether scores on other measures are contingent on these groupings. The common factor model decomposes the variance of a measure into constituent components including contributions of additive and nonadditive genetics and shared environment. The residuals of these models can be used to estimate nonshared environment.

This chapter focuses on the first three of these model types. The regression model is presented first. Its calculation and the type of relationship it can uncover is discussed. Next, strategies using difference scores are presented. These are of particular interest. When the family unit is considered as the unit of analysis, siblings (in fact all family members) can be treated as a repeated measures factor. The difference score for sibling pairs functions in much the same manner as difference scores in analyses of time-ordered data. When the difference score is accepted as a variable, it can be used in follow-up analyses relating it to outcome measures to determine whether degree of nonshared environment has predictive capability.

Once difference scores have been introduced, characteristics of relative and absolute difference scores are presented. These show markedly different hypotheses that are most often not interchangeable.

Scatterplots showing different kinds of relationships are used to illustrate differences in these models. Because scatterplots are easier to interpret when relationships among variables are dramatic, simulated data is used. This allows us to look at prototypical situations that nevertheless have the look and feel of real data.

The analogy to time-ordered repeated measures analysis is used often in this chapter. When the family becomes the unit of analysis, data for different family members within the same family are autocorrelated. This refers to the expectation that when the same measure is repeated across time or family member, the errors for levels of the repeated measure will be correlated. When two siblings are considered, the analogy seems to be a good one. Birth order can function to order the levels of repeated factor much in the way chronological time does. When parents are included as additional levels of the factor, some definition of the levels of the factor other than birth order (e.g., age) could be used to allow the factor to maintain its ordinality. In any case, the variables measured on the different levels of the factor remain autocorrelated.

Probably among the best informed social scientists considering this problem are those who analyze longitudinal data (von Eye, 1990b). Nonshared researchers can make use of their experience handling the modeling problems such data engender. In addition, some of the battles that can be anticipated (e.g., difference scores) have already been fought (even if not to an entirely satisfactory conclusion).

MODELS OF NONSHARED ENVIRONMENT

I first consider two of the basic statistical models for interval–level estimation of nonshared environment: a regression model and a difference score model. After these models are presented contingency table models are discussed. Quantitative genetics models are discussed elsewhere in this volume.

To begin thinking about ways of estimating sibling resemblance (and thus, sibling differences), it is useful to think of the problem as a problem of change. The change is within the family from Sibling 1 to Sibling 2. As in any consideration of change there are at least two computational strategies that can be used to create a discrepancy score for each pair. A regression or stability model (e.g., sibling correlations or stability across siblings) or a difference score model can be used to create a discrepancy score for each pair. These represent ways of testing different hypotheses that have unfortunately been cast as competitors for the best single method for determining differences. I show that they represent appropriate responses to different questions.

The regression model determines the degree of sibling resemblance by predicting one sibling's score on a measure from the other sibling's score. The regression weight reflects the degree of sibling resemblance as measured by the stability of the construct across siblings. The residual of the regression assesses sibling differences to the degree that such differences can be measured as the amount of instability of the construct across siblings. The size of each residual will depend on both the degree of association (the regression weight) and the variance of the measure for both siblings.

The difference score looks at the raw discrepancy between siblings within a family on whatever characteristic is being considered. Depending on whether information about the birth order of the siblings is to be included in the score either relative differences or absolute differences can be computed.

Because different types of scatterplots can be used to best show regression and difference relationships, I present both types in the examples presented here. The regression residual is best represented by a Sibling 1 × Sibling 2 scatterplot. On this type of plot (Sibling 2 on the y-axis) the residual is the vertical distance between the regression line and the Sibling 2 score. The difference score is most easily seen on a sibling × variable plot in which the variable is the environmental variable being considered. On a sibling × variable scatterplot the difference is represented by the slope of a line connecting the scores of each sibling pair.

Our first two figures represent prototypical examples intended to show that the two kinds of discrepancies can tell somewhat different stories. These are followed by three simulated data examples.

Figure 2.1 illustrates a pattern of discrepancies in sibling experience that would generate rank order change. The first plot (Fig. 2.1a) represents rank order change as the crossed lines connecting each sibling pair. The more traditional scatterplot (Fig. 2.1b) shows how these changes in rank order can generate large regression residuals. This pattern of data would generate large variation in both the regression residuals and the difference scores.

Change could occur, however, even when ranks are maintained. A prototypical pattern for this situation is illustrated in Fig. 2.2. The fan-shaped spread of the data (Fig. 2.2a) shows a distribution of difference scores representing raw sibling differences. The rank order is maintained across sibling. The Sibling 1 × Sibling 2 plot (Fig. 2.2b) shows the pattern of residuals generated by the same data. In this case, the rank order change and difference scores are answering different questions regarding change. These two questions may or may not be statistically related to each other.

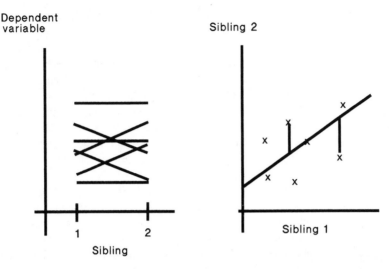

FIG. 2.1. Variability in differences and regression residuals.

To demonstrate that regression residual and difference score approaches can give different indications when applied to the same data, three different patterns representing data measured on two members of a sibling pair were simulated. Each pattern is presented in a figure which shows both the sibling × variable and the Sibling 1 × Sibling 2 scatterplots. Two of these patterns are meant to exemplify situations in which different kinds of discrepancy scores may yield different results. The third represents one in which they are expected to yield the same results.

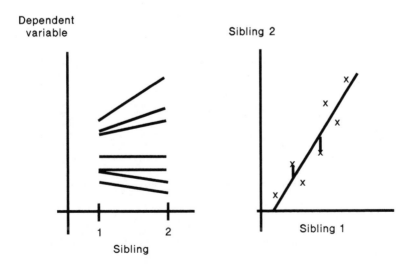

FIG. 2.2. Variability in differences and little in residuals.

Pattern 1 appears in Fig. 2.3 and represents a situation in which moderate stability (r_{xy} = .68) exists along with variation in the Sibling 1–Sibling 2 differences. This data pattern is marked by almost equal variability in the difference scores and the regression residuals. A correlation matrix of and descriptive statistics for the Sibling 1 (X), Sibling 2 (Y), difference score (DIFF), and regression residual (YRES) appears in Table 2.1. As can be seen in this case, the correlation between DIFF and YRES is almost 1. For this pattern, the two discrepancy scores are telling the same story. Table 2.2 shows some of the difference and residual scores for this data set. (Note: To simplify the sibling × variable plots, only some of the cases are shown; residuals are indicated for these points on the Sibling 1 × Sibling 2 scatterplot.)

Pattern 2 also is marked by stability in the data (r_{xy} = .76) along with variability in the differences (Fig. 2.4). This pattern was created by using two subgroups with the following properties. Group 1 had consistent differences across siblings. Group 2 had no differences. The Sibling 1 × Sibling 2 plot shows these two groups as highly stable subsets. The residuals generated by a single regression line for this data would be approximately equal but of opposite sign (depending on which group the pair falls). The slopes of the difference scores on the other hand would reflect the essentially bimodal nature of the difference scores. Descriptive statistics, correlations, and sample points appear in Tables 2.1 and 2.2.

Pattern 3 has no rank order stability (r_{xy} = − .02) and but variability in the differences (Fig. 2.5). The correlation between DIFF and YRES show that they

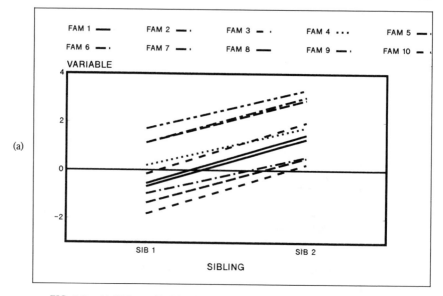

(a)

FIG. 2.3.   (a) Sibling × Variable for Example 1. (b) Plot of Sibling 1 versus Sibling 2 for Example 1.

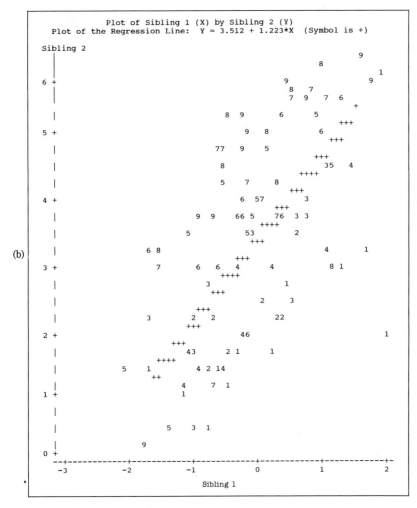

FIG. 2.3. Continued.

share only half of their variation and are thus telling different stories about sibling discrepancies. For this pattern of data notice that YRES is correlated perfectly with Y and uncorrelated with X. On the other hand, DIFF is correlated almost equally with X and Y. This implies that the unshared variance is due to the better job DIFF is doing in describing a characteristic of the sibling pair. YRES is created specifically to be uncorrelated with whichever sibling is placed on the x-side of the regression model. Thus, for the situation in which no rank order stability across siblings exists within the data, the difference score appears to be the better "system" variable. Descriptive statistics, correlations, and selected data points for this example also appear in Tables 2.1 and 2.2.

TABLE 2.1
Descriptive Statistics and Correlations for the Three Data Examples

| Variable | N | Mean | SD | Correlations | | | |
				sib 1 (X)	sib 2 (Y)	DIFF	YRESID
Example 1							
sib 1 (X)	100	−0.053	0.948	1.00	0.68	0.17	0.00
sib 2 (Y)	100	3.447	1.685	0.68	1.00	0.83	0.72
DIFF	100	3.500	1.241	0.17	0.83	1.00	0.98
YRES	100	0.000	1.222	0.00	0.72	0.98	1.00
Example 2							
sib 1 (X)	100	−0.068	1.118	1.00	0.76	0.54	0.00
sib 2 (Y)	100	−0.078	3.311	0.76	1.00	0.95	0.64
DIFF	100	−0.010	2.562	0.58	0.95	1.00	0.83
YRES	100	0.000	2.143	0.00	0.64	0.83	1.00
Example 3							
sib 1 (X)	100	−0.054	0.948	1.00	−0.01	−0.67	0.00
sib 2 (Y)	100	0.500	1.060	−0.01	1.00	0.75	0.99
DIFF	100	0.555	1.436	−0.67	0.75	1.00	0.73
YRES	100	0.000	1.060	0.00	0.99	0.73	1.00

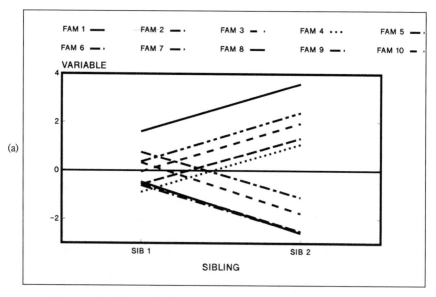

(a)

FIG. 2.4. (a) Sibling × Variable for Example 2. (b) Plot of Sibling 1 versus Sibling 2 for Example 2.

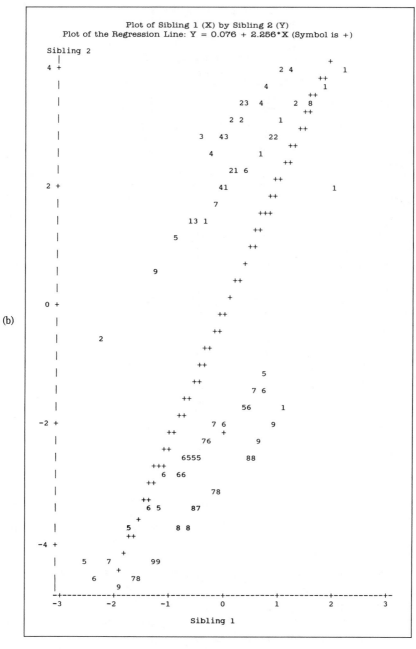

FIG. 2.4. Continued.

TABLE 2.2
Sample Data Points for Three Data Examples

sib 1 (X)	sib 2 (Y)	Difference	Residual
Example 1			
1.141	3.023	1.882	−1.884
−0.966	0.549	1.516	−1.780
−0.549	1.470	2.020	−1.368
−1.350	0.504	1.855	−1.355
−0.159	1.979	2.138	−1.337
−0.674	1.291	1.965	−1.396
1.138	2.899	1.760	−2.004
−1.803	0.238	2.042	−1.067
0.195	1.770	1.574	−1.980
1.717	3.326	1.609	−2.284
Example 2			
1.617	3.593	1.976	−0.130
−0.563	1.339	1.903	2.535
−0.045	1.958	2.004	1.986
−0.879	1.091	1.971	2.999
0.367	2.395	2.027	1.490
0.768	−1.098	−1.867	−2.907
−0.600	−2.544	−1.943	−1.265
−0.462	−2.573	−2.110	−1.606
−0.505	−2.510	−2.000	−1.445
0.331	−1.758	−2.089	−2.581
Example 3			
1.141	0.764	−0.377	0.289
−0.966	−0.967	−0.001	−1.487
−0.549	1.041	1.591	0.530
−1.350	−0.288	1.061	−0.817
−0.159	1.277	1.437	0.775
−0.674	−0.068	0.606	−0.582
1.138	0.521	−0.616	0.046
−1.803	0.085	1.889	−0.452
0.195	0.149	−0.046	−0.345
1.717	−0.780	−2.497	−1.243

These three examples are intended to show that the regression residual and the difference score can give the same or different information depending on the pattern of data being analyzed. Different research questions can generate different expectations regarding which kind of discrepancy one expects to see in the data. Such an a priori notion will suggest the appropriate type of discrepancy to create.

If the question of whether the size of a difference in a particular family on an environmental variable is related to some other variable, the difference score appears to be justified. If the question is whether the difference between the expected and observed rank of Sibling 2 predicted by the rank of Sibling 1 is related to some other variable, the regression residual score will be justified.

When one uses an empirical approach to discern the best model, one must consider what the "best" model is saying about the data. To this end we mention that the regression residual score is not a correction to the difference score. It can be considered an estimate of the difference between siblings one would expect if, for example, all younger siblings had the same score on the variable measured. The investigator will have to decide whether this hypothesis is of interest.

The Regression or Residualized Gain Score Model as an Index of Sibling Discrepancies

When sibling resemblance can be considered to be represented by each sibling having a similar rank order in the individual sibling distribution and a single underlying regression model can be assumed, the regression model can be appropriate for creating the discrepancy score. However, as is probably most often the case, when a single regression model does not adequately describe the sample (when the lack of resemblance in a sibling pair does not depend on the rest of the sample), the difference score model may be more appropriate.

The regression model for sibling pairs is equivalent to what has been termed the residualized gain score model for time ordered data. For two siblings, this

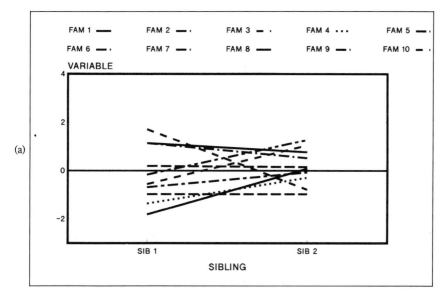

FIG. 2.5. (a) Sibling × Variable for Example 3. (b) Plot of Sibling 1 versus Sibling 2 for Example 3.

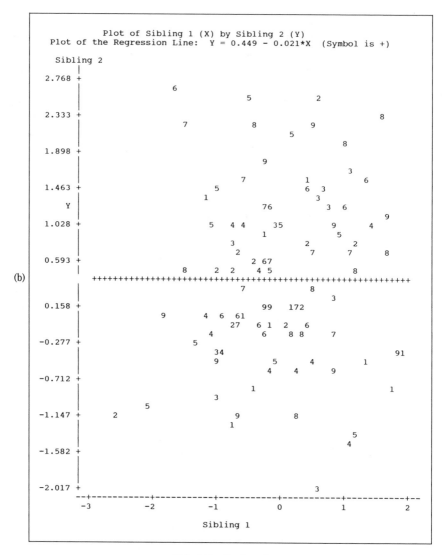

FIG. 2.5. Continued.

model fits a regression line through a scatterplot (Figs. 2.3b, 2.4b, and 2.5b). The regression residuals represent what part of Sibling 2's characteristic on the measure is not predicted by Sibling 1's characteristic. These scatterplots place Sibling 1 along one axis and Sibling 2 along the other. Each point represents the sibling pair for a particular family. The implicit assumption of this score is that a single regression model holds for all pairs in the sample. If the pattern of change differs across pairs, this assumption may not be viable. If this assumption is not met, more than one regression model may be appropriate. Bryk and

Raudenbush (1987) and von Eye and Nesselroade (1992) have suggested methods for determining these separate models for subgroups of individuals.

Consider the regression plots in the three previous examples. When Sibling 1's rank in its distribution is similar to Sibling 2's rank, the stability will be high and the values of the residuals will be small. When the rank of Sibling 1 does not predict Sibling 2, the stability will be low and the residual values will exhibit much more variation. It should be noted that the selection of the sibling that acts as the dependent variable is arbitrary.

The regression model selected creates the residual as the difference between the predicted and actual value for each y-axis sibling. These "vertical" deviations represent the best known solution to the regression problem. However, in addition to this asymmetric regression strategy, other methods of creating regression residuals exist (Isobe, Feigelson, Akritas, & Babu, 1990).

In regression terms the residual can be expressed as

$$E = Y_2 - b^*Y_1 \tag{1}$$

where E is the regression residual that can be used as the measure of non-shared environment under the regression model.

As smaller regression weights tend to produce more variability in the residuals, those weights will lead to a set of scores with more variation that can be ascribed to nonshared environment.

The residual created here includes all variations not predicted. In addition to the systematic variation that can be considered nonshared environment, this value will also include a genetic contribution and error. As a result, if an unadjusted residual is used, it would most likely overestimate the amount of variation due to nonshared environment. Based on this equation alone, the degree of overestimation is impossible to determine.

The regression equation could be fine-tuned by the addition of covariates that could explain systematic variation not considered part of nonshared environment (e.g., systematic error due to siblings talking to each other about the study in which they are taking part). Assuming that all possible covariates are located the equation

$$E = Y_2 - b^*Y_1 - (F(X_1, \ldots, X_n) \tag{2}$$

would generate a residual consisting of nonshared environment, genetic influence, and a stochastic term.

Much of the impetus for the use of the residualized gain score came from the assault by psychometricians on the more simple change (or difference) score. In particular, one characteristic of the change score considered problematic is the apparent negative correlation with the initial status. The residualized gain score is, in part, an attempt to create a discrepancy score that is uncorrelated with initial status. As is discussed later in the chapter, many now believe that this negative correlation is a statistical artifact that does not belie the usefulness of the change score. Because of the controversy regarding its use, recent developments leading to a more general acceptance of the change score are addressed.

The Difference Score as an Index of Sibling Discrepancies

As we have seen, the raw difference between siblings can differ considerably from the residualized gain score. The difference score is defined as

$$\text{DIFF}_{\text{SIB 1} - \text{SIB 2}} = Y_{\text{SIB 1}} - Y_{\text{SIB 2}} \tag{3}$$

and is equivalent to the residualized gain score only when stability is perfect.

If the difference score is to be used, two issues should be considered: (a) whether the birth order of the sibling is part of the hypothesis to be tested, and (b) whether differing variances of the siblings on the measure are to be included as part of the hypothesis test.

When birth order is part of the hypothesis, a relative difference score (maintaining the birth order through the sign of the difference) is appropriate. When any difference is of importance and it does not matter which sibling has more of the characteristic, an absolute difference may be more appropriate. As in the choice of models, these two kinds of differences represent a choice of question rather than just a choice of computational strategy. If the older sibling always has a higher score than the younger sibling (or vice versa) then the absolute and relative difference scores are identical.

When the variances on the target measure differ for the older and younger siblings, interpretive problems may result. The situation can be caused by a measure that, for example, may not apply to the younger sibling (e.g., a yes–no question that is almost always no for the younger sibling but not for the older sibling). In this case the difference score is really a measure of the older sibling.

Relative Versus Absolute Differences

The relative (or raw) difference score is defined by

$$Y_{\text{REL DIFF}} = Y_{\text{SIB 1}} - Y_{\text{SIB 2}}. \tag{4}$$

The sign of the difference indicates which sibling has more of the characteristic. The absolute difference is defined by

$$\begin{aligned} Y_{\text{ABS DIFF}} = Y_{\text{SIB 1}} &- Y_{\text{SIB 2}}. \quad \text{if } Y_{\text{SIB 1}} > Y_{\text{SIB 2}} \\ &\text{or} \\ Y_{\text{SIB 2}} &- Y_{\text{SIB 1}}. \quad \text{if } Y_{\text{SIB 2}} > Y_{\text{SIB 1}} \end{aligned} \tag{5}$$

To see the effects of the two types of difference scores, it is necessary to introduce an outcome variable. This variable appears in the two scatterplots in Fig. 2.6. The scatterplot in Fig. 2.6a was generated by creating a variable,

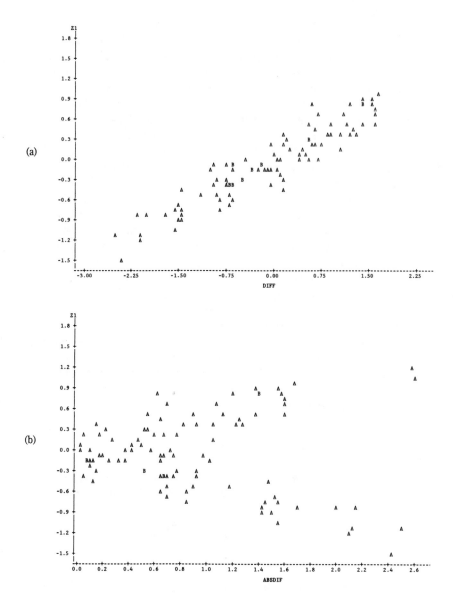

FIG. 2.6. (a) Plot of Z1 versus DIFF. (b) Plot of Z1 versus ABSDIFF.

Z_1, that is highly correlated with the relative difference of the variable shown in Example 3.

This plot represents a strong relationship between a relative difference score as a predictor and a criterion variable. In Fig. 2.6b the relative difference is changed to an absolute difference using the same data. The plot changes as shown. Negative values fold across the x-axis. The relationship that had existed for the relative difference disappears when the absolute difference is used.

Figure 2.7 shows a plot that represents a strong relationship between an absolute difference score and another criterion variable. This scatterplot was generated by creating a variable, Z_2, that is highly correlated with the absolute difference shown in Example 3. If that score were changed to a relative difference, the plot would change as shown. Once again, with the data this time folding across the y-axis, the relationship disappears.

Thus, one cannot necessarily expect to see the same result for relative and absolute difference scores. As noted earlier, they will yield the same results only when each older sibling's score on a measure is in the same direction (either larger or smaller) when compared to the younger sibling. When this is not the case the variance of the absolute difference score will be less than the variance of the relative difference score.

When a strong relationship exists between an absolute difference score and an outcome, the linear regression of that outcome on the relative difference can yield no relationship. It can also be the case that a strong relationship between a relative difference and an outcome can exist in the presence of no relationship between the absolute difference and the outcome. As a result, one who has no a priori notion regarding which score represents the hypothesis of interest (e.g., when no birth order hypothesis exists), may consider using both types of score in an exploratory fashion.

Variance as an Estimate of Discrepancy

Another score that can be derived from the raw scores of family members is the variance of each family on a single measure. The formula for this is

$$X_{\text{FAMVAR}} = \frac{\sum_{i=1}^{N} (X_i - \bar{X})^2}{N - 1} \tag{6}$$

Of the discrepancies mentioned here, this score is most similar to the absolute difference in that it retains no information about the sign of the discrepancy (i.e., birth order). It differs from the absolute difference in at least two important ways. First, because the score is created using squared deviations about the family mean, it gives a somewhat larger weight to the larger discrepancies. One can see the weighting by expanding Equation 7 for two siblings. The expansion yields

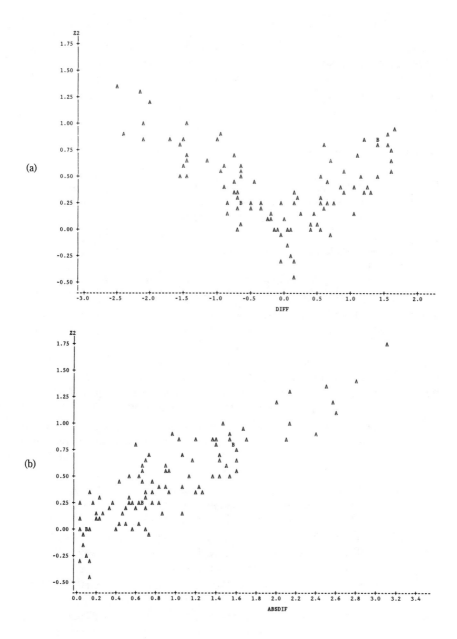

FIG. 2.7. (a) Plot of Z2 versus ABSDIFF. (b) Plot of Z2 versus DIFF.

$$X_{\text{SIBVAR}} = X^2_{\text{SIB 1}} + X^2_{\text{SIB 2}} + 2(\bar{X}^2 - X_{\text{SIB 1}}\bar{X} - X_{\text{SIB 2}}\bar{X}) \qquad (7)$$

Second, the score easily accommodates more than two family members. A variance score for each family could be calculated using the Sibling 1, Sibling 2, Mother, and Father scores. (The characteristics of this score as a measure of family have not to our knowledge been considered; however, the variance as a family score seems intuitively appealing.)

Difference Scores

Difference scores are a useful strategy for representing sibling discrepancies. Because the use of difference scores has elicited much debate in recent years, a discussion of possible objections is important. Although much of the argument has involved change over time, the same arguments can be made regarding change across any repeated measures factor, in this case, across family members.

The attacks against the difference score stem from its use as a measure of incremental increase on a characteristic repeatedly measured. In particular, in the area of education, difference scores have been used to gains in abilities or skills over time, usually due to some kind of treatment. Several respected researchers (Bereiter, 1963; Cronbach & Furby, 1970; Lord, 1958; Werts & Linn, 1970) have suggested that difference scores are so problematic that questions regarding change should be expressed in cross-sectional terms. Difference scores have found champions (Burr & Nesselroade, 1990; Rogosa & Willet, 1983; Zimmerman, Brotohusodo, & Williams, 1981) who suggest that the additional information provided by repeated measures is too much to give up especially since difference scores may not be as problematic as has been supposed.

When difference scores are used to measure growth on a characteristic, the standard two waves of data collection will be insufficient to show any complex patterns of growth. In fact, even the assumption of linear growth requires more than two data points if the assumption is to be tested against a more complex model (Bock, 1975; McArdle & Aber, 1990). Techniques to delineate more complex patterns of change require many times of measurement (Belsky & Rovine, 1989; Bryk, 1977; von Eye & Nesselroade, 1992).

For the researcher expressing nonshared environment as the difference between siblings, the difference score is a measure of differential experience. As there are only scores representing two experiences to be considered, those of Sibling 1 and Sibling 2, the two values comprising the difference score are not attempting to model a continuous function of growth across multiple levels of sibling. Unlike sibling differences, the measurement of individual growth across time needs enough points to show the shape of the function. This suggests at least one distinction in the use of difference scores. They can either be used to model an underlying complex function or they be used to show that experiences as measures by a variable of interest are different.

Rogosa and Willett (1985), among others, have suggested that difference scores are required to search for interindividual differences in intraindividual change. Difference scores calculated on observed variables are, unlike residualized gain scores, direct unbiased indices of intraindividual (in the case of sibling pairs, intrafamilial) change. The distribution of these scores can be used to divide the sample into different subgroups (e.g., when half the group has large positive differences and the other half has large negative differences). They can function as indicators of interindividual (or cross-family) differences. Their utility, however, depends on a certain degree of heterogeneity in the sample. The differences must have some variation in order to function as good predictors or outcomes. In addition, they have other properties (including the tendency to be correlated with the initial level) that have caused some to doubt their usefulness. These problems, both perceived and real, led some to suggest alternatives including residualized gain scores (Cronbach & Furby, 1970), reliability-weighted measures of change (Webster & Bereiter, 1963), and regression-based estimates of "true change" (Cronbach & Furby, 1970; Davis, 1964).

As seen earlier in the chapter, the two levels of a repeated measures factor (e.g., Sibling 1, Sibling 2) can be graphically represented by either a bivariate scatterplot or as individual trajectories (Figs. 2.1 and 2.2). The residualized gain score, which was proposed initially to circumvent a perceived problem in the difference score (the correlation between initial status and the observed difference) seems to follow logically from the bivariate scatterplot. The ease of plotting one level of the factor (e.g., Sibling 1) against the second level of the factor (e.g., Sibling 2) tends to create the impression that the empirical bivariate relationship can be adequately captured by the group level summary statistics (in this case, the correlation or regression weight). This impression may make the move from the difference score to the residualized gain score seem less drastic than it actually is.

This regression model presents the final observed state (i.e., Sibling 2) as conditional on initial state (Sibling 1). As Cronbach and Furby (1970) pointed out, "one cannot argue that the residualized score is a 'corrected' measure of [difference], since in most studies the portion discarded includes some genuine and important change in the person" (p. 74). Instead, as Willett (1987) pointed out for repeated observations, the score answers a question like: If all younger siblings experienced the same degree of paternal affection, how different would the older sibling be from the younger sibling? Of course, all younger siblings do not experience the same degree of affection, and these differences determine, in part, what makes families different.

For any complex well-measured process, Willett (1987) suggested that only when pairs of repeated data points differ at the same rate (or when the rate is dependent on the initial level as the fan pattern in Fig. 2.2) will ranks tend to be maintained. The regression model confuses the difference between stability of rank order (high sibling correlation) and the stability of the construct (reliability) over time. In other words, if the rank order changes, do siblings occupy different places in their respective distributions or is the measure too unstable to allow the ranks to be maintained?

Willett (1987) suggested as an alternative to plotting levels of the repeated measure against each other (Sibling 1 versus Sibling 2), plotting the level of the repeated measure against the value of the measure for each level (e.g., Sibling [1 or 2] versus the environmental measure) is more likely to show different patterns. By connecting the paired sibling scores in each family by lines, one can see individual family difference patterns. Figures 2.3a, 2.4a, and 2.5a show three patterns of within-family differences: (a) Sibling 1 shows more of the characteristic; (b) Sibling 2 shows more of the characteristic; and (c) They are essentially equal. The slope of the change can be used to determine subgroups of families with similar difference patterns. By grouping families with similar patterns, one can show both intrafamilial growth and interfamily differences.

Two major complaints against difference scores that can be carried over to their use as indices of sibling discrepancies are now considered: (a) the apparent unreliability of difference scores, and (b) the correlation of difference scores with the level of one of their components (e.g., Sibling 1).

Difference Scores and Unreliability

Consider a measure, $X_{\text{SIB } i}$, assessed on two siblings from the same family. If the observed score is considered to contain an underlying true score and some degree of measurement error (Lord & Novick, 1968; Nunnally, 1978) the observed score can be written as

$$X_{\text{SIB } ij} = \xi_j (\text{SIB}_i) + \varepsilon_{ij} \qquad (8)$$

where X is the observed score for SIB_i in family j, ξ is the true score for the same child, and ε is the error. If two siblings are measured the difference in their observed scores is

$$D_{\text{SIB } j} = X_{\text{SIB } 2j} - X_{\text{SIB } 1j} \qquad (9)$$

with D_{SIB} the observed difference between siblings. It follows (Willett, 1987) that the difference in true scores is

$$D_{\text{SIB } j} = \Delta_{\text{SIB } j} + \varepsilon_j \qquad (10)$$

with Δ_{SIB} the true difference and ε_j the error.

The reliability of any measure is defined as the proportion of true score variance to observed score variance. For the difference score this can be expressed as

$$\varrho(D) = \frac{\sigma^2}{\sigma D^2} \tag{11}$$

Willet presents the expansion of this as

$$\varrho(D) = \frac{\sigma^2 X_{SIB\,1} \varrho\,(X_{SIB\,1}) + \sigma^2 X_{SIB\,2}\,\varrho(X_{SIB\,2}) - {}^{2\sigma} X_{SIB\,1}\,{}^{\sigma} X_{SIB\,2}\varrho(X_{SIB\,1}\,X_{SIB\,2})}{\sigma^2 X_{SIB\,1} + \sigma^2 X_{SIB\,2} - {}^{2\sigma} X_{SIB\,2}\,{}^{\sigma}\,X_{SIB\,2}\varrho\,(X_{SIB\,1}\,X_{SIB\,2})} \tag{12}$$

The numerator variances are weighted by the separate reliabilities of the measure for each sibling. All else aside, when the reliabilities of the individual scores are less than 1, the reliability of the difference score will be less than 1.

As Willett (1987) pointed out, $\varrho(X_{SIB\,1}\,X_{SIB\,2})$ can take on any value between 0 and 1 and still be valid when there are, as in this case interfamilial differences in sibling differences. He stated that psychometricians have traditionally misinterpreted the correlation between waves as an estimate of construct validity. As a result, they tended to interpret the equation for the situation in which the assumed validity was high (near 1). This is the case in which rank order stability is maintained and variation in the differences does not occur. This interpretation led to the notion that the difference score could not be simultaneously valid and reliable. If one is willing to agree that low correlations across waves can occur on instruments that are valid (as is expected in any statelike measure), then, according to Willett (1987), "when [differences in change] are large, it is possible for the reliability of the difference scores to be greater than the reliabilities of the [individual measures]" (p. 369).

The correlations calculated for data collected on sibling pairs can be expected to range across all possible values. Provided that one has insured the reliability and validity of the instrument for each child, one can expect the difference score to have some degree of reliability.

The calculation of the reliabilities of the difference score requires estimates of the separate reliability for each sibling, along with the estimate of the population correlation between siblings. Studies often depend on poor estimates of reliability (e.g., lower bound internal consistency estimates). If estimates of reliability are to be calculated, these estimates can only be considered approximate, at best, if great care has not been taken in the design of the study to get the best possible estimates. When these estimates are to be used for disattenuate the relationship between the difference score and some other variable for measurement error, particular care must be taken in interpreting the adjusted result because the reliability of difference score will almost certainly be underestimated. Willett (1987) suggested that the true variable-difference score correlation will fall somewhere between the observed correlation and the disattenuated correlation.

Adding Level to the Difference Problem: Minimizing the Correlation Between the Difference Score and an Index of Level

As with other types of difference scores, those reflecting sibling discrepancies do not take into account the level of either of the siblings. Except in the trivial case where one of the siblings has no variance on the measure, the difference score gives no information about the level of the individual. To use level as an additional predictor along with sibling difference in the same analysis, one must choose among three indicators of level: Sibling 1, Sibling 2, or some combination of the two (e.g., the sum or the mean). Other considerations aside, the sum of the sibling scores (created by multiplying the individual scores by the coefficients 1 and 1) would be expected to have the smallest correlation with the difference score (created using coefficients 1 and -1). Either Sibling 1's score (created using coefficients 1 and 0) or Siblings 2's score (created using coefficients 0 and 1) would be expected to be more highly correlated with the difference score.

If one hypothesized an interaction between level and resemblance, one could look at the slope of the difference scores based on levels of one of the same three indicators. This would require categorization of, for example, sibling sum scores followed by a multiple group comparison of the slopes. Suppose a hypothesis including both sibling resemblance and overall level of maternal affection were to be tested. This would be equivalent to looking for an interaction between the level of maternal affection in a family and the individual difference score. If each difference score can be considered a slope, the expectation is that the average slope representing difference in maternal affection differs for the different categories of family maternal affection. This can be tested. If these categories are expected to relate to other variables that are of interest, those relationships can also be determined.

Before moving to a discussion of discrepancies of categorical level measures, I briefly consider what to do if more than one sibling difference is to be used in the same analysis.

Compositing Sibling Difference Scores for Several Environmental Variables

If a multivariate score based on difference scores for a number of environmental measures is desired, some kind of compositing is required. The decision regarding how to composite often involves selecting a scaling model (Allen & Yen, 1979). Much of the work done on creating summary variables has con-

sidered factor analysis. Realizing that much work needs to be done to determine the best scaling model (under particular circumstances) for difference
scores, I mention a rationale for choosing between factor analysis and simple
summation. I realize that other scaling techniques (e.g., multidimensional scaling, Thurstone scaling, etc.) may be more appropriate for particular measures.

One rationale for the use of factor analysis for scaling requires that variables
loading on the same factor be homogeneous. Homogeneity is reflected in the
pattern of correlations among variables. Thus, a pattern of high correlations
among a subset of variables indicates that those variables should be part of the
same factor. In light of this, consider the set of sibling scores represented in
Fig. 2.8. Two variables are shown. Each slope represents a difference score
for a sibling pair on a variable. Figure 2.8a represents a situation in which the

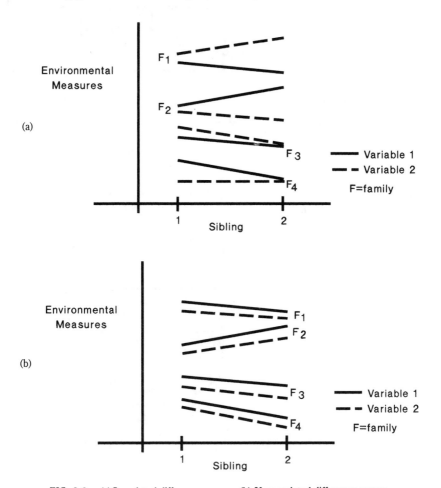

FIG. 2.8.   (a)Correlated difference scores. (b) Uncorrelated difference scores.

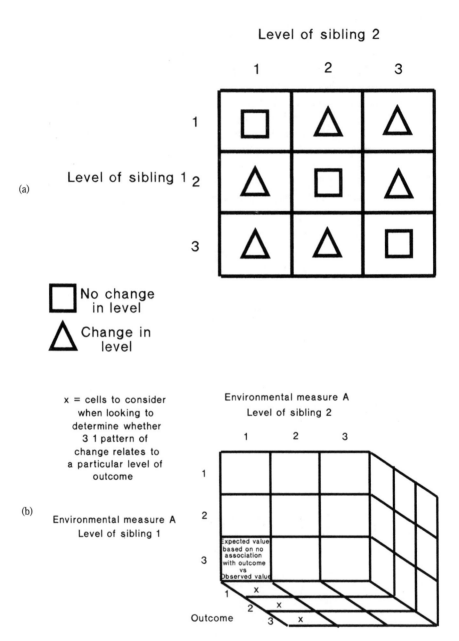

FIG. 2.9. (a) Difference patterns using contingency tables. (b) Relating an outcome to a pattern of change.

slopes on Variables 1 and 2 are essentially the same for each sibling pair. This implies that the pattern of change represented by both variables is essentially the same. A high correlation between the two difference scores would be the result. The two variables in Fig. 2.9b show no such pattern. A low correlation between the differences would be the expectation.

Factor analyzing a set of difference scores (Nesselroade & Bartsch, 1977; Tisak & Meredith, 1990) basically assesses whether the slopes of the scores are similar across a set of variables. If all slopes are similar, they would be expected to load on a single factor. If patterns of similar change exist within subsets of the difference scores, a multifactor solution reflecting patterns of relatively high correlations for the difference scores would be expected. In either case, factor scoring coefficients could be used for generating the individual scores measuring change on the common latent variable. The degree of correlation among multiple latent variables would be estimating by the factor intercorrelations.

The rationale for compositing the two variables in the second set requires that the differences be cumulative, even though a large difference on one score does not necessarily predict a large difference on another. In some sense, those sibling pairs with large differences on both of the variables have more of some characteristic than those who have a large difference on only one of the measures. If these variables were included in a factor analysis, they would be expected to load on different factors.

Models for estimating factor solutions using difference scores along with problems inherent in such estimations have been discussed by Nesselroade and Bartsch (1977) and Tisak and Meredith (1990). They indicate that the requirements for a satisfactory factor analytic solution are certainly more complex than has been started here. Great care must be exercised to generate a measurement model that creates composites that make sense and can be interpreted.

Difference Measures for Noninterval Level Variables

Strategies mentioned here are most appropriate for variables that are at least interval level. In the case of nominal or ordinal measures residualized gain score of difference scores have little meaning. Other strategies for determining the degree of association (and thus indirectly, the degree of nonshared environment) are available. Consider a variable with three nominal categories: 1, 2, and 3. If that variable is repeated on two siblings, the pattern of scores could be placed in a 3 × 3 contingency table (see Fig. 2.9). Off diagonal cells represent discrepancies between siblings.

Each of the cells in the three-way table can be thought of as a pattern of change. In this case expectations may exist regarding how the scores on outcome measures depend on each pattern of change. To estimate this relationship, loglinear strategies could be used to show the association between this cell location and one or a number of categorical outcome variable. To test a hypothesis that a particular pattern of change leads to the increased probability of a particular outcome, one compares the observed frequency of the cell representing that combination with the expected frequency under a particular model (Agresti, 1990; Tabachnick & Fidel, 1989). If the outcome is interval level, it could be categorized to make use of these techniques. Otherwise, ANOVA strategies could look at mean level differences on the outcome based on cell membership.

The diagonals of the three-way table represent siblings with the same level of the repeated measure. Off-diagonal cells represent discrepancies. If those who fall in these cells differ in the level of the outcome as compared to those who fall in the diagonal, then the association may indicate an effect of nonshared environment. As in the case of interval level variables, the effect is probably overestimated and must be interpreted with caution.

One major advantage of this multiway contingency table strategy is that by placing sibling pairs in these cells, it allows one to determine graphically where discrepancies are occurring and how great those discrepancies are. With a single outcome variable, the three-way table (Fig. 2.9) is again a graphically satisfying way to determine which patterns of discrepancy are related to which levels of the outcome.

DISCUSSION

The choice of models for studying sibling differences presents a problem similar to the one facing longitudinal researchers interested in studying change. The problem has been described by Campbell et al. (1986). When a model is available, there is always the danger that the statistical method can determine the substantive question. This can occur either by selecting a question that fits a preexisting technique or by assuming that a technique can be more broadly applied than it should be. Either one causes a mismatch between the question one wants to answer and the question one actually answers. For nonshared researchers, a danger exists in that different models can estimate something that can function as an index of sibling discrepancies, but they involve different and often independent aspects of nonshared environment.

To use discrepancies as an index of the degree to which an environmental measure shows a nonshared component, one must remember that different models are sensitive to different effects. A major choice, then, involves the kind of discrepancy to be created.

For the regression model to be chosen, one must first assume that a single model underlies the complete sample. If no single model can be assumed, some way must be determined to divide the sample into subgroups for the purpose of computing separate regression models. Second, one must assume that the residual is an appropriate index of nonshared environment. In making this assumption it is important to remember that computationally the question being addressed is basically what would the difference between two siblings be if, for example, all younger siblings had the same score on the measure of interest.

For the difference model, one assumes in some sense that there is a separate model for each sibling pair. In the case of sibling differences, this is equivalent to assuming that no single set of family processes determines the degree of difference between siblings in all families. The processes are complex and the best piece of information that can be gleaned from each household is the sum total of all of those effects on the sibling pair, represented by the raw difference.

If the difference score model is selected, a decision regarding the importance of birth order must be made. If order matters, the relative difference may be more appropriate. If order is irrelevant, the absolute difference or the variance score may be more appropriate. Because any one of the models mentioned here may tell you little about any other, in a purely exploratory situation, one may try each of these models. In this exploratory model, two concerns should be considered. First, if absolute and relative difference scores are both used, and one relates to an outcome and the other does not, the relationship that occurs should make sense. The exploratory selection of both scores is an indication that the researcher had no expectations regarding the importance of birth order. Results from such explorations should be considered more descriptive than explanatory and lay the groundwork for attempts at replication. Second, care must be exercised in the interpretation of relationships in the presence of a large number of outcomes. The more scores you use, the more associations you generate. This increases the likelihood that some of those associations will appear statistically significant by change.

A prior decision will regard the level of measurement of both the variable used to create each discrepancy and the score used to create each outcome. The general tendency seems to emphasize interval level variables and to use those variables to create interval level discrepancies. The variables in question may not be able to support that level of measurement. In that case categorization and the use of multiway contingency table strategies (e.g., loglinear analysis) may yield better results. In addition these strategies can lead to results that are somewhat easier to interpret.

If many indices of sibling discrepancies on environmental variables are considered, and some kind of composite is desired, an appropriate rationale for the compositing should be established. Once that has occurred, a measurement model that best conforms to that rationale can be selected (e.g., factor analysis, multidimensional scaling, simple summing, etc.). One warning against making composites that are too general is in order. If the subject of the study is primarily descriptive, compositing can work against a good explanation of the processes one wishes to uncover. If variables have been collected because their separate purposes are considered important, compositing indiscriminately can lose that vital information. However, the investigator will have many more results to look at and interpret. It is important, then, to carefully consider whether the thrust of the study is inferential or primarily descriptive. If the former is the case, compositing is often used to keep the number of hypotheses tested under control. If the latter is the case, compositing should be used primarily to create stronger indices of constructs of interest.

This chapter discusses some of the problems known to exist and anticipates other problems that no doubt will crop up in the use of sibling discrepancies as estimates of nonshared environment. As with any other analysis, it is important to consider the meaning of results generated. In order to respond to the level of significance of a particular statistical test one must understand the underlying models used to generate a specific test. This requires one to determine whether the underlying model matches the question one wishes to answer.

ACKNOWLEDGMENTS

Preparation of this chapter was supported by National Institute of Mental Health Grant MH43373, David Reiss, Mavis Hetherington, and Robert Plomin, principal investigators.

REFERENCES

Agresti, A. (1990). *Categorical data analysis*. New York: Wiley.

Allen, M. J., & Yen, W. M. (1979). *Introduction to measurement theory*. Belmont, CA: Wadsworth.

Belsky, J., & Rovine, M. J. (1989, February). Patterns of marital change across the transition to parenthood: Pregnancy to three years post-partum. *Journal of Marriage and the Family, 52*, 5–19.

Bereiter, C. (1963). Some persisting dilemmas in the measurement of change. In C. W. Harris (Ed.), *Problems in measuring change* (pp. 3–20). Madison: University of Wisconsin Press.

Bock, R. D. (1975). *Multivariate statistical methods in behavioral research*. New York: McGraw-Hill.

Bryk, A. S. (1977). *An investigation of the effects of alternative statistical adjustment strategies in the analysis of quasi-experimental growth data*. Unpublished doctoral dissertation, Harvard Graduate School of Education, Cambridge, MA.

Bryk, A. S., & Raudenbush, S. W. (1987). Application of hierarchical linear models to assessing change. *Psychological Bulletin, 101*, 147–158.

Burr, J. A., & Nesselroade, J. R. (1990). Change Measurement. In A. von Eye (Ed.), *Statistical methods in longitudinal research* (Vol. 1, pp. 3–34). Boston: Academic Press.

Campbell, R. T., Mutran, E., & Parker, R. N. (1986). Longitudinal design and longitudinal analysis. *Research on Aging, 8*(4), 480–504.

Chipuer, H. M., Rovine, M. J., & Plomin, R. (1990). LISREL modeling: Genetic and environmental influences on IQ revisited. *Intelligence, 14*(1), 11–29.

Cronbach, L. J., & Furby, L. (1970). How should we measure "change"—or should we? *Psychological Bulletin, 74*, 86–80.

Davis, F. B. (1964). Measurement of change. In F. B. Davis (Ed.), *Educational measurements and their interpretation* (pp. 234–252). Belmont, CA: Wadsworth.

Falconer, D. S. (1984). *Introduction to quantitative genetics*. New York: Longman Press.

Games, P. (1990). Alternative analyses of repeated measures designs by ANOVA and MANOVA. In A. von Eye (Ed.), *Statistical methods in longitudinal research* (Vol. 1, pp. 81–122). Boston: Academic Press.

Isobe, T., Feigelson, E. D., Akritas, M. G., & Babu, G. L. (1990). *Linear regression in astronomy I*. State College: The Pennsylvania State University, Department of Astronomy.

Loehlin, J. C. (1987). *Latent variable models*. Hillsdale, NJ: Lawrence Erlbaum Associates.

Lord, F. M. (1958). Further problems in the measurement of growth. *Educational and Psychological Measurement, 18*, 437–454.

Lord, F. M., & Novick, M. N. (1968). *Statistical theories of mental test scores*. Reading, MA: Addison-Wesley.

McArdle, J. J., & Aber, M. (1990). Patterns of change within latent variable structural equation models. In A. von Eye (Ed.), *Statistical methods in longitudinal research* (Vol. 1, 151–224). Boston: Academic Press.

Nesselroade, J. R., & Bartsch, T. W. (1977). Multivariate perspectives on the construct validity of the trait-state distinction. In R. B. Cattell & R. M. Dreger (Eds.), *Handbook of modern personality theory* (pp. 221–238). Washington, DC: Hemisphere.

Nunnally, J. (1978). *Psychometric theory*. New York: McGraw-Hill.

Plomin, R., & Daniels, D. (1987). Why are children in the same family so different from one another? *Behavioral and Brain Sciences, 10*, 1–60.

Plomin, R., DeFries, J. C., & McClearn, G. E. (1990). *Behavioral genetics: A primer*. New York: W. H. Freeman.

Rogosa, D. R., & Willett, J. B. (1983). Demonstrating the reliability of the difference score in the measurement of change. *Journal of Educational Measurement, 20*, 335–343.

Rogosa, D., & Willett, J. (1985). Understanding differences in change by modeling individual differences in growth. *Psychometrika, 50*, 203–228.

Tabachnick, B. G., & Fidell, L. S. (1989). *Using multivariate statistics*. New York: Harper & Row.

Tisak, J., & Meredith, W. (1990). Descriptive and associative developmental models. In A. von Eye (Ed.), *Statistical methods in longitudinal research* (Vol. 2, pp.). Boston: Academic Press.

von Eye, A. (1990a). *Introduction to configural frequency analysis*. Boston: Cambridge University Press.

von Eye, A. (1990b). *Statistical methods in longitudinal research*. Boston: Academic Press.

von Eye, A., & Nesselroade, J. R. (1992). Types of change: Applications of configural frequency analysis to repeated observations in developmental research. *Experimental Aging Research, 18*(4), 169–183.

Webster, H., & Bereiter, C. (1963). The reliability of changes measured by mental test scores. In C. W. Harris (Ed.), *Problems in measuring change* (pp. 45–60). Madison, WI: University of Wisconsin Press.

Werts, C. E., & Linn, R. L. (1970). A general linear model for studying growth. *Psychological Bulletin, 73*, 17–22.

Willett, J. B. (1987). Questions and answers in the measurement of change. *Review of Research in Education, 15*, 345–422.

Zimmerman, D. W., Brotohusodo, T. L., & Williams, R. H. (1981). The reliability of sums and differences of test scores: Some new results and anomalies. *Journal of Experimental Education, 49*, 177–186.

3

The Separate Worlds of Teenage Siblings: An Introduction to the Study of the Nonshared Environment and Adolescent Development

David Reiss
George Washington University Medical Center

Robert Plomin
The Pennsylvania State University

E. Mavis Hetherington
University of Virginia

George W. Howe
George Washington University Medical Center

Michael Rovine
The Pennsylvania State University

Adeline Tryon
Salisbury State University

Margaret Stanley Hagan
University of North Carolina—Charlotte

For years, two separate lines of investigations have explored the factors shaping child and adolescent development. In one line, the influence of genetic factors have been investigated. In recent years, behavioral genetics has moved from studying the role of heredity in explaining individual differences at a single point in time to the role of genetics in explaining differences among individuals in their patterns of development. The same evolution can be noted in studies of the influence of the social context on child development. The influences of families and peers, as well as other social systems, is moving beyond their role in individual differences at a single point in time and towards the explanation of variation in developmental trajectories. Most recently, a set of findings from behavioral genetics provides an opportunity to bring these two lines of work together. These are data that strongly suggest particular forms of environmental influences; specifically, experiences that are different for siblings in the same family: the nonshared environment.

This study focuses on the role of the nonshared environment in the development of both competence and psychopathology in adolescence. It is designed to answer three logically related questions. First, what are the differences in the social environments of adolescents, particularly in their families and peer groups? Second, are these differences a product of active environmental processes, or are they a passive response to differences between the siblings in heritable traits? Third, among those environmental differences that are not heavily influenced by genetic factors, which are correlated with differences among our adolescents in competence and in psychopathology? The last of these three questions requires a design that is sensitive to both genetic and environmental influences on development. The question, and research designed to answer it, promotes a significant integration of the genetic and environmental lines of investigation.

Although several studies are currently exploring the role of nonshared environment on children of varying ages, this study is unique because it combines two important design characteristics. On the one hand it is unusually comprehensive in the range of environmental processes which are explored. On the other, the design can detect genetic effects on both the environmental process and on the developmental outcomes we have selected for study. The design is comprehensive in that it encompasses many aspects of the marital, parent-child, sibling, and peer relationships. For each of these areas we explore a range of processes, and for each of these processes we use many methods and many sources of information. For the first three of these four social systems, the family relationships, we also use videotaping for direct observation of social processes. The design can detect genetic effects because it uses an unusual national sample: 720 two-parent families, each with a pair of adolescent siblings of the same gender no more than four years apart in age. This sample is sensitive to genetic effects because these siblings have a known and varying genetic relationship to each other. The sample consists of six groups: families of monozygotic (MZ) twins, dizygotic (DZ) twins, stepfamilies with unrelated siblings (blended families), stepfamilies with half siblings, stepfamilies with full siblings, and nondivorced families with full siblings.

Data collection has been completed on all of the families, but the coding of the videotapes and analysis of the interview and questionnaire data is just beginning. The purpose of this chapter is to introduce the logic of the study, to describe its design and measures, and to report some initial findings, from questionnaires and interviews, on the first 214 families studied. The data are presented not as definite answers to the main questions of the study, but to exemplify the logic of data analysis and to anticipate the form, if not the content, of the major findings that will emerge from this large study over the next 3 years.

Genetic Data and Nonshared Effects

The scientific nucleus of this study is a coherent set of results from a series of studies of genetic influences on behavior and development; these studies have been described in detail elsewhere in this book. To summarize, these genetic studies have reached two conclusions. First, although hereditary is important in explaining differences among individuals in both competent and pathological development, so is environment. Second, the genetic data suggest strongly not only the importance of environmental factors, but specific types of environmental effects that are important. The type of environmental factors that shape development must be those that are different for each sibling in the same family.

There is a surprising corollary to these genetic findings. Factors such as social class, neighborhood conditions, marital conflict, an intellectually enriched home environment, maternal depression, or the general tendency of parents to encourage developmental advances in their children are unlikely to influence development directly, because these are factors shared by all siblings in the same family. Although factors of this kind have often correlated with, or even predicted developmental outcomes, their effects may be mediated by common genes. That is, the set of genes that—in the child—produce the developmental outcome also shape—in the parent—the child rearing or environmental variable that is the predictor. For example, mental and language development in toddlers is probably shaped, in large measure, by the same set of genes in the child as those that, in the parent, lead to encouragement and reinforcement of developmental advances in their children (Plomin, Loehlin, & DeFries, 1985). This fact would explain why the association between these two variables is strong between parents and their biological offspring, but is much weaker between adopting parents and their adopted offspring.

The discovery of nonshared effects, however, was a very mixed blessing. Although the discovery of these effects provided a particularly strong support for their importance in development, Pandora's box had once again, in our science, been opened and with alarming prospects. The first alarm arose from the range of nonshared effects that were possible. Very plausibly, these might include differences in sibling experience in environments about which we developmentalists know very little. In early development these might include differences in intrauterine experience, differences in pre- and postnatal exposure to toxins, bacterial, viral, and fungal pathogens, and differences in exposure to physical accidents. Across the life span these differences might include those of occupational settings, economic circumstances, and nonheritable acute and chronic illness and disabilities.

Even more alarming was the possibility that, from one family to the next, these effects—from familiar or unfamiliar sources—might be random. In one family a child might be born at the time of the death of her mother's mother, whereas another sibling escapes the effects of this acute maternal grief. In another family, one child might spend its earliest years in an economically se-cure household, but a younger sibling might be born into a household swamped with the effects of a sudden family economic disaster. Each of these differences might, for example, lead to the affected child becoming vulnerable to depres-sion, but these nonshared effects could not be studied systematically across fam-ilies. Possibilities of this kind raised a fleeting specter that genetic data concerning nonshared effects might usher in the collapse of systematic developmental psy-chology.

Preliminary Studies of Nonshared Effects

Preliminary studies in this new field provided some reassurance. Some data, for example, have pointed to the systematic importance of differential parent-ing between siblings. For example, Dunn, Stocker, and Plomin (1990) studied variation in internalizing and externalizing in seven year olds who had younger siblings of the same gender. Children who received more affection and less con-trol from their mothers, as determined by interview and direct observation, were less likely to show signs of internalizing as rated by mothers. Two studies of adolescents also suggest that differential parenting, by both their mothers and their fathers, is important (Daniels, 1987; Daniels, Dunn, Furstenberg, & Plo-min, 1985). For example, the sibling who received more paternal affection than the other was the sibling most likely to develop more ambitious educational and occupational objectives. Recent data have suggested that the influence of these differential parental experiences may extend well into adulthood (Baker & Daniels, 1990).

Additional data have clarified and extended these preliminary findings on sys-tematic nonshared effects in two important ways. First, it is clear that differen-tial experiences are not restricted to parenting. All four of the studies cited previously show that differences in the siblings' experiences with one another also constitute a significant part of the nonshared environment. For example, if in a sibling pair one sibling is care-giving and the other sibling is care-receiving, the sibling environment for each is quite different. Indeed, data suggest that the more caretaking of the two siblings is least likely to show patterns of fear-fulness during adolescence and early adulthood (Daniels, 1987). In addition to sibling differences in their experiences with the same parent and with each other, two of the four studies suggested the importance of differential experiences in peer groups (Baker & Daniels, 1990; Daniels, 1987).

A second clarification of these preliminary studies of the nonshared environ-ment illuminated the genetic influence on nonshared effects. In ways that are pre-cisely analogous to shared experiences, nonshared effects may be shaped by genetic factors. A mother may treat one sibling with greater affection than an-other because the first sibling is more socially responsive than the second, a trait which may be heritable. The scientific excitement generated by the genetically-based search for main effects of the nonshared environment must be matched with caution in interpreting these effects; we do not want to build a whole science of the influence of nonshared environmental factors on development only to discover that most of these were due to genes after all. These genetic effects can be detected by comparing groups of sibling pairs whose genetic relationship is known and varying.

Decisions in Research Design

These initial findings led to three major decisions in research design. The first was to focus on adolescence. There were three important reasons for this. First, during this phase, large individual differences in both competence and psychopathology have unquestioned relevance for comparable differences in developmental trajectories later in the life span. Second, traditional, single-child studies suggest that important aspects of adolescent development, as in younger children, remain highly responsive to environmental influences. Third, there is suggestive evidence that the role of genetic factors may shift dramatically during this period (Plomin, 1986; Rose & Ditto, 1983; Scarr & Weinberger, 1983; Wilson, 1983).

Our second decision was shaped by the first efforts to explore the nonshared environment described earlier. In accord with these findings we broadened our concerns beyond that of differences in parenting, and included in our design inventories of sibling and peer group relationships.

Third, we planned our studies to be sensitive to moderate genetic influences on measures of the nonshared environment. This feature of our design will produce its own rich harvest: the most extensive data to date on the role of genetics in shaping family and peer processes. However, our prime intent, following from the preliminary studies of the nonshared environment we have cited, was to uncover systematic relationships between nonshared environments and developmental outcomes that were not mediated by genetics. Adoption and twin designs are frequently used to assess genetic effects. One type of adoption design compares two groups of siblings. One group contains an adopted sibling with either a biological child of the adopting parents, or another adopted child from a different family than the first. The second group contains two biologically related siblings (usually living with their biological parents). Twin designs compare MZ with DZ twins. Although they have rarely been used in genetic research, stepfamilies offer another possible window on genetic processes. In this design we can compare genetically unrelated siblings (blended families), half siblings, and full siblings.

Because of the widespread availability of abortions there have been fewer children given up for adoption to nonrelated families since the late 1970s; combining this factor with the requirement that the adoptee have a same-sex sibling within 4 years of age led us to expect that relatively few suitable adoption-related sibling pairs would be available for study. For this reason, we did not include adoptees in our design. Instead, we included both twins and stepfamilies. Figure 3.1 clarifies this feature of our design. Note that there are still some features of this design that combine traditional adoption studies with the twin and stepfamily methods. For example, as in some adoption designs, the siblings in the blended families are genetically unrelated to each other, and one is unrelated to the mother. Also, in all three stepfamilies, the father is not genetically related to at least one of the children. Note also that we have added a sixth group, derived by random sampling of a national pool, nondivorced families who have full siblings.

Although there have been occasional uses of half siblings in genetically sensitive designs (Cook & Goethe, 1990; Schukit, Goodwin, & Winokur, 1972), this is the first study to exploit fully genetic variation in stepfamilies. In addition, it is one of the few to use a combination of approaches to estimating genetic effects.

There are three major advantages to this design. First, it offers a new approach to disentangling the biological effects of genetics from the social effects of family type. Note in Fig. 3.1, for example, that the difference in genetic relatedness between MZ and DZ twins is the same magnitude as that between blended and full stepfamily siblings. If there are true linear or additive genetic effects on environmental or outcome variables then the differences in these two comparisons should be similar despite the enormous differences between family types being compared. Moreover, a direct assessment of the impact of family type

Design for Separating
Family Structure and Genetic Similarity

Level of Genetic Similarity for Siblings

	0%	25%	50%	100%
Family Structure				
Stepfamilies - No Twins	Blended	Half	Full	
Non-stepfamilies - No Twins			Full	
Non-stepfamilies - Twins			DZ	MZ

FIG. 3.1.   A summary of the research design showing how family structure and genetic similarity are distinguished.

on sibling comparisons, holding genetic relatedness between siblings constant, can be made between DZ twins, full-sibling stepfamilies, and the full siblings in the nondivorced controls. The second major advantage, deriving from the combination of twins and stepfamily design, is that the use of MZ twins is a pure test of the importance of the nonshared environment: Differential environmental factors cannot be caused by genetic differences, and correlations between these differences and differences in outcome cannot be mediated by genetic mechanisms. The third advantage in our design lies in the selection of the nondivorced controls. If findings relating nonshared environmental factors to outcome in the steps and twins are replicated in this group, then the generality of the findings is greatly strengthened.

The Selection of Dependent Measures

We approached the assessment of variation among adolescents, our dependent measures, informed by a life-span perspective. This perspective conceives of adolescence as a critical developmental period where young people can fashion options and opportunities as well as bring upon themselves constraints and obstacles, all of which, in turn, have profound influence on their subsequent development. In accord with this dual perspective, we focused on attributes that play a major role over the life course in predicting high levels of psychological adjustment and occupational satisfaction across the life span. Following Baumrind (1978), we selected two superordinate constructs: social agency and cognitive agency. We also examined three areas of problematic or pathologic functioning, all of which had opposite implications for the life course: forebodings of social and psychological maladjustment, psychological distress, and frank psychiatric disorder. Here, we again studied three domains: depression, conduct disorder, and substance abuse. In this last area we used scaled assessments by the adolescents themselves as well as by parents and teachers.

The Selection of Nonshared Environmental Measures

Two related theoretical perspectives guided our selection of environmental variables. The first was to use existing, traditional studies, almost all of which have used single-child designs, to select environmental or independent variables whose differences between siblings were likely to shape variation in adolescent development in any of the developmental outcomes just outlined. Here, we drew heavily not only on previous studies of adolescents, but, more specifically, on studies of adolescents in stepfamilies. We document these derivations in the section on measurement later in this chapter.

Second, we selected variables that would provide an insight into the factors in families that would shape or separate nonshared worlds for each sibling. Here, we used family systems theory—and some very preliminary empirical data—to fashion a set of hypotheses about the role of parental and sibling conflict. Briefly, our hypothesis is that the resolution of conflict is a fundamental task of all enduring marriages. Marital partners who cannot resolve conflicts by other means utilize their relationships with their children as an ongoing strategy in the resolution of this dilemma: Some children are brought closer into the marriage and others are distanced from it, and this differential distancing forms a core of the nonshared family environment for the siblings (Gilbert, Christensen, & Margolin, 1984). In an analogous fashion, siblings may resolve their own conflict by differentiating themselves from each other and their relationship with each parent (Schachter, 1982; Schachter, Gilutz, Shore, & Adler, 1978; Schachter, Shore, Feldman-Rotman, Marquis, & Campbell, 1976). Further, when one sibling is developing a stigmatized deviance, such as alcoholism, the other sibling may make special efforts to avoid developing the same condition (Cook & Goethe, 1990). It is interesting that, at least in some circumstances, there are clear relationships between marital and sibling conflict (Hetherington & Clingempeel, 1992; MacKinnon, 1988), so that nonshared environments may arise as a family-level strategy for dealing with ongoing conflict within the system. In designing our research, we extended this question about the role of intrafamily stress one step further. We wondered whether stress impinging on the family, particularly if not balanced by adequate external supports, might either enhance conflict and widen the gap between the separate sibling worlds, or whether it might operate to enhance the power, as an interacting factor, of nonshared effects.

SAMPLE

Our major task was to assemble a sample to provide adequate power for detecting moderate genetic effects while at the same time exploring the range and generality of nonshared effects. In Fig. 3.1, we illustrated the six groups of families required by our design. Power analysis revealed that to detect as statistically significant a genetic effect of 20%, at least 80% of the time, we needed at least 100 pairs of siblings in each of our six groups.

The enormous challenge posed by this plan was the extreme rarity of blended-sibling families. We wanted to sample only those blended-sibling families with long marital durations to insure that, like our twin, nondivorced, and half-sibling families, they would be well established and not still in the unstable phases of family formation. Thus, the most critical inclusion criterion of this sample, and the one that drove all other sampling procedures, was to include in our study only those blended stepfamilies where the marital duration was a minimum of 5 years. Because blended families have the highest divorce rates of all stepfamily types, we were searching for a rare species indeed. In order to estimate this rarity precisely, we worked with Dr. James McCarthy and the Current

Population Survey; this survey contains 63,000 households selected at random by the 1980 U.S. Census in order to obtain both household composition and fertility information. This was the only census data that permitted accurate identifications of stepfamilies and clarified the biological relationships of the children and parents in the same household. Of the families in these 63,000 households, less than .05% met our criteria for blended families and only .1% for half siblings. Thus, conventional sampling techniques, where we would search the population at large for our sample, were out of the question. It then became essential to locate a pool of households about which we knew at least the age and number of children and the number and marital status of the adults in the home. A pool of this kind would vastly simplify our search by focusing on a smaller and manageable group that could then be screened, at reasonable cost, for the desired sample.

Two large market panels offered almost ideal resources at reasonable cost. Market panels are assembled by commercial survey companies in order to assess consumer preferences of interest to a variety of business concerns. Lists of households are compiled using "list brokers" who rely on census tract information, warranty lists, magazine subscriptions, and similar sources. The ongoing aim is to make these panels representative of the U.S. population on a number of dimensions, such as geographic region, household annual income, population density of area of residence, age of adults, and household size. Despite these efforts, the panels are slightly skewed toward higher homeownership, higher incomes, and Caucasians. Also, panel members typically are dropped permanently from the panels by Market Facts or National Family Opinion if they fail to respond to two survey attempts.

These skews are reflected in any subsample systematically drawn from these panels. Thus, we attempted to create a truly representative sample of families in our most numerous category: the nondivorced. This sample provides an opportunity to see whether nonshared effects, detected in our other five samples, can be generalized to a truly representative sample. In order to obtain these families, we randomly dialed 10,000 telephone numbers throughout the United States and identified 210 nondivorced families who were eligible for our study. Of these, 96 completed data collection. This 46% response rate could have been substantially increased using the typical, although strenuous, follow-up efforts characteristic of high quality surveys. However, owing to the enormous demands of our protocol and the dispersal of these families in 48 states, these follow-up efforts proved to be extraordinarily expensive. Similar response rates were obtained for our stepfamilies. Sampling proceeded in the following steps.

First, to make our six groups of families as comparable to each other as possible, we specified minimum inclusion criteria for all families: Each family was to have at least two children of the same gender, between the ages of 10 and 18, no further than 4 years of age apart. Further, as mentioned, to assure that none of our stepfamilies was in the unstable, early phases of family formation, we specified that the current marriage in all families be at least 5 years in duration. Finally, to resolve variation in the residence of children in stepfamilies due to custody issues, we required that all children included in the study be residents in the household at least half of the time.

Second, we drew our nondivorced sample from the pool developed by random telephone dialing. Some full-sibling stepfamilies, half-sibling families, and blended families were also drawn in this sample; thus, each of the stepfamily groups have some families obtained from the random digit dialing procedure, which allows for some analyses of the effect of sample source on our data.

Third, we arranged with Market Facts of Oak Park, Illinois to completely review their panel of 275,000 households and National Family Opinion, Inc. of Toledo, Ohio to review the full 400,000 members of their panel. These reviews indicated that 30,730 of the total of 675,000 households were two-parent households with at least two children. These households were surveyed with a brief, mail-back questionnaire that inquired about the current marital status and duration of marriage of the male and female head of household, the birth date and gender of each child in the household, the relationship of each child (biological, step, adopted, or "other") to each adult head of household, and the amount of time each child lived in the household. Eighty-two percent of the Market Facts households responded, as did 74% of the National Family Opinion households. This yielded a potential pool of 760 full-sibling, 229 half-sibling, and 295 blended-sibling families. From this, we drew 181, 110, and 130 families, respectively.

Fourth, to increase the comparability of the stepfamily groups to one another, and before drawing the final sample, we matched the three by age of oldest child and age spacing. Social and educational status could not be a basis for matching because socioeconomic data were not available to us prior to actually interviewing the families. Matching was accomplished by selecting those full-sibling stepfamilies, our most numerous stepfamily type, so that they matched the halfs and blendeds as closely as possible on the age of child variables. The matching was done by stratifying the full-sibling families by age of oldest child and age spacing and then drawing randomly and proportionately from each strata to minimize difference among the means of the age variables of the three stepfamily groups.

Fifth, we also drew our twin sample from the market panel surveys. We began by selecting families with same-sex twins. Because approximately half of same-sex twins are MZ and half are DZ (Plomin, DeFries, & McClearn, 1990), a random selection is likely to yield equal numbers of both types. However, participation rates are often higher for MZ than DZ twins (Lykken, McGue, & Tellegen, 1987); therefore, we monitored the proportion as the sample was drawn to try to assure approximately equal numbers. Zygosity was determined by a self-report questionnaire, designed specifically for adolescent twins whose accuracy, compared to blood tests of zygosity, is over 90% (Nichols & Bilbro, 1966).

The net result of these efforts is a scientific sample that is unusually precious. Clearly, each of the groups is large enough to provide the power necessary to examine our central question about the association of nonshared variables and developmental outcome and to determine the extent to which genetics mediates these associations. Further, the internal validity of the design should be high because of the care in matching the six groups. Also, the external validity should be high given the quasirandom process for drawing the entire sample, its economic and geographic diversity, and the randomly drawn nondivorced sample. Moreover, it is the largest sample of stepfamilies of its kind ever assembled for the direct study of family processes. Particularly rare are the blended and half-sibling stepfamilies and stepfamilies with long marital duration. The sample also permits an extensive exploration of the genetics of adolescent disorders and competence about which little is known as well as the genetic bases of environmental process. Finally, this is one of the largest samples of siblings ever assembled. The study provides an unprecedented opportunity to explore sibling concordances on a range of assessments of competence and psychopathology, as well as to contribute to an understanding of the sibling relationship. Moreover, because it is approximately representative of the U.S. population, this sample should fuel a critical initiative in epidemiology: pairwise prevalence rates. We can answer a question such as, "If one adolescent in the family is depressed what is the probability that the same-sex adolescent closest in age has a conduct disorder?" Pairwise prevalence rates, within and across disorders, are useful clues to the pathogenesis of psychiatric disorder.

This chapter draws on analyses of the first 214 of our families tested. This group consisted of 78 full-sibling families, 71 of which were from our nondivorced group and 6 from stepfamilies; 70 half-sibling families; and 66 blended-sibling families. Table 3.1 presents the demographic characteristics of this "first look" sample. In general, these three samples are very closely matched, even though this sample did not benefit from the planned matching that was carried out only among the full-sibling stepfamilies and the halfs and blendeds. The most consistent differences are those for social status variables: Income, occupational prestige, and education where the half-sibling families are typically a bit lower than the other two. There are also some small age effects. For example, the youngest of the two children (Child 2) was older in the blended group than in the other two groups. Also, the mothers of these blended siblings were younger than the mothers in the other two groups. Finally, because most of the full siblings in this partial sample came from nondivorced families, we expected a major difference in marital duration across our three family types; this, in fact, was observed.

TABLE 3.1

Demographic Characteristics of Sample by Family Types and Sibling Types

(N = 214; 111 boys, 103 girls)

| | Family Type | | | | | | Sibling Type | | | | | | | | |
| | Control | | | Step | | | Full | | | Half | | | Unrelated | | |
Characteristics	N	X	SD	N	X	SD	N	X	SD	N	X	SD	N	X	SD
Age Child 1	71	14.9	1.82	143	14.9	1.99	78	14.9	1.87	70	14.7	1.84	66	15.0	2.10
Child 2	71	12.5	1.86	142	12.6	2.01	78	12.6	1.92	70	12.1	1.73	65	13.1*	2.13
Number of Children in the Family	71	3.3	1.28	143	3.4	1.32	78	3.4	1.31	70	3.2	1.32	66	3.6	1.28
Family Income	71	6.4	1.67	142	6.4	1.33	78	6.4	1.65	70	6.1	1.39	65	6.7*	1.18
Hollingshead's Social Status Index	66	46.4	9.93	129	40.4*	10.07	73	46.7	9.62	61	38.8	9.61	61	41.0*	10.39
Years of Education Father	70	14.6	2.53	141	13.5*	2.59	77	14.5	2.49	68	13.0	2.66	66	14.0*	2.49
Mother	71	13.8	2.34	142	13.2	2.06	78	13.9	2.38	70	13.2	2.13	65	13.1*	1.84
Age Father	71	40.7	5.31	141	39.7	5.65	78	40.5	5.45	68	40.3	5.96	66	39.2	5.21
Mother	71	38.5	4.55	141	36.5*	3.72	78	38.3	4.47	68	36.2	3.94	66	36.8*	3.57
Marital Duration (years)	56	17.9	4.82	133	10.5*	4.11	60	17.2	5.33	67	13.6	2.52	62	7.3*	2.82

| | Family Type | | | | Sibling Type | | | | | |
| | Control | | Step | | Full | | Half | | Unrelated | |
Characteristics	N	%	N	%	N	%	N	%	N	%
Ethnic Identity										
Father Caucasian	66	93.0	129	90.2	72	92.3	64	91.3	59	89.4
Other	5	7.0	14	9.8	6	7.7	6	8.7	7	10.6
Mother Caucasian	66	93.0	131	92.3	72	92.3	65	92.9	60	92.3
Other	5	7.0	11	7.7	6	7.7	5	7.1	5	7.7
Place of Residence										
Father Urban	12	17.1	23	16.3	14	18.2	7	10.1	14	21.5*
Suburban	22	31.4	25	17.7	24	31.2	14	20.3	9	13.9
Small town	17	24.3	42	29.8	18	23.4	27	39.1	14	21.5
Rural	19	27.1	51	36.2	21	27.3	21	30.4	28	43.1
Mother Urban	9	13.2	18	12.9	11	14.7	6	8.8	10	15.4
Suburban	25	36.8	32	22.9	27	36.0	14	20.6	16	24.6
Small town	18	26.5	37	26.4	19	25.3	23	33.8	13	20.0
Rural	16	23.5	53	37.9	18	24.0	25	36.8	26	40.0
Religion										
Father Protestant	38	55.9	62	44.9	41	54.7	34	50.8	25	39.1
Roman Catholic	15	22.1	30	21.7	17	22.7	12	17.9	16	25.0
Other	11	16.2	34	24.6	13	17.3	16	23.9	16	25.0
None	4	5.9	12	8.7	4	5.3	5	7.5	7	10.9
Mother Protestant	36	52.2	73	52.9	38	50.7	38	55.9	33	51.6
Roman Catholic	17	24.6	31	22.5	20	26.7	14	20.6	14	21.9
Other	13	18.8	29	21.0	14	18.7	14	20.6	14	21.9
None	3	4.4	5	3.6	3	4.0	2	2.9	3	4.7

*$p < .05$ for family types and sibling types.

Note: 1. Hollingshead's social status index ranges from 8 to 66 and can be grouped into five social strata, which are presented in Table 3.2.

2. The codes of family income are: 1 = under \$5,000; 2 = \$5,000 to \$9,999; 3 = \$10,000 to \$14,999; 4 = \$15,000 to \$19,999; 5 = \$20,000 to \$24,999; 6 = \$25,000 to \$34,999; 7 = \$35,000 to \$49,999; and 8 = \$50,000 or more.

MEASUREMENT

As indicated earlier, two major objectives shaped our strategy for measurement. The first was to define a set of outcome measures that capture critical aspects of adolescent development, particularly those that play the largest role in the youngsters' successful transition into adult life. The second major objective was to delineate those aspects of the nonshared environment that are likely to play a significant role in shaping these variations in adolescent development.

Beyond these two central foci of our study, measurement was directed at other critical objectives as well. For example, we wanted to learn about features of the family system that might develop and maintain separate worlds for siblings in the same family; in the introduction we pointed to the importance of marital and sibling conflict, within the family as well as stress and supports coming from outside the family. In addition, we wanted to assess assumptions underlying our genetically sensitive model. Can we estimate heritability by comparing groups of siblings that differ in the amount of genetic relatedness, or are these comparisons confounded by nongenetic differences among these groups of siblings? We describe, very briefly, the rationale for the measures we have selected to meet all of these objectives. (A complete list of measures can be found in Appendix A.)

Objective 1: Critical Variation Among Adolescents Central to Their Development Across the Life Span

Our measures here are equally balanced between assessment of competence and psychopathology.

Competence

As already mentioned, we follow Baumrind (1978) in delineating two aspects of competence: social agency and cognitive agency. Social agency has several components. The first is the concept of social maturity developed originally by Gough (1966) in his studies discriminating delinquents from nondelinquents and those of his students distinguishing cheaters and noncheaters on examinations (Hetherington & Feldman, 1964). We use this approach here to focus on variation among adolescents in their internalization of social norms, while at the same time showing a sensitive and flexible regard for the rights and perspectives of others. These assessments played a critical role in understanding resilient youngsters in the Kaui study (Werner & Smith, 1982) as well as adults who achieve a broad range of psychological health and work satisfaction in the Berkeley Guidance and Oakland Growth Studies (Brooks, 1981). Related concepts include social competence as rated by others (Hetherington & Clingempeel, 1992) and as perceived by the adolescent (Harter, 1988, 1990).

The concept of cognitive competence refers to the level of self-confidence a child has in his or her own academic and intellectual ability, as well as more objective ratings of academic and intellectual performance. In the course of adolescent development, school achievement plays a unique broad and critical role in protecting youngsters from psychopathology and promoting positive psychological growth. For example, school achievement is negatively associated with depression (Puig-Antich et al., 1985) and with conduct disorder (Graubard, 1971; Rutter, 1970) and was among the most important protective factors in Werner and Smith's (1982) study of high-risk children.

Social and cognitive agency probably operate jointly to enhance initiative and autonomy in adolescence. Recently, measures have been developed to assess autonomous functioning of adolescents in their families, among friends, and in their own activities and work experiences (Sigafoos, Feinstein, Damond, & Reiss, 1988). Initiative and autonomy in early adolescence has, itself, predicted a broad range of adaptation in adults (Vaillant & Vaillant, 1981). Indeed, the capacity to plan activities with initiative and effectiveness in early childhood was Vaillant's best predictor of mental health in middle-aged men, even when such potent predictors as social class and problematic families were taken into account.

Psychopathology

As the conceptualization and measurement of psychopathology in adolescence has improved, its implication for adult development can be assessed more critically. From studies accumulating across the last two decades, we have the clearest picture of the role of conduct disturbances. A large percentage of children who show severe conduct disorder problems by early adolescence go on to severe psychopathology in adulthood. Antisocial personality disorders are the most frequent outcomes, but a broad range of other psychopathology also is precedented by adolescent conduct disorders including alcoholism, organic brain syndromes, and somatization and conversion disorders (Robins, 1966). A recent study suggests that conduct disorders may be the central gateway to most adult psychopathology (Robins & Price, 1991). We know less about the adult sequelae of adolescent depression. In the Robins and Price study, depressive symptoms functioned quite differently from conduct disorder, predicting psychotic illness rather than adult antisocial or somatoform disorders. In a more recent study (Kandel & Davies, 1986), adolescent depression not only predicted adult depressive symptoms, but significant disruptions in heterosexual ties for men and women. This is notable, insofar as depression is regularly associated with marital distress in adults and has particularly devastating effects in parenting effectiveness. A picture is now just emerging of the developmental consequences of substance abuse in adolescence. For example, heavy alcohol use in adolescence predicts not only adult alcohol abuse, but also difficulties in occupational adjustment. The additional abuse of illegal drugs, in both men

and women, presages more devastating adult developmental outcomes including adult substance abuse, work difficulties, marital disruption, and physical health
difficulties (Kandel, Davies, Karus, & Yamaguchi, 1986).

Objective 2: Important Starting Points
for Characterizing the Nonshared Worlds of Adolescents

As we have indicated, this study is poised between familiar territory and un-
charted terrain. A few pilot studies have specifically examined nonshared environments; their results suggest that there may be systematic, across-family
correlations between nonshared variables and developmental outcome. However,
none of these studies has used a sample of offspring of the age range we have
selected, and only one used direct observational data. Thus, these pilot data
provide more hope than specific guidelines for the selection of variables. Rather
than empirically grounded theory, we have only more general perspectives to
aid us in the selection of measures.

The first general perspective suggested by the preliminary data is the potential
importance of sibling and peer relationships, along with the more traditional measures of parenting processes. Second, a range of empirical work has clarified
the central developmental tasks of adolescence, and gives a strong clue to the
kinds of environmental variables that may be critical; this work has been ampli-
fied by a recent and more precise understanding of the unfolding of adolescence
within stepfamilies. Finally, there have been substantial advances in methods
for measuring parent–child and sibling relationships and, to a much lesser extent, peer relationships. These advances are, of course, of uncertain relevance
for our current design, because few have been utilized in studies of the nonshared environment. However, many of these measures share three important
features. First, they assess the relationship between a parent, sibling, or peer
with a particular or individual child. Thus, it is at least technically possible that
they would show relatively low correlations between siblings, across families.
Second, they reflect processes that are, despite their having no ''track record''
in nonshared studies, good bets as important nonshared variables in adolescent
development. Third, they are psychometrically sound.

Parent–Child Measures

As we indicated in the previous section, adolescence is a time for solidi-
fying developmental gains that make it possible for the youngster to move
effectively into the demands of young adulthood. Our study focuses on the
maintenance and strengthening of self-esteem, along with the capacity for self-
regulation of behavior, the formulation of occupational and educational objectives, and the increasing development of autonomy and self-direction. A range
of previous studies that have used only one child per family suggest that the

following parenting processes may influence these developmental processes in adolescence.

Warmth and Support. This refers to the degree of empathy and rapport between the parent and child as well as the level of affection that is expressed and the degree of mutual involvement in enjoyable activities. Self-disclosure by both parents and children is also an important indicator of this construct (Hetherington & Clingempeel, 1992). In single-child studies, these processes appeared to support social competence and academic achievement as well as buffered against a range of psychopathology in nondivorced and stepfamilies (Hetherington & Clingempeel, 1992). Other data from single-child studies suggests its importance in the maintenance of self-esteem in adolescence (Bell & Bell, 1983). One nonshared study, as noted previously, has examined differences in maternal and paternal affection as recalled by older adolescents and young adults; siblings who received more affection had more ambitious educational and occupational objectives (Daniels, 1987).

Control. Control may begin with attempts by parents to clearly structure their own relationship with their children, as well as to directly shape their behavior. Although this variable reflects clear limit setting, it may have positive developmental outcomes. Indeed, two of the preliminary nonshared studies show positive associations for father's controlling behavior as recalled by late adolescents and young adults (Daniels, 1987) and by older adults (Baker & Daniels, 1990).

Monitoring. This construct reflects the ongoing knowledge parents have about their children's activities, and how this knowledge is used to influence or shape these activities. The activities they monitor may be those related to healthy character development, such as intellectual interests and choice of friends, or deviant behavior, such as promiscuous sexuality, use of drugs, and problem behavior in school. The centrality of monitoring has been shown in a series of nonclinical samples by Baumrind (1978) and in studies of conduct disorder by Patterson and his group (Patterson, 1982). Monitoring may be related to effective parental control or may even, itself, represent a noncoercive form of control. It may also be intrusive and stimulate serious parent–child conflict.

Coercion, Conflict, and Negativity. Across childhood and young adulthood, control has also more negative connotations, probably because it becomes excessive and intrusive and is more aptly termed *coercion*. Thus, one study of young children focusing on differences in maternal control between siblings found the child receiving most control to show greater signs of both internalizing and externalizing (Dunn et al., 1990). Conflict may also belong in this domain; it refers to the frequency and intensity of observed and self-reported disputes in a relationship as well as feelings of anger. As might be expected, it is regularly associated with impaired functioning in both childhood and adolescence. In single studies with one child per family, in both nondivorced and stepfamilies, parental conflict and negativity toward the child was associated with reduced academic and social achievement and increased psychopathology (Hetherington & Clingempeel, 1992).

Our focus, of course, is on sibling differences in the warmth, control, monitoring, and conflict they receive. However, there is another way of understanding and measuring sibling differences that considers the structure of relationships in a family. For example, siblings may be differentially involved in parental conflict. Recently, family researchers (Gilbert et al., 1984, and Vuchinich, Emery, & Cassidy, 1988) have confirmed reports by clinicians that family fights often involve children and, further, that children may be differentially involved. For example, the marital couple may fight more in the presence of one child than another, involve one child in arguments more frequently, or pressure the child to take sides. In this sense, marriage in the family may be quite different for different children. As a consequence of these skewed relationships, one sibling may be more involved in conflicted interaction with the parents than the other. However, a better understanding of these simple differences, ones that would show up in comparing measures of negativity between parent and Sibling 1 and Sibling 2, may be obtained by direct measures of unbalanced, asymmetrical, or differentially involving relationships within the same family. We have developed or adapted some of these in the current study.

Sibling Measures

Compared with a voluminous literature on parent–child relationships and their influence of adolescent development using one child per family, there is much less literature on the impact of sibling relationships. Given that sibling relationships are the most enduring of family relationships, this is a surprising lack. Recent data suggest that the sibling relationship has an impact on individual differences in development across the life span. For example, in childhood and adolescence, sibling relationships are related to the development of social sensitivity (Light, 1979), as well as children's competence in the use of symbols. Likewise, at the other end of the life span, sibling relationships have a significant association with a range of measures of well-being in adults (Cicirelli, 1980, 1982). More recently, Hetherington and Clingempeel (1992) specified the importance of conflictual sibling relationships in the development of externalizing behavior in children in both stepfamilies and nondivorced families. Most recently, several pilot studies of the impact of the nonshared environment have suggested that asymmetrical or differential sibling relationships may have a role equal to that of parents on a range of developmental outcomes. These most recent findings have influenced our selection of measures. Conceptually, we attempted to develop two of the four domains that we used for parent–child measures: (a) warmth/support, control, and care taking, and (b) conflict and negativity.

Warmth/Support. The helping and supporting relationship between one sibling and another has been studied across the life span from early childhood (Dunn & Kendrick, 1982a), to middle childhood (Bryant, 1982), to mid-life (Troll, 1975), and to old age (Cicirelli, 1980). In two studies specifically examining differential care taking, several correlations with developmental outcomes were observed. For example, the sibling who showed the most care taking was the least fearful and shy, on a measure of temperament (Daniels, 1987). In another study focusing on personality differences, the more care-taking sibling showed more masculine personality features during middle adulthood (Baker & Daniels, 1990).

Sibling closeness is a closely related concept. Components of this concept include empathy and involvement and, on the negative pole, avoidance. In assessments of differential sibling closeness, the sibling who felt the closer to the cosibling also was the most sociable and the least shy of the siblings (Daniels, 1987).

Conflict and Negativity. As studied thus far, moderate levels of conflict are endemic in sibling relationships (Dunn & Kendrick, 1982b; Furman & Buhrmester, 1985; Montemayor & Hanson, 1985). However, evidence suggests that these patterns of conflict are generally mixed with more positive feelings and behavior, including care taking as described earlier (Dunn & Kendrick, 1982a). Differential sibling antagonism may, by itself, be an important component of the nonshared environment. However, siblings may transform these feelings into another form of nonshared experience. Because of their ambivalence about conflict with each other, siblings may hide it through a process Schachter called "deidentification" and "split parent identification" (Schachter, 1982; Schachter et al., 1978; Schachter et al., 1976). Siblings seeking to contain conflict with one another develop conceptions of themselves as quite unlike their cosibling and, correspondingly, conceptions of themselves as a parent different from their cosibling. Presumably, these splits allow siblings to tolerate conflict because they diffuse feelings of entitlement to the same sorts of accomplishment, parental praise, and resources as the cosiblings. They serve as self-constructed rationalizations: "I'm different from my sibling so it is no wonder that I have different talents and my parents treat me differently." These processes of resolving conflict may also serve to contain rivalry (see later in chapter). In studies of the nonshared environment, differential antagonism has been correlated with personality outcomes in older adolescents: The more antagonistic twin shows more emotionality on a measure of temperament (Daniels, 1987).

Jealousy may be a quality of sibling relationship closely related to conflict.

In several studies of sibling relationships, jealousy is a dimension that is separable from antagonism, although this concept also includes feelings of rivalry (Daniels & Plomin, 1985). In nonshared studies of differential jealousy, the more jealous sibling also shows greater tendencies, when measured on individual temperament measure, to anger (Daniels, 1987) and to experience all feelings with greater intensity (Baker & Daniels, 1990).

Peer Measures

A sizable literature has developed on peer relationships of adolescents. Most of it views these relationships as outcomes of development. More recently, there have been systematic efforts to understand the role of peer relationships as determinants of adolescent development (Kandel, 1973; Patterson, Capaldi, & Bank, in press). From a logical point of view, peer relationships are a likely source of nonshared influences on development, because siblings are likely to have their own peer networks, which might be quite different from each other along a number of dimensions. One sibling study suggests that there are greater differences between siblings in their peer relationships than in their parent or sibling relationships (Daniels & Plomin, 1985). Further, early sibling studies of the nonshared environment as well as single-child studies suggest four relevant dimensions along which peer systems might differ and that these differences might shape outcome. Because of the immense technical demands of direct observation of peer relationships in a study of this size and geographical dispersion, we relied on three interview and questionnaire measures of peer relationships given to the adolescents themselves, the parents, and teachers. These four domains were examined.

Peer Popularity.   This measure refers to the importance an adolescent peer group attaches to positive social relationships. In two sibling studies of the nonshared environment differential peer popularity was associated with high scores on a personality assessment of sociability (Daniels, 1987) and extraversion (Baker & Daniels, 1990).

Peer College Orientation.   In single-child studies, the impact of peers on academic achievement has been substantiated. This finding has been replicated in sibling studies of the nonshared environment, where it has been associated with higher educational and occupational aspirations (Daniels, 1987).

Peer Delinquency and Substance Abuse.   These two are measured separately. Differences between Sibling 1 and Sibling 2 in the level of delinquency or substance abuse among their peers are each expected to be positively related to variation in conduct disorder and substance abuse in the adolescents and negatively related to levels of their social and cognitive agency.

Objective 3: Detecting the Social Origins and Modifiers, in Social Systems, of the Differential Environments of Siblings

Our study is designed as more than a comprehensive survey of possible non-shared factors and their association with adolescent outcome. We seek to understand the social processes that may give rise to nonshared environmental process and those that may modify their effects on outcome. As beginning work in this field, we have selected three very different areas for preliminary inquiry: marital conflict, dissatisfaction, and instability; parental stress and household disorganization; and child's pubertal status.

Marital Conflict, Dissatisfaction, and Instability. Marital conflict refers to the frequency and intensity of verbal and physical confrontations, arguments, and disputes in marriage. More microscopically, it is manifest in frequent, lengthy, and reciprocal exchanges of negative affect. Although marital conflict is usually associated with marital dissatisfaction, this is not invariably the case. Even more important is to distinguish marital conflict and dissatisfaction from marital instability. The latter refers to active thoughts and steps, by each spouse, directed toward divorce. In our own preliminary analyses, a traditional measure of marital satisfaction, the Locke-Wallace test (Locke & Wallace, 1959), correlated -0.56 with a well-developed index of marital instability (Booth, Johnson, & Edwards, 1983). This suggests that most of the variance assessed by these two measures did not overlap. As indicated earlier, marital dissatisfaction and instability may lead to nonshared environments by their differential impact on the parenting of one child versus the other and by stimulating sibling conflict and the ensuing process of deidentification and split parent identification.

Parental Stress and Household Disorganization. Under conditions of severe stress and disorganization, children may be more sensitive to differences in their treatment from the parents, from each other, and from their peers. Analytically, we expect levels of marital conflict and instability to be positively associated with the magnitude of differences between siblings, across families, in parenting, sibling, and peer variables. However, for parental stress and household disorganization we are expecting moderating effects: These variables will interact with our nonshared variables so that at high levels of stress and disorganization, nonshared effects on adolescent outcome will, we hypothesize, be significantly greater than at low levels of these variables.

Puberty. The literature suggests three different effects of puberty relevant for our study. First are impacts of puberty on family process. Thus, for the subset of our families where one child is well along in puberty but the other is prepubescent, differential levels of puberty may lead to differential parent-child and sibling–sibling relationships. Data from several sources suggest that puberty may increase parent–child conflict and distance, particularly between adolescent children, both boys and girls, and their mothers (Steinberg, 1989). Other observational studies suggest that pubescence may lead to greater inhibition by parents of assertiveness by daughters but more aggressive and assertive behavior by boys with their parents (Hill, 1988). A precious scientific opportunity should be noted in our sample of dizygotic twins. A small but richly informative subset of these families will have children discordant for pubescent status. This allows a precise test of the differential impact of the status of puberty on nonshared family relationships while controlling for family, age, and gender.

A second consideration is that puberty may itself contribute to variation in outcome measures. For example, anorexia nervosa in girls shows a distinct spurt in incidence and prevalence in early adolescence, a rise that may be linked to pubertal changes. The same is true for depression in girls (Cantwell & Baker, in press) and conduct disorder in boys (Brooks-Gunn & Reiter, 1990). In these instances, regression techniques and covariance analyses will be important to separate the contributions of nonshared environmental and differential pubertal status on variations in outcome measures.

Third, puberty may influence the impact of parental behavior (and possibly sibling and peer behavior) on outcome. In this case, it may serve as a moderating or interacting variable.

Objective 4: Testing the Assumptions of Our Genetically Sensitive Design

In addition to these three major objectives, we developed measures to help us detect possible artifacts in our design. Many developmental investigators have argued that comparisons made among groups of families by behavioral geneticists are open to several interpretations. For example, it is often argued that families may treat identical twins more similarly than fraternal twins for entirely social reasons, rather than genetic ones. Likewise, differences between families with adopted children and those with biological children may be due to social rather than genetic causes. These concerns have been examined in detail (Loehlin & Nichols, 1976; Scarr & Carter-Saltzman, 1979; Scarr, Scarf, & Weinberg, 1980). Nonetheless, it is good to raise them again in the current study, because we are the first to use stepfamilies in a design that is sensitive to genetic influences. Might there be differences among our three types of stepfamilies that are more properly attributable to social rather than genetic influences?

One major artifact might arise from parents' beliefs about their genetic relatedness to their children. For example, in blended families, each child is biologically related to one parent and not to the other. Thus, each parent may treat the child who he or she believes is biologically related to him or her differently than the one who is believed to be biologically unrelated to that parent. For this reason alone, the blended siblings may have very different developmental outcomes. To examine the question about the role of biological beliefs or labeling, we have designed two new instruments. The first measures parents' beliefs about characteristics that might be inherited. These include physical characteristics, such as hair color, height, and weight; personality characteristics; and psychopathology. The second measures parents' perceptions of their similarity to Sibling 1 and Sibling 2 on each of these characteristics. Taken together, these instruments are designed to tap the parents' subjective construction of their own genetic relationship to each child. For example, if a mother believes that physical appearance is highly heritable and rates herself as very similar in appearance to her son, we can assume that she believes that she is genetically related to her son. We expect considerable variation in these beliefs about genetic relatedness within each of our subsamples. For example, many people believe that children get all or most of their genes from their mother; thus, in our blended families, fathers may differ in their beliefs of how related their child is to them, even though we know that they share 50% of their genes. Along these same lines, parents often believe that there is a great deal of difference in the proportion of their genes that they transmit to their different children. We take advantage of natural variation in these beliefs to determine the role of subjective genetic linkages in comparison to objective ones.

A third measure assesses parents' attitudes about the relative parental roles and responsibilities of biological and adopting parents in order to determine the role that these expectations, in contrast to genetic differences, may have on contrasts among our three groups of adoptive parents. Here, we do not do a fine-grained analysis of variation in beliefs about genetic relatedness; rather, we inquire about more global attitudes toward biological and step-parenting.

ANALYSIS AND RESULTS

Sequence of Analyses for Nonshared Effects

Our research design requires that we ask a series of logically ordered questions of our data. The first question reflects the sensitivity of any estimates of the effects of the nonshared environment to reliability of measurement. Our initial query, then, is what is the reliability of each of our measures *in this sample*? Second, do our measures of the environment, in fact, show that siblings live in different social worlds; are siblings really different? Third, for those measures that do show a sizable and reliable difference between siblings, to what factors can these differences be attributed? It is possible for example, that the difference may simply reflect birth order with the older child always receiving more of X than the younger; in this case we would do well to study birth order directly. It is also possible that differences reflect differences in heritable characteristics of the child. The fourth step in our analysis is to relate differences between Sibling 1 and Sibling 2 to developmental outcome. For every adolescent in our sample we can compute, for any independent variable, a difference between his or her score and that of the sibling (Sibling 1 – Sibling 2). This difference is then compared to that adolescent's score on any theoretically appropriate outcome measure. A knowledge of the possible genetic basis for nonshared environmental processes permits us to estimate the extent to which genetic factors may mediate these associations. A fifth question follows naturally from these first four: Which comes first, variation in environmental difference or variation in outcome? The answer to this question depends on longitudinal data that we plan to collect but do not, as yet, have in hand. Analyses of these data would begin to resolve questions about causal priority between environmental and outcome variables.

An Example of the Links Between
the Nonshared Environment and Adolescent Development

In the current exemplification of our analytic strategy we have picked two outcome measures and a single environmental measure. For our dependent measure, we have selected two broad-band measures of psychopathology on a shortened version of the well-known Achenbach Child Behavior Checklist (Achenbach & Edelbrock, 1983) developed by Zill and Peterson (Peterson & Zill, 1986). This checklist was given to each parent to rate each of the two siblings in the study and was also given to each of the two children in the family for them to report on their own symptoms. We use two scores: "Internalizing" sums items reflecting anxiety, depression, and social withdrawal, and "externalizing" reflects antisocial behavior, temper tantrums, and argumentativeness.

The nonshared environment variable is the difference in magnitude between siblings in their experience of threatening behavior from their parents as measured by the Symbolic Aggression subscale of the Conflict Tactics (CT) scale (Straus, 1979). The CT scale was used to query both children and parents about the frequency with which they used certain behaviors to resolve conflict. A Reasoning subscale included such items as "discussed calmly," and a Violence subscale included such items as "slapped other." The Symbolic Aggression subscale included intermediate items, such as "insulted other" and "threatened to hit." The CT scale is one of several instruments we used in which each family member reported on his or her own behaviors to each of the other members in the study (e.g., father reported on his own behavior toward his wife and each of the two siblings) as well as on the behavior of each of the others toward him or her (e.g., father reported on the behavior of mother and each sibling toward him). In addition, for all children in the study who had a nonresidential parent, the child and residential parent reported on the child's behavior toward the nonresidential parent and that parent's behavior toward the child. This strategy of measurement allows an unusually comprehensive comparative assessment of perceived behaviors in the family. For example, it allows for round-robin analysis that asks whether interaction behavior, observed or reported, is a unique product of a particular relationship or, rather, reflects a general trait or interactional style of one or the other individual in that relationship (Kenny & La Voie, 1984). In the current exemplification, we focus on each residential parent's behavior toward each of the two children as reported by both the children and the parents.

Reliability

Self-report measures, when used the way they are in this study, allow two forms of reliability assessment. By examining interitem correlations we can compute internal consistency reliability using coefficient *alpha*, which is a very conservative estimate of reliability.

A second approach to reliability is to measure interrater agreement. Where investigators can train raters according to exacting standards, interrater agreement can be considered a test of the reliability of the instrument and its scores. When the raters are untrained members of the family, interrater agreement is less informative about the instrument and more informative about the family itself. Where family members show agreement this suggests that what they are rating is conspicuous. However, where they disagree we might reason that members are observing different behaviors as a basis for their ratings or that the behaviors in question are more apparent to some members than others. An interesting case arises when all three or more members of the family are all rating the same behavior, feeling, or interaction. Some dyads may consistently show high levels of agreement—for instance, parents—whereas other dyads do not, as in the case of parents and children; a pattern of this kind may reflect a coalition. Whatever the reasons, if interrater agreements are low for any score, then one would be hesitant to aggregate scores on the same scale, across raters, in any multivariate procedure.

The internal consistency reliability and interrater agreements of the internalizing and externalizing subscales of the Zill symptom checklist for each child are shown in Table 3.2. The table also shows internal and interrater agreements of the Symbolic Aggression subscale. It suggests that internal consistency reliability is adequate for these measures. It also shows that the agreements are low between mother and child and father and child for the mother's symbolic aggression toward the child, the father's aggression, and the child's aggression toward the parents.

The interrater agreements on the Zill provide additional information. As on the Symbolic Aggression subscale, they show low parent–child agreements. The

TABLE 3.2
Interrater Correlations for Symbolic Aggression on the Conflict Tactics Scale
and Internalizing and Externalizing on the Zill Problem Behavior Scale
(May 14, 1990)

| | CTS—Symbolic Aggression | | | |
| | Child to Others | | Others to Child | |
	Child 1	Child 2	Child 1	Child 2
Mother	.16*	.29*	.27*	.27*
Father	.19*	.18*	.28*	.26*
Sibling	.30*	.40*	—	—

| | Zill—Internalizing Behavior | | | |
	Mother	Father	Child 1	Child 2
Mother	—	.52*[a]	.23*	.33*
Father	.46*[b]	—	.20*	.20*

| | Zill—Externalizing Behavior | | | |
	Mother	Father	Child 1	Child 2
Mother	—	.59*[a]	.25*	.34*
Father	.57*[b]	—	.26*	.19*

	Internal Consistency (α) CTS—Symbolic Aggression
Child's Perception**	α
Mother → Child	.72
Child → Mother	.81
Father → Child	.85
Child → Father	.75
Parent's Perception	
Mother → Child	.77
Child → Mother	.73
Father → Child	.77
Child → Father	.74

Zill Symptom Checklist

	Internalizing (6 items)	Externalizing (20 items)
Father**	.80	.91
Mother**	.79	.91
Child**	.75	.87

[a]Indicates correlation between mother and father reports of Child 1.
[b]Indicates correlation between mother and father reports of Child 2.
*Indicates $p < .05$.
**Psychometric analyses for Child 1 only.

Zill data also show mother–father agreements (not possible on symbolic aggression because we did not ask mothers to rate father aggression toward the child or vice versa). These agreements are substantially higher than the parent–child agreements; this pattern has been quite consistent for most measures in which we have mother, father, and child all rating the same scale (e.g., the Child Depression Inventory). In a limited sense, there is evidence for a coalition with parents perceiving their child's psychopathology somewhat differently than does the child. In subsequent analyses (not shown here) this pattern of findings has led to speculation on the distinction between public (depressive symptoms that are clearly apparent to both parents, hence their agreement) and private depression (depressive symptoms, such as suicidal thoughts, which may be known only to the adolescent). A similar distinction fits data about antisocial behavior: conspicuous versus concealed.

Sibling Differences in the Experience of Symbolic Aggression

For any measure of the environment, there are three approaches for characterizing differences between two siblings. The first is the correlation between siblings across families. This gives a good estimate of sibling similarity and, because it is standardized, is particularly effective for comparing different sources of ratings—parents with children, for example—as well as different environmental variables. However, the correlation coefficient does not provide a suitable statistic describing sibling environmental differences for an individual family and hence cannot be used to compare variation in these differences across families with variation in adolescent outcome variables. Here, we have two choices.

Relative difference scores require picking some invariant property of each sibling, such as birth order, and systematically subtracting the score of Sibling 2 (the youngest) from Sibling 1 (the oldest) across all families.

Absolute difference scores are the unsigned differences between the two siblings. Absolute and relative difference scores can be uncorrelated with each other and each positively correlated with the same criterion variable. As we note later, relative and absolute difference scores also index very different environmental processes, and thus interpretations drawn from one will be very different from interpretations drawn from the other.

A complete discussion of computational presentations of the nonshared environment can be found in chapter 2 of this volume, by Michael Rovine. That chapter describes a greater range of analytic options that we can explore in this chapter. For example, it shows how correlations between Sibling 1 and Sibling 2 can be incorporated into a residualized regression analysis, which specifies the unique contributions of Sibling 1's environment[1] to Sibling 1's outcome, its

---

[1]For example, the level of symbolic aggression shown by mother to Sibling 1.

effect on Sibling 2's outcome, and the comparable findings for Sibling 2's environment.

Table 3.3 presents data on absolute and relative difference scores for symbolic aggression, as well as the correlations between Sibling 1 and Sibling 2 scores. Note that the correlations are very low—nearly zero—for the children's perceptions of how they are treated by their parents but that the correlations are much higher for parents' perceptions of how they treat their children. Some of this difference may be due to the fact that a correlation of fathers' reports, for example, relates two different sets of reports, one for each sibling, by the same father. The children's reports are always correlating reports from two different children. As we show in the next section, it is unlikely that—in this case—this difference is entirely attributable to this effect of one versus two raters. For both parents and children, correlations are higher for how children treat their parents than for how parents treat their children. As expected from the correlations, parents as sources of ratings show lower absolute difference scores than do children as sources.

Note also that the mean relative difference scores are almost zero for all informants, indicating that there is no systematic birth order effect across families on threatening behavior of parents toward their children or children toward their parents.

We explored further this intriguing difference between parents, who make claims for great consistency, and children, who do not. Figure 3.2 shows that for 97 difference scores, parents' reports show very high levels of correlations between the siblings, whereas the children's correlations are much lower. This is true whether the targeted behavior is parenting or between-sibling interaction.

The Determinants of Sibling Differences

Clearly, there are sizable differences in how siblings are treated in the same family. A difference score of 5, for example, is 21% of the entire range of the Symbolic Aggression subscale. Three determinants of difference are of interest but for very different reasons.

First are differences due to simple family structural effects. We know from examining the relative difference scores that birth order is not an important contribution to differences, but the age of the siblings, their difference in age, their gender (whether the sibling pairs are male or female—we had no mixed pairs in this sample), and the number of other siblings in the residential household may be important. These variables could account for the tendency of siblings to be similar in the treatment they receive, particularly according to parents' accounts, or they could account for differences in sibling treatment. Family structural effects on nonshared environmental variables are important to isolate. Where these effects are large they are potentially important causes of nonshared environmental effects and should be studied as main effects in their own right.

TABLE 3.3

Correlations, Relative and Absolute Difference Scores for Symbolic Aggression

Variable	N	Older sib Mean (SD)	Young. sib Mean (SD)	Mean Relative Diff. Score (SD)	Mean Absolute Diff. Score (SD)	Correlation
Child's perception of:						
M's aggress to child	212	14.5 (5.4)	14.2 (5.5)	0.25 (7.4)	5.54 (4.9)	.08
Child's aggress to M	212	13.3 (5.8)	12.2 (5.3)	1.03 (6.9)	5.01 (4.8)	.24
F's aggress to child	214	11.4 (4.4)	11.4 (4.4)	0.66 (6.3)	4.68 (4.3)	.09
Child's aggress to F	209	10.1 (4.5)	10.1 (4.5)	0.81 (6.3)	4.11 (4.9)	.20
Parents' perception of:						
M's aggress to child	212	14.8 (5.8)	14.3 (5.7)	0.52 (5.9)	4.36 (4.0)	.48
Child's aggress to M	214	11.6 (5.8)	9.8 (4.2)	1.73 (2.9)	2.35 (2.4)	.77
F's aggress to child	209	13.4 (5.1)	12.7 (4.6)	0.59 (5.1)	3.87 (3.4)	.44
Child's aggress to F	212	11.0 (4.2)	9.1 (3.2)	1.85 (3.3)	2.44 (2.9)	.62

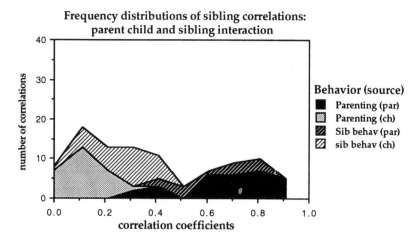

FIG. 3.2.   A comparison between the correlations for parents in their reports
on C1 and C2 and the correlations between the reports of C1 and C2. The figure
shows these comparisons for measures of parenting and for measures of the
siblings' interactions with each other. For both parenting and sibling interaction
measures the correlations for parent reports are much higher than those for child
reports.

For example, suppose that age spacing between the two siblings were highly
correlated with the difference in how much parental threatening behavior each
perceived. Then, difference in age should be studied for its impact on developmental outcomes; those nonshared environmental variables—in this instance
parental threatening behavior—would then be explored as mediators.

The second source for differences is indicators of family dynamics that might,
under most or under selected circumstances, lead to differences in how siblings
are treated. As already indicated, we have designed our study to explore the
extent to which the magnitude of differences between siblings, in environmental experience, reflects strategies or responses of the family in managing conflict.

A third source of differences is genetic effects. These are estimated by comparing between-sibling differences across our six groups of families, as we have
explained previously. Analytic models for determining genetic influence on within-
family (Sibling 1–Sibling 2) differences are still being developed; results of our
analyses of these effects will be reported elsewhere.

We examined the effects of genetic processes by comparing the correlation
between siblings of threatening behavior across our three groups of families as
shown in Table 3.4. Note that correlations of mothers' and fathers' reports of
their threatening behavior toward their children are higher for full siblings than
for other siblings, suggesting genetic effects on this behavior. In more detail,
mothers' correlations show a stepwise decline from full to half to blended sib-

TABLE 3.4
Sibling Correlations on the Conflict Tactics Scale (CTS) Threatening Behavior
for Full Siblings, Half-Siblings, and Unrelated Siblings

	Relationship		
Respondent	Full Sib	Half-Sib	Unrelated
Mother to child:			
Mother report	.67*	.47*	.16
Child report	.10	.04	.09
Father to child:			
Father report	.55*	.35*	.41*
Child report	.24*	−.07	.15
Sibling to child:			
Child report	.41*	.25*	.29*

*Indicates significance at $p < .05$.

lings, whereas fathers' correlations primarily involve a difference between the full siblings and the other two groups. Although the fathers' data may suggest nonadditive genetic variance (Plomin et al., 1990), it is equally likely that variable results such as these are to be expected given the small size of our preliminary sample. Model fitting techniques, described elsewhere (Plomin et al., 1990), estimate that the 78% of the total variance in symbolic aggression among mothers' reports is accounted for by additive genetic effects and 57% among fathers' reports. These findings, like others we are reporting here, are illustrative only and may be revised significantly when the full sample is available for analyses. They do, however, suggest genetic effects on environmental measures and the social processes that underlie these measures. As such, they are consistent with an emerging body of data from several studies (Plomin & Bergeman, in press).

The relatively low correlations between siblings' descriptions of the same behavior suggests virtually no genetic control of their reports but a very substantial nonshared effect. In this instance, nonshared effects are a form of residual. What is directly estimated are genetic effects, which must be small because of the small differences across the three groups, and shared environmental effects, which are directly estimated by the very small correlations for the genetically unrelated blended siblings, .09 and .15 for children's reports of maternal and paternal aggression. Because genetic and shared environmental effects are small, the only thing left are nonshared environmental effects and error of measurement. Because the reliability of the measures are reasonably high, we conclude that nonshared effects must be large. Model fitting provides estimates that they account for 90% of variation in children's reports of maternal aggression and 71% of variation in their reports of paternal aggression. However, the relatively high correlations between blended siblings for parental reports, particularly for fathers, suggests very substantial shared environmental influences on these measures. Model fitting suggests shared environmental influences account for 22% of variation in mothers' reports of their aggression toward their children and 41% of variation in fathers' reports.

In summary, these data suggest that child reports of parental symbolic aggression are more likely to uncover nonshared effects of symbolic aggression on internalizing and externalizing, as well as on other outcome measures. This is because there is substantial genetic influence on parental reports. As noted in Table 3.2, the correlations between children's ratings and their parents' ratings of the same dimension of symbolic aggression correlated less .30 in all cases. This suggests that parents and children may be responding to different interactional phenomena. Also these data, particularly on mothers' reports, illuminate further the possible reasons for the contrast between parent ratings and child ratings on the same scale; the former showed much higher Sibling 1–Sibling 2 correlations than did the latter. This, in turn, suggests that the higher Sibling 1–Sibling 2 correlations in parents' reports is not due entirely to simple rater effects (i.e., one rater, in the case of the parent's rating of each child, versus two). For blended-sibling families the sibling–sibling correlation for mothers' reports is as low as that for the children. To put the matter another way, some portion of the increased Sibling 1–Sibling 2 correlations in parents may reflect a genetic influence on these ratings.

Differential Symbolic Aggression Toward Siblings and Variation in Internalizing and Externalizing

As mentioned earlier, correlations of environmental variables between siblings, across families, does not provide a suitable metric for relating nonshared environmental experiences to outcome variables. We need a metric that provides us a measure for sibling difference for each family. As already outlined, there are two: relative and absolute difference scores. However, there is more than a computational difference between the two; indeed, they imply very different environmental mechanisms.

As indicated, we computed relative difference scores by subtracting the environmental score for the youngest sibling from the corresponding score for the oldest. The next step was to compare the size of these relative difference scores with developmental outcome. We began with the older siblings and asked how much variation in outcome (e.g., depressive symptoms) could be explained by the relative difference in symbolic aggression received by the older child in comparison to that received by the younger. We then repeated these analyses for the full sample of younger siblings.

Before examining the actual findings, let us anticipate the meaning of this analysis by supposing that a relative difference in symbolic aggression toward children correlates with variation in externalizing. If the correlation is positive for our analysis of older siblings and negative for younger siblings, this means that the child who, in any siblingship, receives more symbolic aggression than the other sibling will also be more likely to show externalizing symptoms; this is true whether the child is the older or the younger sibling. Let us further suppose that these relationships between relative differences in symbolic aggression and externalizing are comparable across three types of families: those with relatively low aggression (as measured by parental means), moderate levels of aggression, and high levels. In other words, the main effect of the relative Sibling 1–Sibling 2 differences does not interact with the magnitude of aggression from the parents when parents are compared across families. If findings of this kind are, in fact, observed they would suggest that the nonshared environment, sibling differences in aggression received from parents, and developmental outcome, internalizing, and externalizing, are linked in two ways.

First, a risk or causal factor, such as parental aggression, can have unique or focused effects on the child who is the target of that factor. In other words, within a family, one child can be singled out for harsh treatment while the other, in a relative sense, is spared. Second, it is this relative difference between the siblings that matters most. In other words, even in families where there is hardly a harsh word by the parents to either child (as represented by a very low Sibling 1 + Sibling 2 mean), if one child is victimized by an occasional parental aggression, while the other is not, the first will be at risk for psychopathology and the second will be protected from it. Indeed, findings of the kind we are discussing would suggest that this child in a nonaggressive household who is treated relatively worse than his or her sibling is at the same risk as a child in a very aggressive household where the magnitude of the relative Sibling 1–Sibling 2 difference is the same. Findings of this kind would suggest that social comparison processes in the family play a surprisingly important role in development. Both children must have a keen appreciation of the family norm, and each must know that he or she is receiving treatment that is harsher or more benign than that norm. Comparisons by each child with that norm and with one another must lie at the core of the pathogenic effect of this form of nonshared effect.[2]

Absolute difference scores, and their correlation with outcome variables, imply a very different form of social comparison. Again, let us assume that these are positively correlated, say with externalizing. (For these analyses we do not expect a reversal in sign when we analyze the relationship for older and then younger siblings, because the absolute difference score is unsigned and has the same meaning for both.) Let us also assume, again, that this effect is not moderated by variation among families in mean levels of parental aggression. Findings of this kind would not suggest that a child who is a special target of parental patho-

---

[2]Difference scores are complex computational entities. They contain information about differences but also, when correlated with other variables, can reflect the effects of magnitudes of the component scores. Our team is developing analytic models to parse these effects, but a description of these models is beyond the scope of this chapter. See chapter 2, by Michael Rovine, for a further explication of these analytic issues.

genic behavior is at worse risk than his or her sibling; rather, the finding suggests that if *either* child is targeted, *both* are at risk. Here, the social comparison processes are quite different and may take one of at least two forms. The first might be called the *potential risk* factor. In effect, a child who is protected from harsh parental treatment, while his or her sibling is the target of much of it, thinks, "If one child in this family can be singled out for this treatment now, then I might be the next one." Being *singled out* is the potential risk factor. If *both* children are harshly treated, then *neither* is at risk. Another, related type of social comparison might also explain findings of this kind. This might be called the *different boat comparison process*. Large absolute differences may convey to each child in the family that there is a family norm that allows for two children to be treated very differently. This may lead to psychopathology in either child because each child feels adrift in stormy seas but in separate boats.

It should be noted that absolute differences constitute a nonshared effect only if one child (either the victim or the protected one) in each family is negatively affected. If both children are equally affected, across families, then absolute differences represent a shared rather than a nonshared effect.

The most straightforward approach to reporting our initial findings are simple zero order correlations between absolute and relative difference scores for symbolic aggression, on the one hand, and variations among our adolescents in internalizing and externalizing scores, on the other. However, because fathers, mothers, and children serve as reporters of both parental aggression and child symptoms, this creates a matrix of $12 \times 8 = 96$ correlations, as shown in Table 3.5.

The most informative of these correlations is the submatrix formed by children's reports of their parents' aggression and the parents' reports of their children's symptomatology. As we have indicated, children's reports of parental aggression do not seem very much determined by genetic influences, and thus their relationship to outcome variables are least likely to be mediated by genetic processes. Because children's reports of the independent variable are selected for this genetic reason, the reports from different sources for the outcome variable should be given greater weight to be sure that common method variance plays as small a role as possible in the associations. The only other source available in our data now are parents, although teachers' reports are currently being analyzed. These submatrices, of children's reports of aggression and parents' of symptoms, are indicated by a solid black border. Note that none of the correlations for relative difference scores are significant, but 6 out of 16 correlations are significant for absolute difference scores.

Three other submatrices, where parents are the reporters of their own aggression, are also of interest. These are the submatrices where one source reports on the aggression and another reports on the symptomatology. These matrices are demarcated with a dotted border. Here, 9 out of 16 correlations are significant for the absolute difference scores, and 5 of the 16 for the relative

TABLE 3.5

Correlations Between Internalizing and Externalizing Behaviors on the Zill Problem Behavior Scales and Absolute and Relative Differences (Child 1–Child 2) on the Conflict Tactics Scale (CTS)

| Zill Problem Behavior | Absolute Differences[1] | | | | Relative Differences | | | |
| | Parent | | Child | | Parent | | Child | |
	Father	Mother	Father	Mother	Father	Mother	Father	Mother
Father report:								
Internal: Child 1	.16*	.22*	.12	.04	.26*	.25*	.11	.08
Child 2	.17*	.16*	.11	.02	-.19*	-.13	-.06	-.06
External: Child 1	.27*	.21*	.19*	.12	.26*	.25*	.11	.08
Child 2	.19*	.18*	.11	.08	-.19*	-.13	-.06	-.06
Mother report:								
Internal: Child 1	.08	.19*	.16*	.10	.32*	.26*	.10	.03
Child 2	.17*	.25*	.02	.02	-.15*	-.14*	-.02	-.03
External: Child 1	.18*	.33*	.15*	.16*	.32*	.26*	.10	.03
Child 2	.16*	.20*	.13*	.16*	-.15*	-.14*	-.02	-.03
Child report of self:								
Internal: Child 1	.09	.03	.22*	.15*	.00	.00	.11	.16*
Child 2	.15*	.15*	.12	.14*	-.06	-.10	.03	-.02
External: Child 1	.00	.02	.06	.13*	.00	.00	.16*	.11
Child 2	.09	.06	.15*	.11	-.06	-.10	.03	.00

[1]$N = 214$.

*Significant correlation, $p < .05$.

difference scores. These findings need to be interpreted with great caution; because they involve parent reports, they may be genetically mediated. Of the remaining correlations for both absolute and relative difference scores, the great majority are significant. Note that for relative difference scores, in all cases where the correlation is significant, the sign is positive for older siblings and negative for younger siblings, suggesting that the within-family risk factor operates in the same way (more risk is associated with more pathology) for younger and older siblings. Several additional analyses help to clarify these basic findings.

First, what are the correlations between the relative and absolute difference scores? Table 3.6 shows the intercorrelations among all the difference scores with the most informative data in the main diagonal. Here, the most important correlation is between child absolute and relative difference scores: It is zero, suggesting that each provides different information about the family environment. The other three correlations are significant but quite small.

Second, are these relationships moderated by the magnitude of symbolic aggression as reflected in mean parental aggression scores? As a first and straightforward approach to answering this question, we divided our sample into three approximately equal subgroups according to the mean parental level of aggression. The contrasts across the three groups were not striking for absolute difference scores but showed a tendency to decline: There were 8, 6, and 4 significant correlations for low, mid-level, and high aggression families, respectively. For those particularly informative correlations, based on children's reports of aggression and parents' reports of symptoms, the number of significant relationships were 3, 2, and 0 for the low, mid-level, and high aggression families. For the relative difference scores, there was a distinct increase in the number of significant relationships across the three groups: a total of 9, 6, and 20 for all

TABLE 3.6
Correlations Between Absolute and Relative Difference Scores
(Older Sibling–Younger Sibling) for Symbolic Aggression
on the Conflict Tactics Scale

| | Relative Difference Scores | | | |
| | Parent Self-Reports | | Child Reports | |
Absolute Difference Scores	Mother	Father	Mother	Father
Parent Reports:				
Mother Report	.22*	.02	– .02	.00
Father Report	– .05	.16*	.01	.07
Child Reports of:				
Mother	.09	.08	.00	.06
Father	.02	.16*	.19*	.27*

*$p < .05$.

correlations and 1, 0, and 3 for the child/aggression and parent/symptomatology correlations.

A similar analysis was performed comparing findings from the full, half, and blended siblings groups. This analysis showed a sharp drop in the number of significant relationships for absolute difference scores for the blended siblings (only 4 significant, as compared to 8 for the fulls and 10 for the halfs) but a jump in the number of significant relationships for relative difference scores (15 significant relationships for blended vs. 10 for the fulls and 9 for the halfs). These contrasts, however, did not hold for the correlations built on children's reports of aggression and parents' reports of psychiatric symptomatology; these were approximately the same across the three types of families.

Finally, we analyzed the data according to gender. Here, the findings were clear: Absolute difference scores showed many more frequent relationships for boys than did relative difference scores (17 vs. 8 for all correlations and 4 vs. 0 for the child/aggression, parent/symptomatology correlations) whereas girls showed more effects due to relative difference scores (8 vs. 3), but there were no significant correlations in the child/aggression, parent/symptomatology submatrix for girls.

In these analyses the correlations were, in almost every case, in the same direction: the greater the absolute difference score, the more symptomatology, and the greater the relative difference score the more symptomatology for the older sibling and the less for the younger sibling. Likewise, there was little difference between their associations with externalizing or internalizing as outcome variables (internalizing and externalizing correlate .52, .51, and .58 for child, mother, and father reports, respectively).

Taken together, these findings suggest an interesting comparison between absolute and relative difference scores. In this very preliminary analysis they share three important features. First, the larger the difference scores, the more symptomatology is reported for or by the child. Second, there is no conspicuous difference between their effects on internalizing and externalizing symptoms. Third, their effects seem to be the same, across families, for the younger and older child in the sibling pairs we sampled.

There are also important differences. First, relative differences seem more important at high overall levels of aggression, whereas absolute differences are more conspicuous at low levels. Second, absolute differences are most important for full and half siblings and least important for blendeds, whereas the reverse is true for relative difference scores. Third, boys show larger effects of relative and girls of absolute difference scores. These findings might all be explained, although very speculatively at this early stage of our data analysis, by considering relative and absolute difference scores as if they were relatively uncorrelated signals that can be detected by children under different receiver operating characteristics. Considered as receiver characteristics, what do low levels of aggression in the family (as indexed by combined parent scores), half or full siblings and girls all have in common? All are receiver characteristics that enhance the detectability of absolute difference scores.

All three conditions may convey a quality of intimacy, embeddedness, or connectedness of relationships between parents and children. For example, relationships between parents and children are more secure or more intimate in low-aggression homes. Likewise, full and half siblings have spent almost a full lifetime together with the same mother. Finally, data on gender difference in adolescence does suggest that girls remain more emotionally tied into the family system than boys during this period (Hill, 1988).

If a child is close to or very embedded in a relationship with a parent, that child may be exquisitely sensitive to any shift of positive or negative feeling to or from himself or herself to a sibling. These shifts to or from the sibling are potentially disruptive, we speculate, because they suggest to the child the probable instability of the Parent–Child 1–Child 2 triad. This possibility is less threatening where the Parent–Child 1 or Parent–Child 2 ties are more attenuated. Hence, the absolute difference score is a signal that can more readily be ignored.

Relative difference scores may be very different signals. Our data suggest that they depend less on the special sensitivity of the receiver than on the power of the signal itself. That is, relative difference scores seem most important when the absolute levels of both the lower and higher scores are high.

DISCUSSION AND SUMMARY

This chapter has presented the logic underlying a large-scale study of the association of nonshared environment, using parental, sibling, and peer variables, on the one hand, and adolescent adjustment, on the other. More than in most studies, it was essential to detail the logic of the research design itself as well as our approach to the analysis and interpretation of findings. This is because the logic derives from several lines of behavioral genetic evidence that have not, as yet, been incorporated into the design of developmental studies; further, our choices of analytic procedures depend on assumptions about how the nonshared environment actually works—assumptions that require continuing critical review. Thus, at this stage in our work, it was important to open our choices of design and analytic approaches for careful inspection by our scientific colleagues so that the assumptions and derivatives of the basic logic can be examined critically. We review here some of the most important issues of design and analysis. Interpretation of the substance of our findings must wait until we can analyze many more variables in our full sample.

The logic of our method centers on two important and intimately linked objectives. The first, of course, is to detect—with sensitivity—nonshared environmental effects on adolescent development. The second objective is to separate genetic from environmental components of these nonshared effects. Both objectives are derived from two distinct but related lines of evidence from behavioral genetics. The first, the search for nonshared environmental effects, rests on a line of data, reviewed exhaustively in chapter 1 of this book, which is now becoming widely accepted among developmentalists. Indeed, we suspect that the cumulative effect of all the chapters in this book will be to encourage our colleagues to add siblings to their studies of the impact of the environment on development. The importance of siblings in these designs should become as important as control groups were in a previous generation of studies. Indeed, siblings might be regarded as another form of control, this one within families.

Our second objective, to separate the genetic from the environmental, has led to strenuous and expensive efforts to recruit a highly specialized sample of families with siblings: three types of stepfamilies and families of MZ and DZ twins. This feature of our design rests on another line of genetic evidence that is less well known by many of our developmental colleagues. These data indicate, as we have mentioned briefly, that genes influence variables that developmentalists have ordinarily considered strictly environmental. In this study we are concerned with genetic influences on parenting behavior, sibling interaction patterns, and the nature of peer groups. As Plomin and Bergeman (in press) pointed out in a recent review, genes may influence variation in these domains by one of two mechanisms. Genes may operate directly by influencing, let us say, parenting style or behavior; or genes may operate indirectly on variables in these domains by influencing the target child's characteristics. For example, with respect to our design, genes may have an effect on children's cognitive or social agency. These effects may, in turn, shape parenting or sibling or peer variables. Our design is centered on detecting influences of the second, or indirect kind, as we have already indicated. However, influences of direct genetic influence on our environmental measures can be explored by our design, as we showed in our example of symbolic aggression.

Our approach to data analysis was, like our research design, shaped by these two major objectives: the search for nonshared effects and the parsing of genetic and environmental components of these effects.

Selecting appropriate analytic models for the detection of nonshared effects requires us to go beyond the genetic data and to call upon our understanding of how family systems operate. For example, in the analyses we have presented in this chapter, we have relied on raw difference scores as our independent variable. The critique and defenses of difference scores in our science have been, for a generation, a major industry. However, our choice of these scores as an initial analytic tool rests on theoretical and not technical grounds. We are aware that when we correlate difference scores with outcome measures we cannot separate the unique effects of the absolute levels or variance of each score used to construct the difference score or the correlation between the two component scores. All of these may influence the magnitude and/or significance of the basic correlation. Further, although in the example of data analysis we provided in the chapter, absolute difference scores had little or no correlation with relative difference scores, this might not always be the case, and the unique variance due to each may have to be analyzed. However, all of these potentially confounding factors depend on between-family effects. The assumption behind the use of simple or uncorrected difference scores is that these scores reflect what each child actually perceives. That is, the child has firsthand knowledge of how he or she is being treated and how his or her sibling is being treated. The child, according to this assumption, cannot know or perceive levels of the same variable in other families, and thus to correct for these between-family differences may not only be unnecessary but distorting.

To our knowledge, the form of analysis we have used in this chapter to explore the effects of the nonshared environment has only one precedent. In a study of much younger children (Dunn et al., 1990), relative difference scores were used to compare nonshared maternal and sibling variables with psychiatric symptoms in school-age children. It may be, however, that adolescents are much more sensitive to between-family as well as within-family effects and that additional models, which we are now exploring, may be necessary to most effectively represent our data.

One further note on data analysis illustrates the potential for insight on adolescent development offered by this design. As we have mentioned, this design permits us to estimate indirect genetic effects on environmental variables. It also permits us to estimate the direct genetic effects on all of our dependent measures. This will not only provide a wealth of information on the heritability of competence and psychopathology in adolescence, much of this *terra incognita* in developmental studies but, through this capacity for detecting genetic effects, our design promises to provide a more accurate estimate of environmental models as well.

For example, let us say that we estimate the heritability of externalizing behavior as 40%. This means that the most that any environmental model (probably composed of a set of interrelated independent and mediating variables) could account for is 60% of the total variance in externalizing. However, most environmental models in traditional studies are evaluated for their capacity to account for 100% of any outcome variable or dependent measure. This, it can now be seen, is too stringent a test and may lead to the rejection of environmental models where they should be accepted. Indeed, in the case of a dependent measure that is 40% heritable and an environmental model that is not confounded by genetic effects, the amount of variance accounted for—as computed by traditional formulae—should be divided by 0.6.[3]

---

[3]It is certainly premature, however, to apply a formula of this kind. Heritability scores are estimates often associated with significant error. At this stage in our knowledge it is best to use heritability estimates of dependent measures as guides to the interpretation of tests of environmental models rather than as the quantitative bases for correcting the attenuation of effects.

Behavioral genetic data have infused new insights into the design and interpretation of developmental studies. We might say it centers our attention on these important new issues: First, what are the similarities and differences between siblings in their experience of the social world? Second, what social forces account for these differences? Third, how are these differences perceived by the individuals affected? Fourth, what is the relationship between these differences and psychological and social development? Fifth, what portion of these associations are mediated by genetic processes? Sixth, what proportion of the nongenetic variance in development is explained or accounted for by our models of the nonshared environment?

APPENDIX A: LIST OF MEASURES

I. Child Outcome Measures

Reference   *Respondent*[1]

A. *Mental Health/Illness Indicators*

1. Child Depression Inventory (Kovacs, 1985)   P, C
2. Jessor Substance Abuse Survey (Jessor & Jessor, 1977)   C
3. Behavior Events Inventory (Hetherington & Clingempeel, 1992) P, C, T
4. Child Behavior Checklist—Social Competence Scale (Achenbach & Edelbrock, 1983) P, C
5. Child Behavior Checklist—Teacher Report Form (Entire Form) (Achenbach & Edelbrock, 1983) T
6. Zill Behavior Items (Zill, 1985)   P, C

B. *Personality and Development Strengths*

1. California Psychological Inventory (Megargee, 1972)   C
2. EAS Temperament Survey (Buss & Plomin, 1984)   P, C, T
3. Autonomous Functioning Checklist (Sigafoos et al., 1988)   P, C
4. Physical Development Scale (Peterson, Toben-Richards, & Boxer, 1983) P, C
5. Harter Self-Perception Profile (Harter, 1982)   P, C, T
6. Optimism Scale (Scheier & Carver, 1985)   C

---

[1]P = Parent, C = Child, T = Teacher, O = Observer.

II. Measures of Child Environment

Reference   *Respondent*[1]

A. Parent–Child

1. Household Routines (this chapter)   P, C
2. Child-Rearing Issues, Part One (Hetherington &
   Clingempeel, 1992)   P, C
3. Child-Rearing Issues, Part Two (Hetherington &
   Clingempeel, 1992)   P, C
4. Expression of Affection (Hetherington &
   Clingempeel, 1992)   P, C
5. Family Conflict Inventory—Child Involvement
   (Hetherington & Clingempeel, 1992)   P, C
6. Child Monitoring (Hetherington & Clingempeel, 1992)   P, C
7. Parent–Child Relationship (Hetherington &
   Clingempeel, 1992)   P, C
8. Conflict Intensity Scale (this chapter)   P, C
9. Conflict Tactics Scale (Straus, 1979)   P, C
10. Sibling Inventory of Differential Experience—
    Sections 7 and 8 (Daniels et al., 1985)   C
11. Behavioral Observation (Hetherington &
    Clingempeel, 1992)   O

B. Sibling

1. Sibling Inventory of Behavior (Hetherington &
   Clingempeel, 1992)   P, C
2. Semantic Differential for Deidentification (Schachter
   et al., 1978)   C
3. Sibling Inventory of Differential Experience—
   Section 11 (Daniels et al., 1985)   C
4. Sibling Interaction Task (this chapter)   C
5. Conflict Tactics Scale—Sibling Forms (Straus, 1979)   C
6. Conflict Tactics Scale—Sibling Version (Straus, 1979)   C
7. Behavioral Observation (Hetherington &
   Clingempeel, 1992)   O

C. Non-Custodial Parent

1. Child's Relationship with Non-Residential Parent
   (Hetherington & Clingempeel, 1992)   P, C

---

[1]P = Parent, C = Child, T = Teacher, O = Observer.

Reference   *Respondent*[1]

D. Peer

1. Parent Perception of Child's Peers (this chapter)   P
2. Sibling Inventory of Differential Experience—
   Sections 9 and 10 (Daniels et al., 1985)   C

E. Other

1. Life Events Checklist—Child Version (Hetherington
   & Clingempeel, 1992)   C
2. Social Support (this chapter)   C

III. Moderators of Non-Shared Environment

A. General Stressors

1. Life Events Checklist—Parent Version (Hetherington
   & Clingempeel, 1992)   P

B. Marital Stressors

1. Locke-Wallace Marital Adjustment Test (Locke &
   Wallace, 1959)   P
2. Conflict Intensity Scale—Spouse Ratings (this chapter)   P
3. Marital Relationship Questionnaire (this chapter)   P
4. Family Conflict Inventory—Spouse Items
   (Hetherington & Clingempeel, 1992)   P
5. Conflict Tactics Scale—Spouse Ratings (Straus, 1979)   P
6. Marital Instability Scale (Booth et al., 1983)   P
7. Child-Rearing Issues—Self and Spouse (Hetherington
   & Clingempeel, 1992)   P
8. Behavioral Observation (Hetherington & Clingempeel,
   1992)   O

C. Parent Beliefs

1. Parent Perception of Child Similarity (this chapter)   P
2. Opinions About Genetic Inheritance (this chapter)   P
3. Opinions About Parenting Responsibilities
   (this chapter)   P

---

[1]P = Parent, C = Child, T = Teacher, O = Observer.

IV. Parent Functioning

Reference   *Respondent*[1]

1. Center for Epidemiological Studies Depression
   Scale (Radloff, 1977)   P
2. Alcohol and Drug Abuse Survey (Jessor &
   Jessor, 1977)   P

---

[1]P = Parent, C = Child, T = Teacher, O = Observer.

REFERENCES

Achenbach, T. M., & Edelbrock, E. (1983). *Manual for the Child Behavior Checklist and Revised Child Behavior Profile*. Burlington, VT: University of Vermont.

Baker, L. A., & Daniels, D. (1990). Nonshared environmental influences and personality differences in adult twins. *Journal of Personality and Social Psychology, 58*, 103–110.

Baumrind, D. (1978). Parental disciplinary patterns and social competence in children. *Youth and Society, 9*, 239–276.

Bell, D. C., & Bell, L. G. (1983). Parental validation and support in the development of adolescent daughters. In H. D. Grotevant (Ed.), *Adolescent development in the family* (pp. 27–42). San Francisco: Jossey Bass.

Booth, A., Johnson, D., & Edwards, J. N. (1983). Measuring marital instability. *Journal of Marriage and the Family, 45*, 387–393.

Brooks, J. B. (1981). Social maturity in middle age and its developmental antecedents. In D. H. Eichorn, J. A. Clausen, N. Haan, M. P. Honzik, & P. H. Mussen (Eds.), *Present and past in middle life* (pp. 244–269). New York: Academic Press.

Brooks-Gunn, J., & Reiter, E. O. (1990). The role of pubertal processes in the early adolescent transition. In S. Feldman & G. Elliott (Eds.), *At the threshold: The developing adolescent* (pp. 16–53). Cambridge: Harvard University Press.

Bryant, B. K. (1982). Sibling relationships in middle childhood. In M. E. Lamb & B. Sutton-Smith (Eds.), *Sibling relationships: Their nature and significance across the lifespan* (pp. 87–121). Hillsdale, NJ: Lawrence Erlbaum Associates.

Buss, A. H., & Plomin, R. (1984). *Temperament: Early developing personality traits*. Hillsdale, NJ: Lawrence Erlbaum Associates.

Cantwell, D. P., & Baker, L. (in press). Manifestations of depressive affect in adolescence. *Journal of Youth and Adolescence*.

Cicirelli, V. G. (1980). Relationships of family background variables to levels of control with the elderly. *Journal of Gerontology, 35*, 108–114.

Cicirelli, V. G. (1982). Sibling influence throughout the lifespan. In M. E. Lamb & B. Sutton-Smith (Eds.), *Sibling relationships: Their nature and significance across the lifespan* (pp. 267–284). Hillsdale, NJ: Lawrence Erlbaum Associates.

Cook, W. L., & Goethe, J. W. (1990). The effect of being reared with an alcoholic half-sibling: A classic study reanalyzed. *Family Process, 29*(1), 87–93.

Daniels, D. (1987). Differential experiences of children in the same family as predictors of adolescent sibling personality differences. *Journal of Personality and Social Psychology, 51*, 339–346.

Daniels, D., Dunn, J., Furstenberg, F. F., Jr., & Plomin, R. (1985). Environmental differences within the family and adjustment differences within pairs of adolescent siblings. *Child Development, 56*(3), 764–774.

Daniels, D., & Plomin, R. (1985). Differential experiences of siblings in the same family. *Developmental Psychology, 21*(5), 747–760.

Dunn, J., & Kendrick, C. (1982a). Siblings and their mothers: Developing relationships within the family. In M. E. Lamb & B. Sutton-Smith (Eds.), *Sibling relationships: Their nature and significance across the lifespan* (pp. 39–60). Hillsdale, NJ: Lawrence Erlbaum Associates.

Dunn, J., & Kendrick, C. (1982b). *Siblings: Love, envy, and understanding.* Cambridge, MA: Harvard University Press.

Dunn, J., Stocker, C., & Plomin, R. (1990). Nonshared experiences within the family: Correlates of behavioral problems in middle childhood. *Development and Psychopathology, 2,* 113–126.

Furman, W., & Buhrmester, D. (1985). Children's perceptions of the personal relationships in their social networks. *Developmental Psychology, 21,* 1016–1024.

Gilbert, R., Christensen, A., & Margolin, G. (1984). Patterns of alliances in nondistressed and multiproblem families. *Family Process, 23,* 75–87.

Gough, H. G. (1966). Appraisal of social maturity by means of the CPI. *Journal of Abnormal Psychology, 77,* 236–241.

Graubard, P. S. (1971). The relationship between academic achievement and behavior dimensions. *Exceptional Children, 37,* 755–757.

Harter, S. (1982). The perceived competence scale for children. *Child Development, 53,* 87–97.

Harter, S. (1988). *The self-perception profile for adolescence.* Unpublished manuscript, University of Denver, Denver, CO.

Harter, S. (1990). Causes, correlates, and the functional role of global self-worth: A life-span perspective. In R. J. Sternberg & J. Kolligian, Jr. (Eds.), *Competence considered* (pp. 67–97). New Haven: Yale University Press.

Hetherington, E. M., & Clingempeel, W. G. (1992). Coping with marital transitions: A family systems perspective. *Monographs of the Society for Research in Child Development, 57*(2–3, Serial No. 227).

Hetherington, E. M., & Feldman, S. E. (1964). College cheating as a subject of subject and situational variables. *Journal of Educational Psychology, 55,* 212–218.

Hill, J. P. (1988). Adapting to menarche: Familial control and conflict. In M. R. Gunnar & W. A. Collins (Eds.), *Development during the transition to adolescence* (pp. 43–77). Hillsdale, NJ: Lawrence Erlbaum Associates.

Jessor, R., & Jessor, S. L. (1977). *Problem behavior and psychosocial development: A longitudinal study of youth.* New York: Academic Press.

Kandel, D. B. (1973). Adolescent marijuana use: Role of parents and peers. *Science, 181,* 1067–1070.

Kandel, D. B., & Davies, M. (1986). Adult sequelae of adolescent depressive symptoms. *Archives of General Psychiatry, 43,* 255–262.

Kandel, D. B., Davies, M., Karus, D., & Yamaguchi, K. (1986). The consequences in young adulthood of adolescent drug involvement. *Archives of General Psychiatry, 43,* 746–754.

Kenny, D. A., & La Voie, L. (1984). The social relations model. In L. Berkowitz (Ed.), *Advances in experimental social psychology* (pp. 141–182). New York: Academic Press.

Kovacs, M. (1985). The Children's Depression Inventory (CDI). *Psychopharmacology Bulletin, 4*(21), 995–998.

Light, P. (1979). *The development of social sensitivity.* Cambridge: Cambridge University Press.

Locke, H., & Wallace, F. (1959). Short marital adjustment and prediction tests: Their reliability and validity. *Marriage and Family Living, 21,* 251–255.

Loehlin, J. C., & Nichols, R. C. (1976). *Heredity, environment, and personality.* Austin, TX: University of Texas Press.

Lykken, D. T., McGue, M., & Tellegen, A. (1987). Recruitment bias in twin research. *Behavior Genetics, 17,* 343–362.

MacKinnon, C. E. (1988). Influences on sibling relations in families with married and divorced parents: Family form or family quality? *Journal of Family Issues, 9*(4), 469–477.

Megargee, E. I. (1972). *The California psychological inventory handbook*. Washington, DC: Jossey-Bass.

Montemayor, R., & Hanson, E. (1985). A naturalistic view of conflict between adolescents and their parents and siblings. *Journal of Early Adolescence, 5*, 23–30.

Nichols, R. C., & Bilbro, W. C. (1966). The diagnosis of twin zygosity. *Acta Genetica, 16*, 265–275.

Patterson, G. R. (1982). *Coercive family process: A social learning approach*. Eugene, OR: Castalia.

Patterson, G. R., Capaldi, D., & Bank, L. (in press). An early starter model for predicting delinquency. In D. Pepler, K. H. Rubin, & L. Bank (Eds.), *The development and treatment of childhood aggression*. Hillsdale, NJ: Lawrence Erlbaum Associates.

Peterson, A. C., Toben-Richards, M., & Boxer, A. (1983). Puberty: Its measurement and its meaning. *Journal of Early Adolescence, 3*, 47–62.

Peterson, J. L., & Zill, N. (1986). Marital disruption, parent–child relationships, and behavior problems in children. *Journal of Marriage and the Family, 48*(5), 295–307.

Plomin, R. (1986). *Development, genetics, and psychology*. Hillsdale, NJ: Lawrence Erlbaum Associates.

Plomin, R., & Bergeman, C. S. (in press). The nature of nurture: Genetic influences on "environmental" measures. *Behavioral and Brain Sciences*.

Plomin, R., DeFries, J. C., & McClearn, G. E. (1990). *Behavioral genetics: A primer* (2nd ed.). New York: W. H. Freeman.

Plomin, R., Loehlin, J. C., & DeFries, J. C. (1985). Genetic and environmental components of "environmental" influences. *Developmental Psychology, 21*(3), 391–402.

Puig-Antich, J., Lukens, E., Davies, M., Goetz, D., Brennan-Quattrock, J., & Todak, G. (1985). Psychosocial functioning in prepubertal depressive disorders. *Archives of General Psychiatry, 42*(5), 500–507.

Radloff, L. S. (1977). The CES-D scale: A self-report depression scale for research in the general population. *Applied Psychological Measurement, 1*, 385–401.

Robins, L. N. (1966). *Deviant children grown up*. Baltimore: Williams and Wilkins.

Robins, L. N., & Price, R. K. (1991). Adult disorders predicted by childhood conduct problems: Results from the NIMH epidemiological catchment area project. *Psychiatry, 54*, 116–132.

Rose, R. J., & Ditto, W. B. (1983). A developmental-genetic analysis of common fears from early adolescence to early adulthood. *Child Development, 54*, 361–368.

Rutter, M. (1970). *Education, health, and behavior*. New York: John Wiley.

Scarr, S., & Carter-Saltzman, L. (1979). Twin method: Defense of a critical assumption. *Behavior Genetics, 9*(6), 527–542.

Scarr, S., Scarf, E., & Weinberg, R. A. (1980). Perceived and actual similarities in biological and adoptive families: Does perceived similarity bias genetic inferences? *Behavior Genetics, 10*(5), 445–457.

Scarr, S., & Weinberg, R. A. (1983). The Minnesota Adoption Studies: Genetic differences and malleability. *Child Development, 54*, 260–267.

Schachter, F. F. (1982). Sibling deidentification and split-parent identification: A family tetrad. In M. E. Lamb & B. Sutton-Smith (Eds.), *Sibling relationships: Their nature and significance across the lifespan* (pp. 123–151). Hillsdale, NJ: Lawrence Erlbaum Associates.

Schachter, F. F., Gilutz, G., Shore, E., & Adler, M. (1978). Sibling deidentification judged by mothers: Cross-validation and developmental studies. *Child Development, 49*, 543–546.

Schachter, F. F., Shore, E., Feldman-Rotman, S., Marquis, R. E., & Campbell, S. (1976). Sibling deidentification. *Developmental Psychology, 12*, 418–427.

Scheier, M. F., & Carver, C. S. (1985). Optimism, coping, and health: Assessment and implications of generalized outcome expectancies. *Health Psychology, 4*(3), 219–247.

Schukit, M. A., Goodwin, D. A., & Winokur, G. (1972). A study of alcoholism in half siblings. *American Journal of Psychiatry, 128*(9), 1132–1136.

Sigafoos, A., Feinstein, C. B., Damond, M., & Reiss, D. (1988). The measurement of behavioral autonomy in adolescence: The autonomous functioning checklist. *Adolescent Psychiatry, 15*, 432–462.

Steinberg, L. (1989). Pubertal-maturation and parent–adolescent distance: An evolutionary perspective. In G. R. Adams, R. Montemayor, & T. P. Gullotta (Eds.), *Biology of adolescent behavior and development* (pp. 71–97). Newbury Park, CA: Sage.

Straus, M. A. (1979). Measuring intrafamily conflict and violence: The conflict tactics (CT) scale. *Journal of Marriage and the Family, 41,* 75–85.

Troll, L. E. (1975). *Early and middle adulthood.* Monterey, CA: Brooks/Cole.

Vaillant, G. E., & Vaillant, C. O. (1981). Natural history of male psychological health: Work as a predictor of positive mental health. *American Journal of Psychiatry, 138*(11), 1433–1440.

Vuchinich, S., Emery, R. E., & Cassidy, J. (1988). Family members as third parties in dyadic family conflict: Strategies, alliances, and outcomes. *Child Development, 54,* 1293–1302.

Werner, E. E., & Smith, R. S. (1982). *Vulnerable but invincible.* New York: McGraw-Hill.

Wilson, R. S. (1983). The Louisville Twin Study: Developmental synchronies in behavior. *Child Development, 54,* 298–316.

Zill, N. (1985). *Behavior problems scales developed from the 1981 Child Health Supplement to the National Health Interview Survey.* Washington, DC: Child Trends, Inc.

4

Young Children's Nonshared Experiences: A Summary of Studies in Cambridge and Colorado

Judy Dunn
Shirley McGuire
Pennsylvania State University

My mother had a good deal of trouble with me but I think she enjoyed it. She had none at all with my brother Henry, who was two years younger than I, and I think that the unbroken monotony of his goodness and truthfulness and obedience would have been a burden to her but for the relief and variety which I furnished in the other direction.

—Mark Twain, *Autobiography*

Mark Twain (1966) is very clear indeed about the differences between himself and his brother Henry, who became Sid in *The Adventures of Tom Sawyer*: The famous occasions in which Sid repeatedly lands Tom in trouble come straight from their childhood together. Likewise, George Eliot (1979) in *The Mill on the Floss* vividly brings us the experiences of her childhood with her strikingly different brother Isaac—Tom in the novel. And to Henry James, he and his three brothers and sister were all so different "We were, to my sense . . . such a company of characters and such a picture of differences, and withal so fused and united and interlocked, that each of us . . . pleads for preservation" (James, 1913, p. 12). Henry repeatedly contrasts himself unfavorably with his brother, William James, characterizing himself as unadaptive, aloof, lacking William's gregariousness, his effortless talents, and savoir faire.

These writers explore in an illuminating way the differences between themselves and their siblings, and they vividly expose the differences in the patterns of family life that children growing up within the same family can experience. They, and many other writers, show us with penetrating clarity and sensitivity, just how differently they saw their childhood experiences from those of their siblings (Dunn & Plomin, 1990). Are such notable differences between siblings just the unusual divergence of outstanding individuals? Clearly, we have much more extensive information about these illustrious and exciting people than we have about more ordinary individuals, both from their fictional writings and from the industry of their biographers. Yet the striking finding that emerges from every systematic study of siblings in the general population is that the differences between siblings—in personality, in psychopathology and adjustment, in depression, even in intellectual ability—are substantial (for overview see Dunn & Plomin, 1990).

The average correlation between siblings in personality, for example, derived from a large range of studies is only .15, which implies that about 85% of the variance in personality is not shared by two children growing up in the same family. In the largest study yet completed that focuses on the two major clusters of personality dimensions, extraversion and neuroticism, the sibling correlations are .25 for extraversion and only .07 for neuroticism (Ahern, Johnson, Wilson, McClearn, & Vandenberg, 1982). As other chapters in this volume discuss, the differences between siblings are notable too in areas such as mental illness and developmental psychopathology (e.g., see chapter 6).

It is these differences that challenge those of us who study the family. The variables that we have assumed are the all-important family influences on children's development—for example, the quality of the marital relationship, the parents' child-rearing attitudes, their mental health, personalities, educational levels and socioeconomic status—appear to be shared by siblings. Yet the siblings develop to be so very different from one another. Mark Twain and his brother shared the same childhood home in that "almost invisible village" in Missouri, the same mother (Aunt Polly in *Tom Sawyer*), yet they were distinctively different from one another. Henry and William James, who differed so dramatically in personality, style, sociability, and self-confidence, spent much of their childhood and adolescence together in Albany, New York, and wandering Europe with their family; yet their family experiences clearly differed greatly (Edel, 1953; James, 1913, 1914). The question that students of family process have to answer, in terms of siblings within the general population, is this: In what ways do the family worlds of siblings differ, and which of these differences in experiences within the same family are influential in their development?

The behavior geneticists have demonstrated from their studies of adopted siblings and from twin studies that the environmental influences on siblings are working to make them different rather than similar. What similarity there is between siblings—and there is, of course, some—is attributable to heredity, as the research on twins and adopted siblings shows (see chapter 1). The behavior geneticists' focus is on identifying the chief sources of influence on variance in individual outcome; for environmental variance, they have demonstrated, such influence is not shared by two children within the same family. The concern of behavior geneticists is not to specify the processes through which such environmental influence affects children. But this is indeed the concern of those of us who hope to understand how family experiences affect children's development. Growing up in the same family makes children different, not similar. How can we identify the microenvironments within the family that are experienced differently by siblings within the same family? And which of these differential experiences are influential in their development?

There are some obvious candidates for powerful differential experiences within families. First, it is clear that siblings may experience different relationships with their mothers and fathers—a topic that is amply documented by writers drawing on their childhood experiences in fiction or in autobiography. A second possibility is that, within the sibling relationship itself, each individual child experiences the relationship differently from the other. The acid criticism and effortless superiority shown by William James, who mercilessly mocked his younger brother Henry, was very painful to Henry, who showed no such behavior to William; the pattern of teasing reflected how profoundly different the sibling relationship was for the two brothers (Edel, 1987). A third possibility is that children may have different relationships and experiences with peers or teachers, outside the family; and a fourth possibility is that chance incidents may affect one child but not the other, or that life events that are apparently ''shared'' by family members in fact impact more heavily on one sibling than the other. A first step toward understanding the nature and influence of nonshared experiences within families must be to document the extent of each of such differential experiences, and a second step is to examine how far these are related to individual outcome. In a recent book (Dunn & Plomin, 1990) we discuss these issues at length, drawing on both systematic research and the insights of writers; in this chapter we summarize how, in a series of studies in England and the United States, we are beginning to take these steps. (For an extended discussion of the issues, argument, and evidence the reader is referred to Dunn & Plomin, 1990.)

Siblings in Cambridge and in Colorado

Since the late 1980s, we have examined the nature and extent of differential experiences of siblings in a variety of ways, with longitudinal studies of siblings studied within their families. In England, in Cambridge and surrounding villages, we conducted three studies of very young siblings; these included a longitudinal study of firstborn children followed from before the birth of their sibling through the infancy of the secondborn (Dunn & Kendrick, 1982), and two further studies that focus on secondborn children followed from their second year (e.g., Dunn, Brown, & Beardsall, 1991; Dunn & Munn, 1985; see also Dunn, 1988). In each study the research strategy included naturalistic, unstructured observations of children at home with their mothers and older siblings during infancy and early childhood, with audiotapes of family conversation, and interviews with mothers about differential parental treatment and the siblings' relationship. At the follow-up stage in middle childhood and early adolescence, the siblings were assessed on a variety of tests of sociocognitive development and of perceived self-competence, and were interviewed about their sibling relationship; data on life events over the preceding 3 years were gathered from the mothers.

The second set of studies to be summarized is based in Colorado, where around 100 sibling pairs whose families were participants in the larger Colorado Adoption Project (CAP) (Plomin, DeFries, & Fulker, 1988) have been studied with their mothers, together as dyads, and as individuals, initially as 4- and 7-year-olds (Dunn, Stocker, & Plomin, 1990b; Stocker, Dunn, & Plomin, 1989), then as 7- and 10-year-olds. In this study, again, a variety of methods were employed, including interviews with family members and teachers, videotapes of the children engaged in playing games with their mothers as triads, and the siblings alone together as dyads, and a variety of outcome assessments were included. Because the CAP includes an extensive array of assessments of individual development on each child, the opportunities to examine the relative importance of differential family experiences to different domains of outcome are considerable.

In the next section we consider the first general question raised in the introduction: What is the nature and extent of differential experience within the family? We look in turn at the four chief candidates for differential experience, namely differences in parent–child relationships, differences within the sibling relationship, differences in peer relations and experiences with teachers, and in the impact of life events on siblings growing up together. It should be noted at the outset that, as in other studies with siblings, in both the Cambridge and the Colorado samples the siblings differed notably from one another in personality, in self-esteem, and in adjustment. It is these differences that form the challenge for family researchers.

Differential Experiences of Siblings Within Their Families

Differences in Parent–Child Relationships?   Both parents and children report that there are differences in the relationships parents have with the different children within their families. Children as young as 5 years report differences in perceived treatment of themselves and their siblings by their parents (Koch, 1960; for interview studies of older siblings see Daniels & Plomin, 1985), as do their parents. Children's sensitivity to differential parental behavior is revealed to us not only in their responses to interview questions, but in their actions. The naturalistic observations that we carried out in Cambridge showed that extremely early in childhood the children responded very directly to their parents' interactions with their siblings.

Observations of Children's Responses to Parent–Sibling Interaction. A number of lines of evidence highlight the salience to young children of their siblings' relationships with the shared parents. For example, in the months that follow the birth of a sibling, the interaction between mother and baby has a marked effect on the behavior of the firstborn. Many firstborns responded to as many as three out of four of the interactions between their mothers and baby siblings—most commonly with a protest or demand for the same attention, as in the example that follows, which is drawn from a study of firstborn children followed over the birth and infancy of a sibling (Dunn & Kendrick, 1982):

Example 1:

14-month-old Malcolm was playing with his mother, while his older sister, 3-year-old Virginia, watched vigilantly:

Mother to Malcolm (playing with Legos): I'll make you a little car, Malcolm.

Virginia: Well, I want one.

Mother to Malcolm: Shall I make you one? Mmm?

Virginia: Don't let him have the red pieces.

Mother to Malcolm (picking him up and imitating his noises): Wawwaw! Wawwaw!

Virginia: Can I sit beside you? Can I sit on knee?

Mother to Virginia: Is that just because Malcolm's up here?

Virginia: Yes.

Mother to Virginia: Come on then.

Often the firstborn children in the study imitated the action of the baby to which the mother was responding, or copied "naughty" actions of the baby, when these drew maternal attention. Sometimes they tried to join in the play between baby sibling and mother, sometimes they tried to disrupt it. Sometimes, most poignant of all, they simply broke down in unhappiness and cried. These responses varied, in part according to the temperament of the firstborn, and in part according to the kind of interaction in which mother and sibling were engaged. But what was incontrovertible was the salience to the children of the exchanges between their mother and the younger sibling.

This sensitivity to the relationship between mother and sibling was not solely a firstborn phenomenon, or a response to displacement. In our other studies the target children were secondborn, and here we found that as early as 14 months, when they were first observed, the secondborn children were extremely attentive to any interaction between their mothers and older siblings, especially disputes or animated play (Dunn, 1988; Dunn & Munn, 1985). Interactions in which emotions were expressed were of especial interest to them, and were relatively rarely ignored. In disputes between mother and sibling, for instance, they frequently attempted to support either one of the antagonists; as early as 24 months they made judgmental comments on their siblings, and tried to aid or punish either mother or sibling.

A third line of evidence from our observational work further confirmed how closely children monitor the interaction between their mothers and siblings. This was an analysis of the development of children's conversational participation (Dunn & Shatz, 1989). Much of the talk in families is not directed to the youngest members, and the development of the ability to join effectively in the talk between others is an important acquisition. Our results showed that the children monitored very closely the talk between their mothers and siblings, and over the course of the third year became increasingly effective at intervening in such conversation to draw attention to themselves and what interested them. In summary, each of these different lines of study highlights how closely children attend to and react to the relationship between their mothers and siblings; such prompt and insistent reaction makes it unsurprising that in interviews children so often report that they perceive differential attention given to their sibling.

Perceived Differences in Parent–Child Relationships. Many phenomenologically oriented researchers have reminded us that although the actual behavior of others toward children is important, children's perceptions of others' actions and intentions may be equally or more important in influencing their development. In relation to children's perceptions of parental differential treatment, Plomin and Daniels (1987) point out that small differences in perceptions may lead to very large differences in their development. Studies that have asked both children to rate how they are treated by their parents relative to their sibling (Daniels, Dunn, Furstenberg, & Plomin, 1985; Daniels & Plomin, 1985), have found that siblings do not agree on the nature and extent of parental differential treatment. We asked the Colorado siblings to rate how they are treated compared to their sibling, with respect to positive aspects of the relationship (e.g., "Does more things with me") and negative aspects (e.g., "Is more strict with me"). As Table 4.1 shows, on average, about 50% of the children said that they are treated differently from their siblings. About an equal number of siblings said that they are treated better than their sibling, or worse than their sibling. It is not the case that each child complained "I am treated worse." The children admitted that sometimes they were better off than their sibling. However it is interesting to note that there was little to no agreement between the two children within a family about the differential treatment. We also compared these

TABLE 4.1
Siblings' Reports of Mothers' and Fathers' Differential Treatment:
Colorado Sample (n = 90)

| | Parent's Treatment | | |
	Younger Sibling More	Same	Older Sibling More
Older Sibling			
Mother's involvement	23%	54%	23%
Mother's negativity	19%	43%	38%
Father's involvement	23%	45%	32%
Father's negativity	22%	52%	26%
Younger Sibling			
Mother's involvement	18%	55%	27%
Mother's negativity	25%	37%	38%
Father's involvement	35%	38%	27%
Father's negativity	18%	53%	29%

data with the mother's report of her own behavior with each sibling, and did not find significant agreement among the three family members. These different perspectives make the investigation of parental differential treatment even more complicated.

In addition to these observations and interviews, we interviewed the mothers in each of our studies directly about the quality of their relationships with their different children, and the extent to which they treated the siblings differently. Somewhat to our surprise, given the socially acceptable view that parents should treat children similarly, only a third of the Coloradan mothers described feeling a similar intensity and extent of affection for their two children, and only a third said they gave similar attention, when the siblings were 4 and 7 years old, and the observations told a similar story (Fig. 4.1).

The differences in reported discipline were particularly striking in the Cambridge sample, in which only 12% said they found discipline equally easy or problematic with their two children, and only 12% said they disciplined the siblings equally frequently. It is worth noting that the mothers who were interviewed were in both sets of studies very much at ease, and did not seem to hesitate to describe frankly aspects of their relationships with their children which were socially unacceptable. Here, for example, are the comments of a Cambridge mother about her behavior with her two children—older sister Sue, and new baby brother: "I was very miserable. I smacked Sue all the time. I was screaming and shouting at her. *He's* very easy in the day. Very undemanding. If he'd been like her, I'd be in the hospital." The validity of the interview material is further supported by the evidence that there was some agreement between what the mothers said about their behavior to their children and what we observed (Dunn, Stocker, & Plomin, 1990a).

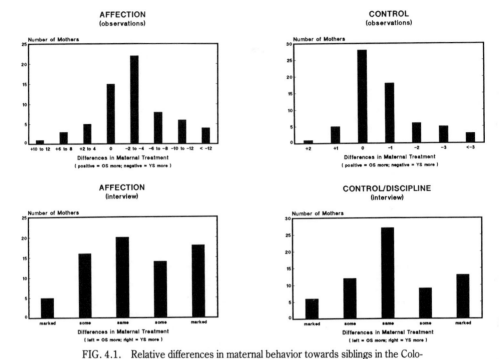

FIG. 4.1.   Relative differences in maternal behavior towards siblings in the Colorado Adoption Project (from Dunn, Stocker, & Plomin, 1990b).

Differential Parental Treatment: The Significance of Children's Ages.
The data from the Colorado Adoption Project gives us a particularly interesting
perspective on how the mothers in the sample behaved toward their two children. As each child was studied as an individual with the mother at 12, 24, and
36 months, we were able to examine how mothers behaved to their different
children when they were at particular and comparable ages (Dunn & Plomin,
1986; Dunn, Plomin, & Daniels, 1986; Dunn, Plomin, & Nettles, 1985). The
results here were initially rather unexpected. We found that mothers were in
fact quite consistent (relative to other mothers) in their behavior to their successive children when they were at the same age, although they did not behave
very consistently to the same child as that child grew up. For example, a mother
who was relatively responsive and affectionate to her first child as a 12-month-
old was not, when compared with other mothers, particularly affectionate to
that same child 1 year later. However, she was relatively affectionate to her
secondborn child when that child was 12 months. It appeared that the particular
stage of development that a child had reached had a rather strong influence on
the mothers' behavior for children within the toddler and preschool-age period—
at least under the conditions in which we were studying them.

One implication of these results for the issue of differential parental behavior
is key: At any one time point in real life the siblings within a family are, of course,

different ages and at different developmental stages. What the evidence from the Colorado data shows is that mothers behave very differently to children of different stages, even to the same child at different stages. Some mothers are "turned on" by babies, others are especially interested in children when they begin to talk. In a family in which the mother is especially affectionate to her children when they are 1-year-olds, but less interested in argumentative 3-year-olds, the older sibling at 3 will daily be the witness of his mother's special affection for his young sibling. A further implication of the findings is that although two children may each have had rather similar relationships with their mother at particular stages in early childhood, it is witnessing *differential* behavior to self and to sibling that may be more important in a child's development than the fact that the siblings experienced *similar* affection or attention when at a certain stage of childhood. Witnessing your sibling being loved may override the experience of affection you yourself received at that age. It is an idea rather at odds with conventional views on what is important in parent–child relationships, but one which should clearly be pursued, if we are to explain why siblings develop to be so different.

Differences Within the Sibling Relationship? Perceived Differences Within the Sibling Relationship. Psychologists studying the sibling relationship generally describe and categorize the quality of the relationship in terms of broad dyadic dimensions, such as "affection," "conflict," "rivalry," or "hostility." One implication of this focus on the dyad is that both partners in the relationship are affected similarly by the relationship. Such research has shown that conflict, affection, and control are relatively independent dimensions: A sibling pair can be endlessly fighting, yet affectionate with one another, for instance. But the issue of whether the two siblings within the relationship experience that relationship differently has not often been considered—in contrast to the attention psychologists have shown to whether a marriage is experienced differently by the two partners (Bernard, 1982), or a parent–child relationship is experienced differently by child and parent. Yet for our concern with differential experiences within the family, the issue of whether two siblings experience that relationship differently is clearly important. Consider the following comments made by two siblings in a Cambridge study concerning their relationship:

Example 2:

Nancy, 10 years old, talks about her brother Carl, who is 6:

Nancy: Well, he's nice to me. And he sneaks into my bed at night time from Mummy. I think I'd be very lonely without Carl. I play with him a lot and he thinks up lots of ideas and it's very exciting. He comes and meets me at the gate after school and I think that's very friendly . . . He's very kind . . . Don't really know what I'd do without a brother.

Carl: She's pretty disgusting and we don't talk to each other much. I don't really know much about her.

Interviewer: What is it you particularly like about her?

Carl: Nothing. Sometimes when I do something wrong she tells me off quite cruelly.

Such differences in perceptions of the sibling relationship are not uncommon. In the Cambridge study, the children were asked open-ended questions about their relationship: Tell me about X . . . What is it you particularly like about X? . . . What is it you particularly dislike about him/her? Their responses were analyzed both in terms of the specific content of the replies, and in terms of the degree of "closeness" the siblings expressed. Only 23% of the siblings were rated as expressing similar degrees of closeness as their sibling expressed. Carl and Nancy were not exceptions.

In addition to this open-ended approach, a number of studies now use the Sibling Inventory of Differential Experience (SIDE) in which children are asked to compare their experiences within the sibling relationship (Anderson, 1989; Baker & Daniels, 1990; Daniels, 1986; Daniels & Plomin, 1985). The extent of differences they report is remarkable, and is much greater in fact than the differences siblings report in their parent–child relationships. In one study, 20% of the children described, on average, "much difference" in their own and their siblings' behavior in the relationship.

A similar picture of differences in the children's experiences within the sibling relationship comes from our second source of information—the parents. In both the Cambridge and the Colorado studies we interviewed the parents about their children's behavior and feelings toward each other, with very similar results. The parents were asked detailed questions about a number of features of the children's relationship with one another, and from their replies two general dimensions of the relationship were derived, one positive and one negative. According to the parents, 60% of the Colorado children differed from their sibling in the extent and expression of their friendly feelings toward their sibling; that is, 60% of siblings experienced differing degrees of friendliness within the relationship. The siblings were rather more similar in their negative hostile feelings, but even so, 40% were thought by their parents to differ in their hostile feelings and behavior from their siblings, and thus to experience different degrees of hostility.

Observed differences in sibling relationships. In both the Cambridge and the Colorado studies we also have observational data on the children together: unstructured naturalistic observations of the preschool-aged siblings in the Cambridge data, with auditotaped recordings of family conversation, and rather more structured videotaped observations of the (slightly older) siblings and mothers playing a series of games in the Colorado study. In the former observations, differences between the siblings' behavior were clear, especially in the friendly aspects of their relationship. The younger siblings, especially, often approached their older siblings hoping to play, or trying to "help," only to be met with a hostile or uninterested response. The findings from the videotaped observations of the siblings in the Colorado study also showed differences in some sibling pairs, in their friendly behavior and interest in cooperation, in the dominance within the pair, although these were less extensive than the differences seen in the unstructured Cambridge observations, perhaps because of the age differences of the two samples. Conflict behavior was more evenly matched; this seemed to us not surprising, given the constrained circumstances of the videotaped games.

Social Comparison. There is a further, less direct way in which the presence of a sibling can lead to different, but developmentally significant experiences for two children who grow up together in the same family. The daily presence of another child who is different from oneself, with whom one can compare oneself, and with whom one competes for parental affection and interest, may be enormously important in the development of a sense of self, and in understanding of others. Here the data in the Cambridge study shows us that processes of social comparison between the siblings begin astonishingly early, in the emotional atmosphere of the family. It is not just that parents make frequent implicit and explicit comparisons between their children, but children themselves make such comparisons even as preschoolers. In the example that follows, Andy, a sensitive and rather anxious 30-month-old overhears his mother's proud comment about his exuberant younger sister Susie, who has just succeeded in achieving a (forbidden) goal in the face of prohibitions from their mother:

Example 3:

Mother to Susie (affectionately): Susie you *are* a determined little devil!

Andy to Mother (sadly): *I'm* not a determined little devil.

Mother to Andy (laughing): No! What are you? A poor old boy!

Andy is already aware of how his sister is seen, of how different he is from her. Younger siblings often compare themselves favorably with their older siblings, eagerly commenting on any reference made by their siblings to their own incapacities or inadequacies.

Differences in Experiences With Peers and Teachers

The third possible source of differential experience for siblings that we will consider takes us beyond the family. It seems very likely that when children begin to have a life outside their family world, with their school friends and peers, that important new experiences which may be different for the two siblings will influence their development. To what extent do siblings in fact have different experiences at school, with peers and teachers? They do, after all, often attend the same schools, and share the same neighborhood and social background. Two different studies have employed questionnaires that focus on differences in siblings' experiences with peers, and the results indicate that these differences are as great as those that they report in their relationship with their siblings. In one, for example, 20% of the children report their sibling's peer group and peer experiences and their own are "much different," whereas a further 42% report "a bit of difference." The extent of difference depends on the particular aspect of the peer group experience considered, with more similarity in delinquency and use of alcohol and drugs than in attitude to school work and popularity.

In our current study of the Colorado siblings, both children are in middle childhood, a period when peer and school relationships have an important impact on development (Hartup, 1983). Such extrafamilial experiences were noted by Rowe and Plomin (1981) as underexplored yet possibly important sources of nonshared experience. Using information gathered from mothers, children, and teachers we pursued the question of whether siblings did in fact have very different experiences outside the family (McGuire, Dunn, & Plomin, 1990). Each sibling was asked about the positive and negative aspects of their relationship with their teacher. Teachers were given a parallel scale to complete about their relationship with the child. For both teacher and sibling accounts, the correlations between the two siblings' experiences were non-significant (ranging from $r = .06$ to $r = -.26$), showing that the experiences the siblings had at school were very different, in this sample. We also interviewed the mother and each child about the negative and positive aspects of the child's relationship with his or her best friend. The correlation between the maternal reports for each sibling were positive, but low ($r = .22$ and $r = .14$ for positive and negative dimensions of the relationship respectively). Mothers, that is, tended to see their children as experiencing different kinds of friendships outside the family. However, there were for same-gender sibling pairs significant correlations between the children's accounts of the quality of their best friendships, though not for different-gender siblings. In other words, two sisters or two brothers were more likely to report similar kinds of friendships than were a sister and brother. This finding is perhaps not surprising. It could be that there are gender differences in how boys and girls talk about their relationships; it could also be that there are gender differences in the quality of best friendships. Still, the data show us that on average there were considerable differences in the experiences of the siblings.

Differences in Experiences of Life Events

The final source of differential experiences for siblings growing up together that we will consider concerns the impact of life events. In our Cambridge study, we examined the prevalence and the impact on each sibling of life events over a 3-year period; the scenarios of 256 events were rated by a child psychiatrist for their negative impact on each sibling (Beardsall & Dunn, 1992). Only 1 of the 80 children had not experienced at least one major event. The most commonly experienced events concerned accidents and illness, school problems, and bereavement. Some events, such as death of a grandmother or illness of the mother were likely to affect both siblings, others such as school-related events affected only one sibling directly. The results of the analysis highlighted two issues. First, the events that were apparently "shared," such as paternal unemployment or maternal illness, frequently affected the two siblings differently: 60% of such "shared" events had a different impact. Second, the number of events in total that had the same degree of negative impact on both siblings was relatively small: Only 31% had shared impact, whereas 69% had differing impact on the two siblings.

The general point that stands out from these results is that within the same family two children will usually experience differing degrees of stress. The individual family histories show us, moreover, that these events can often have a cumulative effect, in which one sibling suffers increasingly from a series of events, becoming apparently more and more vulnerable. For example, in one family the father had to be away for a 3-month period; his son missed him considerably, more so than his daughter. During the next 18 months the family suffered two car accidents, a burglary, and a house move, and the boy again was more disturbed by each of these events, becoming particularly anxious about his parents when they were out. The family were then burgled for a second time, and finally the paternal grandfather, to whom the boy was especially attached, died. The boy showed increasing disturbance in response to these events, in contrast to his sister, who coped with the events with little sign of upset other than a brief immediate response. Such data are based, of course, on a small sample, but they give us the first indication of the considerable extent to which such life events are not shared by siblings.

Associations Between Nonshared Experiences of Siblings and Outcome Measures

The data from these studies in Cambridge and Colorado, which differ in their methods and their samples, converge in the picture they give of the extent and nature of the differences in experiences of siblings in early and middle childhood in their relationships with their parents, and within the sibling relationship itself. The Colorado study shows us, moreover, that there are marked differences too in siblings' experiences in their peer relationships, and the Cambridge study highlights the differences in the impact upon siblings of life events. This documentation of the extent of differential experiences is, as we noted, the first step toward answering the challenge with which we began. The second step is to examine whether and how these differential experiences are related to the children's developmental outcome. In both studies we have begun to examine this issue, and in this section the preliminary findings are commented on briefly.

In the Colorado study, the emotional adjustment of each child is assessed when the child reaches 7 years, with the Child Behavior Checklist (Achenbach & Edelbrock, 1983). When we examined the relation of the children's adjustment to their experiences of differential treatment from their mothers, and to differential experiences within the sibling relationship, the results showed that differential maternal affection and control were linked to children's worrying, anxiety, and depression (Dunn et al., 1990b). Children who experienced more maternal control or less affection than their siblings were more likely to be anxious or depressed. Differential maternal behavior was also linked to children's antisocial behavior; the older siblings in families in which the mother controlled the older much more than the younger were likely to show relatively high levels of problem behavior. In these analyses, we cannot draw any conclusions about causal direction: it could be that the mothers were attempting to exert control over these older siblings because they were difficult—that the differential parental behavior is a response to child behavior and does not make an independent contribution to the adjustment. This issue of the direction of causal influence is clearly one of the chief topics to be addressed in future research (see later). However, the data do demonstrate that there is a clear association between differential experiences and outcome that is independent of the particular level of affection and control that the children received as individuals.

In the Cambridge study we have gone some way towards taking account of the contribution of child personality differences in the patterns of differential experience. We examined, for example, the differences between the siblings in their sense of self-worth and perception of their own self-competence—centrally important in children's emotional development. Children who feel that they are disliked by their peers and inadequate in their social relationships are more likely to describe themselves as depressed as they grow older. Little is known about the early family correlates of these differences in children's feelings of self-worth—though it is clearly important that we should understand what features of family life are linked to their development.

As we noted earlier, the Cambridge siblings were very different in their sense of self-competence and self-worth (Beardsall & Dunn, 1992). And the features of family experience that were correlated with the marked differences in their perceived self-competence included differential maternal and paternal behavior, both at the time that the children were assessed (aged on average 6½ and 9 years), and at the observations conducted 3 to 4 years earlier. Of particular importance is the finding that this contribution of differential parental behavior to the variance in self-esteem was independent of earlier differences in the siblings' temperament. Children whose mothers had shown relatively more affection to their siblings had a lower sense of self-competence than the children whose mothers had shown them more affection than their siblings. This effect remained after we took account of the variance in self-worth correlated with earlier temperamental differences between the siblings.

Differences in the siblings' experience within the sibling relationship was also related to the outcome measure of perceived self-competence. The greater the disparity between the negative behavior that the older siblings meted out to their younger siblings, and the hostility that they received from those siblings, the lower their own self-esteem. Children who behaved more negatively to their siblings than vice versa felt better about themselves than the children who received more hostility than they gave.

Are differences in peer experiences also related to child outcome? As yet, the information that we have comes chiefly from the cross-sectional studies employing the SIDE questionnaire. Associations are reported in these studies between these differential peer experiences and individual differences in personality and adjustment; these connections are not just associations between differences in sibling personality (with the more sociable sibling enjoying more peer popularity) but with the personality of the individual compared to other individuals in the wider population. That is, the implication is that if we want to explain why individuals in the general population differ, we should take account of their experiences with peers that are not shared with their siblings. Because these data are cross-sectional we are not, of course, able to draw conclusions about directions of causal inference. It seems likely that causal processes will go in both directions: Children who are easygoing and sociable will probably be more popular when they first move into the world of peers than their shyer, worrying siblings, but good experiences with peers are likely, too, to have a positive effect on children's feelings of self-worth and their confidence with other children.

Finally, we have already seen that the impact of life events differed for the siblings within the Cambridge study. The relation between the impact of school problems, parental illness, and so on and children's outcome was clear (Beardsall & Dunn, 1992). There were, for example, correlations between the experience of such stressful events and children's perceived self-competence. For the older siblings in the sample, the experience of negative life events was correlated $r(40) = -.36$ with perceived self-competence; for the younger siblings the correlation was $r(40) = -.38$, both $p < .05$. Siblings not only had differential experience of these events, but these experiences were systematically related to differences in outcome. It is of course a familiar problem with research on the influence of life events that the impact of an event is not independent of the personality of the person affected. We cannot therefore regard such events as purely "external," influencing the children's emotional adjustment in an independent way. It could be argued, for example, that accidents, illnesses, and school problems of the children themselves should be considered as "controllable" events, and where these have negative impact this reflects personality or vulnerability effects that are in part what we wish to explain. However two points should be noted: First, the proportion of clearly "noncontrollable" events with negative impact on the children (such as paternal absence due to employment problems, or bereavement) was high. Second, in this sample, no link was found between the frequency of events with negative impact and the children's temperament. The key observation is that within the same family, children experience stressful events to differing degrees, and these events can have a cumulative effect; initial personality differences may make the siblings vulnerable to different extents, but the experience of a series of such events may lead to very different outcomes for the two siblings. In considering the origins of sibling differences we must include not only the different relationships in which siblings are involved, but the impact of a broader range of experiences.

Directions for Research

What are the lessons from these first steps in examining differential experiences within the family? Where can our research efforts most usefully be focused in the future? We have learned that siblings experience very different relationships with their parents, with each other, and with their peers, and that they are differently affected by the dramas that beset families. It is much too early to judge how important each of these is for the children's developmental outcome in particular domains. But a number of points are highlighted by the studies in Cambridge and Colorado, which deserve emphasis.

First, there are suggestions from these first results that each of the sources we have studied makes a contribution to sibling differences. In inquiring about the origins of individual differences we need to move from general to more specific and focused questions—to ask not about whether the major source of nonshared environmental influence is parent–child relationships, or sibling relationships, or the world beyond the family, but rather, about the extent to which each of these sources and the components within each source affect a specific outcome at a particular stage.

Second, we should not expect to find simple associations between differential experiences of siblings and outcome measures. We know that developmental processes operate at many and interacting levels, and that there are complex patterns of mutual influence between family members. How a child behaves towards her sibling is affected by how each parent relates to each child in the family, and to make matters even more difficult for the investigator, these patterns of mutual influence are likely to change with development. Until now, we have hardly begun to consider how children's developmental stage affects the significance of the various kinds of differential experience within the family.

The third point concerns the importance of perceptions of relationships and of events within the family. The Cambridge research has shown just how early children notice and respond to the relationships and behavior of others within the family, and indeed compare themselves with those other family members

(Dunn, 1988). The results of systematic study confirm what the autobiographies of writers tell us so vividly: that children are extremely sensitive to perceived injustices, and differences in affection, esteem, and approval. The sophistication of even quite young preschool children's understanding of other people, and their relationships, draws attention to a fourth issue. We believe it is likely that the processes of influence that are important in the microenvironment of the family—the salient nonshared influences that lead to one child being different from his or her sibling—operate at a very subtle level. With research conducted on large numbers, and with the standardized methods that we try to use, our tools for studying such processes, the complexities of relationships and their differences, the significant incidents that shape children's development are inevitably extremely clumsy. With our simple descriptive tools and standardized procedures we run the risk of missing what matters in children's lives, in the microenvironments of their family worlds. At the very least, we need to be aware of the "epiphanies of the ordinary" in family lives, to use Joyce's phrase. And one lesson here is that we should listen to our subjects, and take their perceptions seriously. Finally, if we are to make progress in understanding how differences in children's personalities play a part in the trajectories of their different experiences within the family, we need to focus on children as active builders of their own worlds, within the family and outside. From Piaget onward, it has been acknowledged in theoretical discussion that children actively select and act on their environments, but there has been little empirical work that shows how such ideas can be tested. How can children's active construction or exploitation of their environments be described, and measured? Facing up to such intractable questions appears to be centrally important if we are to capture the key aspects of nonshared experience.

ACKNOWLEDGMENTS

The studies of siblings from the Colorado Adoption Project were conducted with support from NSF (BSN-782604 and BNS-8200310) and NICHD (HD-10333 and HD-18426). The Cambridge studies were supported by the Medical Research Council, and NIMH (MH46535-02).

REFERENCES

Achenbach, T. M., & Edelbrock, C. S. (1983). *Manual for the Child Behavior Checklist and revised Child Behavior Profile.* Burlington: University of Vermont, Department of Psychiatry.

Ahern, F. M., Johnson, R. C., Wilson, J. R., McClearn, G. E., & Vandenberg, S. G. (1982). Family resemblances in personality. *Behavior Genetics, 12,* 261–280.

Anderson, S. L. (1989). *Differential within-family experiences as predictors of adolescent personality and attachment style differences.* Honors thesis, Department of Psychology, Harvard University, Cambridge, MA.

Baker, L. A., & Daniels, D. (1990). Nonshared environmental influences and personality differences in adult twins. *Journal of Personality and Social Psychology, 58,* 103–110.

Beardsall, L., & Dunn, J. (1992). Adversities in childhood: Siblings' experiences and their relations to self esteem. *Journal of Child Psychology and Psychiatry, 33,* 349–359.

Bernard, J. S. (1982). *The future of marriage.* New Haven: Yale University Press.

Daniels, D. (1986). Differential experience of siblings in the same family as predictors of adolescent sibling personality differences. *Journal of Personality and Social Psychology, 51,* 339–346.

Daniels, D., Dunn, J., Furstenberg, F., & Plomin, R. (1985). Environmental differences within the family and adjustment differences within pairs of siblings. *Child Development, 56,* 764–774.

Daniels, D., & Plomin, R. (1985). Differential experiences of siblings in the same family. *Developmental Psychology, 21,* 747–760.

Dunn, J. (1988). *The beginnings of social understanding.* Cambridge, MA: Harvard University Press.

Dunn, J., Brown, J., & Beardsall, L. (1991). Family talk about feelings and children's later understanding of others' emotions. *Developmental Psychology, 27,* 448–455.

Dunn, J., & Kendrick, C. (1982). *Siblings: Love, envy and understanding.* Cambridge, MA: Harvard University Press.

Dunn, J., & Munn, P. (1985). Becoming a family member: Family conflict and the development of social understanding. *Child Development, 56,* 480–492.

Dunn, J., & Plomin, R. (1986). Determinants of maternal behavior toward three-year-old siblings. *British Journal of Developmental Psychology, 4,* 127–137.

Dunn, J., & Plomin, R. (1990). *Separate lives: Why siblings are so different.* New York: Basic Books.

Dunn, J., Plomin, R., & Daniels, D. (1986). Consistency and change in mothers' behavior to two-year-old siblings. *Child Development, 57,* 348–356.

Dunn, J., Plomin, R., & Nettles, M. (1985). Consistency of mothers' behavior towards infant siblings. *Developmental Psychology, 21,* 1188–1195.

Dunn, J., & Shatz, M. (1989). Becoming a conversationalist despite (or because of) having an older sibling. *Child Development, 60,* 399–410.

Dunn, J., Stocker, C., & Plomin, R. (1990a). Assessing the sibling relationship. *Journal of Child Psychology and Psychiatry, 31,* 983–991.

Dunn, J., Stocker, C., & Plomin, R. (1990b). Nonshared experiences within the family: Correlates of behavioral problems in middle childhood. *Development and Psychopathology, 2,* 113–126.

Edel, L. (1953). *Henry James: A biography. Vol. 1, The untried years.* London: Hart Davies.

Edel, L. (1987). *Henry James: A life.* London: Collins.

Eliot, G. (1979). *The mill on the floss.* Harmondsworth: Penguin Books.

Hartup, W. W. (1983). Peer relations. In P. H. Mussen (Series Ed.), E. M. Hetherington (Ed.), *Handbook of child psychology: Vol. 4. Socialization, personality, and social development* (pp. 103–196). New York: Wiley.

James, H. (1913). *A small boy and others.* New York: Charles Scribner's Sons.

James, H. (1914). *Notes of a son and brother.* New York: Charles Scribner's Sons.

Koch, H. L. (1960). The relation of certain formal attributes of siblings to attitudes held toward each other and toward their parents. *Monographs of the Society for Research in Child Development, 25* (Serial No. 4).

McGuire, S., Dunn, J., & Plomin, R. (1990). *Siblings' nonshared experiences with teachers and friends.* Manuscript submitted for publication.

Plomin, R., & Daniels, D. (1987). Why are children in the same family so different from each other? *The Behavioral and Brain Sciences, 10,* 1–16.

Plomin, R., DeFries, J. C., & Fulker, D. W. (1988). *Nature and nurture during infancy and early childhood.* New York: Cambridge University Press.

Rowe, D. C., & Plomin, R. (1981). The importance of nonshared (EI) environmental influences in behavioral development. *Developmental Psychology, 17,* 517–531.

Stocker, C., Dunn, J., & Plomin, R. (1989). Sibling relationships: Links with child temperament, maternal behavior, and family structure. *Child Development, 60,* 715–727.

Twain, M. (1966). *Autobiography.* New York: Harper & Rowe.

5

Sibling Relationships and Their Association With Parental Differential Treatment

Gene Brody
Zolinda Stoneman
University of Georgia

Children's relationships with their siblings can be important sources of influence in their lives, along with those they form with their parents, teachers, and friends. Siblings can serve as playmates, companions, agents of socialization, advocates with the peer group, and allies in dealing with parents, as well as models of both positive and negative behavior. As siblings compare themselves with one another, they develop ideas about their own abilities and worth (Tesser, 1980). Their behavior toward one another has been found to be associated with aspects of their social and cognitive development, personalities, and personal adjustment (Daniels, Dunn, Furstenberg, & Plomin, 1985; McHale & Gamble, 1987). Feelings that siblings develop toward one another in childhood have been found to persist into their adult lives (Ross, Dalton, & Milgram, 1981; Ross & Milgram, 1982). The sibling relationship, therefore, is an important area of study.

As both child development professionals and experienced parents have noted, children growing up within the same family can be remarkably different in their personalities and behavior. These differences, to some extent, can be attributed to environmental influences that the children do not share. Researchers have identified such factors as siblings' experiences with each other, their relationships with peers and teachers, and disparate life events as contributors to their personality differences (cf. Dunn & Stocker, 1989). In this chapter we examine an important source of nonshared family experience, parental differential treatment, in terms of its associations with sibling relationship quality.

Differences in the ways in which parents treat their children have been clearly documented. Children ranging in age from 5 years to adolescence have reported that their parents treat them differently from their siblings (Brody & Stoneman, 1990; Daniels et al., 1985; Koch, 1960). Observational studies, indicating that mothers direct different rates of affectionate, controlling, and responsive behavior toward their children (Abramovitch, Pepler, & Corter, 1982; Brody, Stoneman, & Burke, 1987; Bryant & Crockenberg, 1980; Dunn & Kendrick, 1982; Dunn & Munn, 1985, 1986; Hetherington, 1988; Stocker, Dunn, & Plomin, 1989), support their perceptions. Dunn and her colleagues found mothers to treat their children differently based on the children's age differences, on such dimensions as affection, control, play behavior, and disciplinary approaches (see Dunn & Stocker, 1989). Other researchers have found mothers to be more responsive, verbal, controlling, and emotionally expressive with their younger children than with their older children (Brody et al., 1987; Bryant & Crockenberg, 1980).

Differences such as these in parental behavior have been linked to sibling relationship variables. Specifically, differential treatment from a parent, usually the mother, is associated with higher than average levels of conflict and negativity between siblings (Brody et al., 1987; Bryant & Crockenberg, 1980; Furman & Buhrmester, 1985). The cross-sectional designs used in these studies, however, do not allow the conclusion that parental differential treatment causes difficult sibling relationships; parents may treat their children differently in response to the behaviors the siblings have enacted throughout their lives. Nevertheless, the fact that these variables are significantly related suggests the importance of parental differential treatment to siblings' personality differences and interactions.

RESEARCH STUDIES

Differential Treatment and Child Temperament

We have conducted several studies designed to identify further the associations among sibling relationship characteristics, parental differential treatment, and other nonshared influences. In our first project we investigated two divergent aspects of children's environments in terms of their associations with sibling behavior: one personal attribute, temperament, and one family influence, maternal differential behavior (Brody et al., 1987). Forty mothers and their same-gender children, 20 pairs of boys and 20 pairs of girls, participated. The mothers and two children were observed in triadic interactions, playing the board game Trouble (Gilbert Industries) and building with a set of Legos (Interlego, AG). We chose the Legos as a semistructured task and the Trouble game as a structured one, to enable us to observe parent–child interaction in different kinds of contexts. On a separate occasion the siblings played with these toys together, without the mother present. All toy interactions were videotaped, and the participants' verbal, prosocial, and agonistic behaviors were coded using a 10-second interval coding procedure. One week after the interactions were taped, mothers completed the activity, emotional intensity, and persistence subscales of Martin's (1984) Temperament Assessment Battery. These particular subscales were used because the personality dimensions they are designed to assess have been associated with antisocial behavior among school-aged children (Buss & Plomin, 1975). Further, in sibling pairs in which one child demonstrated these temperamental traits, both children were found to behave negatively toward one another, and to experience conflict with one another to a greater extent than did a group of control siblings (Arnold, Levine, & Patterson, 1975; Mash & Johnson, 1983).

Our results indicated that, for sisters, high activity, high emotional intensity, and low persistence levels in either child were associated with increased negative behavior between them. For brothers, high activity and low persistence levels among younger siblings were associated with the exchange of more negative behavior. When the mother's behavior favored the younger child, the siblings talked to each other less, and exchanged less of both positive and negative behaviors. These results indicated that both child temperament and parental differential treatment were associated, in the ways that we predicted, with the amount and quality of the behavior that siblings exchange.

Sibling Relations and Direct and Differential Treatment

Our next study (Brody, Stoneman, & McCoy, 1992) focused exclusively on parental behaviors as they are associated with sibling relations. We again examined parental differential treatment, because of its negative associations with sibling expressiveness and relationship quality in the previous study. In addition to re-examining the mothers' role in sibling relations, we included fathers in this study. Fathers' behavior toward their children has seldom been examined, especially as it is expressed through differential treatment. It is possible that parent gender also may be associated with differential treatment patterns, because parents of different genders have been found to interact with their children in distinct ways. Most American fathers have been found, for example, to assume a secondary caregiver role with their children, and to play with them more often than do mothers (Lamb, 1981; Parke, 1978). These differences in the ways in which fathers relate to their children, and in the amount of time that they spend with them, may be associated with differences in the patterns of sibling relations that are associated with fathers' differential treatment. In view of these factors, the major purposes of this study were to examine the associations of paternal, as well as maternal, differential behavior with differences in sibling relationships, and to examine the unique contributions of maternal and paternal direct and differential behavior to variations in sibling relationships.

In addition to continuing our exploration of differential treatment, we also wanted to see how direct parental behavior is associated with the ways in which siblings behave toward one another. Direct behavior is that which a parent addresses to an individual child, without regard to the behavior the parent enacts with the child's siblings. We hypothesized that direct parental behavior would influence sibling relationships by influencing the behaviors of the individual children who comprise the relationship. For example, we expected a child to whom a parent directs frequent positive and prosocial behavior to direct much the same behavior to his or her siblings, thus making for a harmonious relationship. Perspectives such as social learning (Parke, MacDonald, Beitel, & Bhavnagri, 1988) and attachment (Sroufe & Fleeson, 1986) theories predict such an association. Researchers have found such direct maternal behaviors as responsiveness (Dunn & Kendrick, 1982; Howe, 1986; Stewart, Mobely, Van Tuyl, & Salvador, 1987), control (Brody, Stoneman, & MacKinnon, 1986; Brody et al., 1987; Stocker et al., 1989), and positivity/negativity (Brody et al., 1987; Stocker et al., 1989) to be associated with siblings' behavior toward one another. We specifically hypothesized that high rates of parental positive and responsive behavior would be associated with more positive sibling relations, that more negative and controlling parental behavior would be related to more negativity in the sibling relationship, and that a higher degree of parental differential treatment would be associated with poorer sibling relations.

The participants in this study were 109 Caucasian, intact, middle-class, nonclinic families with same-gender children, 56 pairs of boys and 53 pairs of girls. As in the previous study, only same-gender sibling pairs were recruited for participation in order to control for gender effects. The older siblings' ages ranged from 6 to 11 years at the beginning of the study, and the younger siblings' from 4 to 9 years. Most of the pairs were separated in age by 2 or 3 years.

The procedures followed in this study are similar to the ones we used in our previous project. Again, two visits were made to each participating family's home, scheduled 1 week apart. These visits also were repeated 1 year later, so that longitudinal assessments could be made. As before, parents and children were videotaped interacting with one another while participating in activities that the research team provided. The board game Trouble was again used, and several new activities were added in place of the Lego construction task. Each parent and the siblings shared a Viewmaster, selecting together the program they wanted to watch and coordinating their turn taking. An anagram/computer task, based on one developed by Zussman (1980), was also provided, in which each parent and the siblings sat together while working on different tasks; the parent mentally solved a scrambled word puzzle while the siblings took turns playing with a hand-held video game. These two activities were added in order to simulate situations that occur every day in the home: one in which the parent is concentrating on the children and is involved in their activity, and one in which the parent's attention is devoted to something else. As in our previous study, the siblings were also observed interacting alone, without parents present. They played Trouble and Viewmaster together, and shared snacks.

The videotapes were coded using a 5-second interval recording system through which verbal, controlling, responsive, positive, and negative behaviors were recorded. For the purposes of this study, the controlling and responsive behaviors from the triadic interactions were examined, as were the positive and negative behaviors from both the parent–child triadic and dyadic sibling interactions. The proportion of time during which each subject directed each behavior to the others was computed by dividing counts of each behaviors' occurrence by the number of intervals in the interaction. These proportions were averaged across activities.

In order to supplement the information gained from objective observation, we included a self-report measure of sibling relationship quality. Eighty-three of the older siblings in the sample used Furman and Buhrmester's (1985) Sibling Relationship Questionnaire (SRQ) to report their perceptions of the quality of their sibling relationships. This instrument was added later in the study, hence 26 of the older siblings did not have the opportunity to complete it; younger siblings were not administered the questionnaire because not all of them were able to respond to it reliably when it was introduced. As with the observational assessments, the self-report instrument was administered both years.

Two sets of analyses were conducted. First, we executed descriptive analyses to compare rates of maternal and paternal direct and differential behavior. Second, we used hierarchical multiple regression analyses to determine each parent's unique contributions to the contemporaneous and longitudinal assessments of sibling relationship quality. The first set of analyses revealed differences and similarities in the ways in which mothers and fathers interact with their children. We found that the mothers in our sample directed more positive behavior to both their children than did the fathers. Both parents directed more of their interactive behaviors toward the younger sibling than toward the older sibling, and mothers and fathers did not differ significantly in the degree of differential treatment they enacted with their children. Preliminary analyses, designed to determine which direct and differential behaviors were associated with variations in the quality of sibling relationships for each parent, indicated that a mixture of such behaviors from the father were associated significantly with the sibling relationship measures; this indicates the importance of including data on parental behavior from both parents, rather than from the mother only, when studying its association with sibling relations.

The results of the preliminary analyses also provided support for our hypotheses concerning direct and differential parental behavior. Direct positive and negative behavior from the parents to the children was associated with the children's enactment of the same kind of behavior with their siblings, and

TABLE 5.1
Concurrent Parental Behavior Predictors of Sibling Relationship Measures
from Hierarchical Multiple Regression Analyses

Sibling Relationship Measures, Year 1	Parental Behavior	p	R^2
Younger sibling positive behavior	Paternal direct responsive behavior to younger sibling (−)	.005	.07
	Paternal direct positive behavior to younger sibling (+)	.03	.04
Older sibling positive behavior	Maternal direct positive behavior to older sibling (+)	.04	.03
Younger sibling negative behavior	Paternal direct negative behavior to younger sibling (+)	.02	.03
	Paternal direct control behavior to younger sibling (+)	.002	.06
	Paternal differential responsive behavior (+)	.002	.06
Older sibling negative behavior	Paternal direct negative behavior to older sibling (+)	.0001	.18
	Paternal differential control behavior (+)	.03	.03
SRQ positive scale	Paternal direct control behavior to older sibling (−)	.03	.03
	Paternal differential positive behavior (−)	.005	.09
SRQ negative scale	Maternal direct control behavior to older sibling (+)	.005	.08
	Paternal differential negative behavior (+)	.02	.06

differential treatment, particularly from fathers, was associated with negative sibling behavior.

In Tables 5.1 and 5.2 we present the results of the hierarchical multiple regression analyses through which we examined the unique contributions of maternal and paternal behavior to contemporaneous and longitudinal assessments of sibling relationship quality. Table 5.1 presents the contemporaneous, and Table 5.2 the longitudinal, data. In these analyses, the contribution of each parent's direct and differential behavior is computed after the contribution of the other parent's behavior has been statistically controlled. For each sibling relations measure reported in Tables 5.1 and 5.2, first the maternal predictors were added after the paternal predictors. Each paternal predictor then was added after the maternal predictors, in order to determine the unique variance each parent's behavior contributed to the prediction of the sibling relationships. Such analyses remove any variance that both parents contribute; the resulting R-squared statistics are usually modest.

Several interesting patterns are revealed in the tables. For the contemporaneous analyses, 10 of the 12 parental predictors were paternal and 2 were maternal. Four of the paternal predictors were differential treatment measures, whereas neither of the maternal predictors was such. Paternal differential responsive and controlling behavior were associated with higher rates of negative

TABLE 5.2
Longitudinal Parental Behavior Predictors of Sibling Relationship Measures
from Hierarchical Multiple Regression Analyses

Sibling Relationship Measures, Year 2	Parental Behavior	p	R^2
Younger sibling positive behavior	Maternal differential control behavior (−)	.002	.08
	Maternal differential responsive behavior (+)	.009	.06
	Paternal direct positive behavior to younger sibling (+)	.01	.05
	Paternal differential negative behavior (−)	.02	.05
Older sibling positive behavior	Paternal differential negative behavior(−)	.01	.06
Younger sibling negative behavior	Maternal direct negative behavior to younger sibling (+)	.05	.03
Older sibling negative behavior	Paternal direct negative behavior to older sibling (+)	.01	.06
	Paternal direct positive behavior to older sibling (−)	.05	.03
SRQ positive scale	(None significant)		
SRQ negative scale	Maternal differential positive behavior (+)	.03	.04
	Paternal differential negative behavior (+)	.05	.04

behavior from younger and older siblings, respectively. Paternal differential positive and negative behavior were associated with fewer positive and more negative perceptions of the sibling relationship.

Those maternal and paternal direct and differential behaviors that contributed to the longitudinal prediction of sibling relationship quality were more evenly distributed. Of the 10 uniquely contributing maternal and paternal predictors, 6 were differential treatment measures. Mothers' differential control forecast lower levels of positive behavior from younger siblings, and their differential positive behavior was longitudinally linked with older sibling's negative perceptions of the sibling relationship. Fathers' differential negative behavior forecast lower rates of positive behavior from both younger and older siblings, and more negative perceptions of the sibling relationship from older siblings.

Although rates of direct and differential behavior are similar for fathers and mothers, fathers' behavior appears to be associated especially strongly with their children's behavior and sibling relationships. This result may be related to the relative scarcity of fathers' attention compared to that of mothers in everyday settings. Because fathers have been found to spend less time than do mothers with school-age youth (Baumrind, 1982; Noller, 1980; Patterson, 1982; Russell & Russell, 1987), the types of relationships that children form with each of their parents may vary in ways are related to these unique associations with differential treatment. Future research therefore should focus on the relation of parental availability to the relative salience of parental behavior.

Sibling Conflict and Differential Treatment

Because this study revealed that some differential treatment variables were linked to siblings' positive and negative behavior and feelings toward each other, we next explored the association of differential treatment with sibling conflict (Brody, Stoneman, McCoy, & Forehand, 1992). This time, we chose a context in which to assess differential treatment that even more closely resembles family interaction in its natural setting, a family discussion about problems that the siblings were experiencing in their relationship. We proceeded from a systems theory perspective (P. Minuchin, 1985; S. Minuchin, 1974), that family subsystems are influenced by one another. In our study, we investigated the interconnections among sibling conflict, marital satisfaction, conflict between spouses, family emotional climate, and problem-solving strategies.

This study was performed with some of the same families who participated in the one described earlier. Seventy-six families, 36 with female and 40 with male children, participated. The negative behavior observational codes and the SRQ negative scale from the previous investigation were used as indicators of sibling conflict for the present study. (In this smaller sample, 56 of the 76 older siblings had completed the SRQ.) Rather than using triadic play interactions among parents and siblings to gauge differential treatment, the discussion activity described above was designed to involve both parents and both siblings in the resolution of problems that the children were experiencing in their relationship.

During the second home visit that took place each year during the previous study, each sibling was asked privately by a researcher to name a problem that the child had with the other sibling, one that he or she would feel comfortable discussing on tape with the family. The researchers then presented the problems to the assembled family group, asking them to discuss the problems and try to arrive at solutions. The families were limited to 15 minutes in which to do this; if they were finished sooner, they informed the researchers. Most of the families quickly became highly involved with the task.

To code the discussions, we designed a system especially for this study, using global ratings of *family harmony, parenting style,* and *equality of treatment of siblings*, the variables that we proposed to be associated with sibling conflict. These dimensions were rated on Likert-type scales by trained student coders, who watched the entire interaction and then rated it. The family harmony construct was rated on a 7-point scale ranging from conflicted to harmonious; the parenting style and equal treatment variables were rated along 4-point scales ranging from overcontrolling to moderately controlling and younger sibling clearly favored to equal treatment, respectively. The higher ends of these latter scales, indicating undercontrol and favoritism toward the older sibling, were dropped, because few families scored in these areas.

Each year, about a week after the visit in which the problem-solving interaction took place, a third home visit was made during which the parents completed self-report instruments. They completed the Dyadic Adjustment Scale (Spanier, 1976) and the O'Leary-Porter Scale (Porter & O'Leary, 1980) as measures of the extent of harmony and conflict in the parents' relationship, and the Family Relationship Inventory (Moos & Moos, 1981) as an indicator of the total family's social climate. Each parent completed these reports privately, to insure independent responses.

Modest correlations emerged among the contemporaneous family relationship constructs. Based on mothers' reports, marital quality was positively related to family expressiveness and cohesion, and negatively related to interparental and family conflict. Family cohesion was further related, positively, to family expressiveness, and negatively to family conflict. Family conflict was itself positively related to interparental conflict. The same associations of marital quality with interparental conflict, family expressiveness, and family cohesion emerged when fathers' reports were used, as did the relation of family cohesion to family expressiveness. In addition, family cohesion was also related, negatively, to interparental conflict according to the fathers' reports.

Other significant associations were found both at the contemporaneous and longitudinal levels. Two of the family relationship variables as reported by mothers showed significant contemporaneous relationships with two of the observed problem-solving behaviors. Mothers' reports of interparental conflict were negatively related to harmonious family interaction and to equality of sibling treatment; the latter behavior was also negatively related to family conflict. In addition, sibling conflict levels were stable across 1 year, as measured by both the siblings' observed negative behavior and the older siblings' reports of conflict on the SRQ.

Our first hypothesis, concerning the association between sibling conflict and family relations variables, received considerable support, particularly from associations with mothers' family environment reports. Contemporaneously, negative sibling behavior was positively associated with interparental conflict and negatively associated with marital quality. The SRQ conflict score also was positively related to interparental conflict; in addition, it was related positively to family conflict and negatively to family cohesion. The associations with the SRQ conflict measure remained significant in the longitudinal assessment. Significant associations emerged only longitudinally with the fathers' measures. Negative sibling behavior was negatively related to family cohesion, and the SRQ conflict score was positively related to interparental conflict and negatively associated with marital quality.

The second hypothesis, concerning the association of sibling conflict with problem-solving behaviors, received both contemporaneous and longitudinal support. Contemporaneously, negative sibling behavior was found to be positively associated with both maternal and paternal overcontrol, and negatively with maternal and paternal equal treatment and family harmony. SRQ conflict scores

TABLE 5.3
Variance in Sibling Conflict Measures Explained by Family Relationship
Measures and Family Problem Solving for Contemporaneous and
Longitudinal Stepwise Regression Analyses

Sibling Conflict Measures	Predictors	p	R^2
Contemporaneous Negative Behavior	Paternal Equality of Treatment (−)	.0003	.17
	Family Harmony (−)	.04	.05
Contemporaneous SRQ Scale	Maternal FRI–Conflict (+)	.002	.16
	Family Harmony (−)	.008	.11
Longitudinal Negative Behavior	Paternal Equality of Treatment (−)	.001	.14
	Paternal FRI–Cohesion (−)	.02	.06
Longitudinal SRQ Scale	Maternal FRI–Cohesion (−)	.005	.11
	Maternal Equality of Treatment (−)	.05	.05

also were negatively associated with family harmony and with equal treatment from each parent. The associations of negative sibling behavior with family harmony and paternal equal treatment, and of SRQ conflict with family harmony and maternal equal treatment, were also significant in the longitudinal analysis.

Table 5.3 presents those pairs of predictors that most parsimoniously accounted for variance in the sibling conflict measures. For negative sibling behavior, paternal equal treatment and family harmony together accounted for 22% of the variance in the contemporaneous analysis, whereas paternal equal treatment combined with paternal reports of family cohesion accounted for 20% of the variance in the longitudinal assessment. For the SRQ conflict measure, maternal reports of family conflict and ratings of family harmony together accounted for 27% of the contemporaneous variance, and maternal reports of family cohesion combined with maternal equal treatment of siblings accounted for 16% of the longitudinal variance.

These findings both corroborate and extend those that have emerged from previous research. School-age siblings whose fathers treated them impartially during problem-solving discussions, whose families are generally harmonious even when discussing problems, and whose parents consider their family relationships to be generally close, were less likely to develop conflicted relationships. This study also indicated that fathers' unequal treatment of siblings during problem-solving discussions was especially significant to sibling conflict, a finding that is similar to the one that emerged from our previous study, in which fathers' direct and differential behavior was found to be strongly associated with more general sibling relationship quality. Further, open family discussion of school-age siblings' disputes, during which the children were able to assertively voice their opinions while the parents considered each sibling's perspective equally and used moderate levels of control, was associated with less conflicted sibling relationships.

The longitudinal associations indicated that unequal treatment from mothers was associated with siblings' reports of conflicted relationships, whereas such treatment from fathers was associated with conflicted sibling behavior. This provides new information on the associations between parental differential treatment and sibling conflict. As noted in our previous study, the associations of unequal treatment by fathers with sibling behavior and unequal treatment by mothers with perceptions of conflict may have to do with the parents' relative availability. Because fathers spend less time than do mothers with school-age youth, we may speculate that unequal treatment from fathers could be more salient, and could possibly induce more anger and rivalrous feelings that are actualized during sibling interactions. Unequal treatment from mothers could, instead, contribute to the children's perceptions of their relationship across time.

The stability of sibling conflict levels across one year may have special significance from a developmental perspective. Ross and Milgram (1982) found that rivalrous feelings between siblings that originated in childhood persist into adulthood, and that such feelings are associated with the closeness of adult sibling relationships. This suggests the importance of understanding early sibling conflict, given the degree to which siblings can serve as sources of emotional support across the life span.

IMPLICATIONS FOR RESEARCH AND PRACTICE

Taken together, the results of the studies we have presented in this chapter have implications for continued research, as well as practical applications for families. Both studies on the associations of parental behavior with sibling relations brought out the importance of examining both parents' behavior in this context. Family researchers customarily have focused only on the mother; our data indicate that both mothers and fathers must be included in studies of family dynamics, because the associations that each parent's behavior has with sibling relationships may differ. We have found that mothers and fathers are not interchangeable, and one cannot be used as a proxy for the other.

Our data further revealed that both child behavior and child attitudes are associated with parental behavior. Both the observations of sibling interactions and the self-report SRQ measure demonstrated significant associations with the parent behavior measures. The fact that attitudes as well as behavior are associated with parental treatment suggests the possibility of a long term association that goes beyond the siblings' immediate interactions, by establishing a particular frame of reference from which siblings interact with each other. The effects of siblings' attitudes on their long term behavior and relationship quality should receive further research attention.

Finally, it must be acknowledged that, the emergence of negative associations between differential treatment and sibling relationship measures notwithstanding, it is impossible for parents to treat their children completely equally; even if it were possible, it would not be desirable. For example, in most families the siblings differ in age, and parents have in fact been found to treat their children differently on the basis of age (Maccoby & Martin, 1983). Not to do so would insure that the parents' behavior would be developmentally inappropriate for at least one of the children; one cannot maintain the same standards, and enact the same type of behavior, with a 2-year-old and a 6-year-old. Our studies, as well as others (Brody et al., 1987; Brody, Stoneman, & McCoy, 1992; Brody, Stoneman, McCoy, & Forehand, 1992; Bryant & Crockenberg, 1980; Stocker et al., 1989), have indicated that parents consistently direct more of their behaviors to younger siblings than to older siblings. This type of parental behavior appears to be normative, and is based on the fact that younger siblings are usually less mature, less cognitively competent, and less physically and socially skilled than their older brothers and sisters. The differential treatment observed in this context therefore is a response to the children's individual needs, rather than a manifestation of some sort of parental "favoritism." Differences in children's needs and personalities arising from genetic influences, unique life experiences, and events occurring outside the family context may also make it necessary for sensitive and responsive parents to treat their children differently from one another.

From our perspective, parents and siblings operate in unison to maintain balanced interactions that include appropriate amounts of parental behavior directed to each child. The specific behaviors and amounts are probably derived from the interaction of such factors as the temperaments of children and parents, family members' thoughts about particular behaviors' meanings, and the histories of positive and negative contingencies that family members provide for particular behaviors, as well as parental sensitivity to their children's needs. Each family thus establishes the type of interaction that each member feels is equitable; the resulting "comfort zone" is one in which each child receives an age-appropriate balance of parental behavior, and no child feels that his or her own individual needs are being neglected in favor of a sibling.

The type of differential treatment that appears to be associated with sibling relationship difficulties is not based on responses to the children's individual needs. Some recent data from our lab indicate that the balance of the comfort zone can be disrupted when parents bring emotion from situations that do not involve children (such as anger with a spouse) into situations that do involve them. Such a practice can hamper parents in their efforts to maintain balanced interactions with their children by interfering with the monitoring of their own behavior, possibly fostering higher levels of non-need-based differential treatment. Our ongoing research efforts in this area are addressing these processes.

REFERENCES

Abramovitch, R., Pepler, D., & Corter, C. (1982). Patterns of sibling interaction among preschool-age children. In M. E. Lamb & B. Sutton-Smith (Eds.), *Sibling relationships: Their nature and significance across the lifespan* (pp. 61–86). Hillsdale, NJ: Lawrence Erlbaum Associates.

Arnold, J., Levine, A., & Patterson, G. R. (1975). Changes in sibling behavior following intervention. *Journal of Consulting and Clinical Psychology, 43*, 683–688.

Baumrind, D. (1982). Are androgynous individuals more effective persons and parents? *Child Development, 53*, 44–75.

Brody, G. H., & Stoneman, Z. (1990). Sibling relationships. In I. Sigel & G. H. Brody (Eds.), *Methods of family research: Biographies of research projects* (pp. 189–212). Hillsdale, NJ: Lawrence Erlbaum Associates.

Brody, G. H., Stoneman, Z., & Burke, M. (1987). Child temperaments, maternal differential behavior, and sibling relationships. *Developmental Psychology, 23*, 354–362.

Brody, G. H., Stoneman, Z., & MacKinnon, C. (1986). Contributions of maternal childrearing practices and interactional contexts to sibling interactions. *Journal of Applied Developmental Psychology, 7*, 225–236.

Brody, G. H., Stoneman, Z., & McCoy, J. K. (1992). Associations of maternal and paternal direct and differential behavior with sibling relationships: Contemporaneous and longitudinal analyses. *Child Development, 63*, 82–92.

Brody, G. H., Stoneman, Z., McCoy, J. K., & Forehand, R. (1992). Contemporaneous and longitudinal associations of sibling conflict with family relationship assessments and family discussions about sibling problems. *Child Development, 63*, 391–400.

Bryant, B., & Crockenberg, S. (1980). Correlations and dimensions of prosocial behavior: A study of female siblings and their mothers. *Child Development, 51*, 529–544.

Buss, A. H., & Plomin, R. (1975). *A temperament theory of personality development.* New York: Wiley-Interscience.

Daniels, D., Dunn, J., Furstenberg, F., & Plomin, R. (1985). Environmental differences within the family and adjustment differences within pairs of adolescent siblings. *Child Development, 56*, 764–774.

Dunn, J., & Kendrick, C. (1982). *Siblings: Love, envy and understanding.* Cambridge, MA: Harvard University Press.

Dunn, J., & Munn, P. (1985). Becoming a family member: Family conflict and the development of social understanding in the second year. *Child Development, 56*, 480–492.

Dunn, J., & Munn, P. (1986). Sibling quarrels and maternal intervention: Individual differences in understanding and aggression. *Journal of Child Psychology and Psychiatry, 27*, 583–595.

Dunn, J., & Stocker, C. (1989). The significance of differences in siblings' experiences within the family. In K. Kreppner & R. M. Lerner (Eds.), *Family systems and life-span development* (pp. 289–301). Hillsdale, NJ: Lawrence Erlbaum Associates.

Furman, W., & Buhrmester, D. (1985). Children's perceptions of the qualities of their sibling relationships. *Child Development, 56*, 448–461.

Hetherington, E. M. (1988). Parents, children, and siblings six years after divorce. In R. A. Hinde & J. Stevenson-Hinde (Eds.), *Relationships within families* (pp. 311–331). New York: Oxford University Press.

Howe, N. (1986). *Socialization, social cognitive factors, and the development of sibling relationships.* Unpublished doctoral dissertation, University of Waterloo, Canada.

Koch, H. L. (1960). The relation of certain formal attributes of siblings to their attitudes held towards each other and towards their parents. *Monographs of the Society for Research in Child Development, 25*(No. 4).

Lamb, M. E. (1981). *The role of the father in child development* (2nd ed.). New York: Wiley.

Maccoby, E. E., & Martin, J. A. (1983). Socialization in the context of family: Parent-child interaction. In P. H. Mussen (Series Ed.) & E. M. Hetherington (Vol. Ed.), *Handbook of child psychology: Vol. 4. Socialization, personality, social development* (4th ed., pp. 1–101). New York: Wiley.

Martin, R. P. (1984). *Manual for the temperament assessment battery.* Unpublished monograph, University of Georgia, Athens.

Mash, E. J., & Johnson, C. (1983). Sibling interactions of hyperactive and normal children and their relationship to reports of maternal stress and self-esteem. *Journal of Clinical Child Psychology, 12,* 91–99.

McHale, S. M., & Gamble, W. C. (1987). Sibling relationships and adjustment of children with disabled brothers and sisters. *Journal of Children in Contemporary Society, 19,* 131–158.

Minuchin, P. (1985). Families and individual development: Provocations from the field of family therapy. *Child Development, 56,* 289–302.

Minuchin, S. (1974). *Families and family therapy.* Cambridge, MA: Harvard University Press.

Moos, R., & Moos, B. (1981). A typology of family social environments. *Family Process, 15,* 357–371.

Noller, P. (1980). Cross-gender effect in two child families. *Developmental Psychology, 16,* 159–160.

Parke, R. D. (1978). *Fathers.* Cambridge, MA: Harvard University Press.

Parke, R. D., MacDonald, K. D., Beitel, A., & Bhavnagri, N. (1988). The role of the family in the development of peer relationships. In R. D. Peters & R. J. McMahon (Eds.), *Social learning and systems approaches to marriage and the family* (pp. 17–44). New York: Bruner-Mazel.

Patterson, G. R. (1982). *Coercive family process: A social learning approach.* Eugene, OR: Castalia.

Porter, B., & O'Leary, K. D. (1980). Marital discord and childhood behavior problems. *Journal of Abnormal Child Psychology, 80,* 287–295.

Ross, H. G., Dalton, M. J., & Milgram, J. (1981). *Older adults' perceptions of closeness in sibling relationships.* (ERIC/CAPS Document Reproduction Service No. ED 201 903)

Ross, H. G., & Milgram, J. (1982). Important variables in adult sibling relationships: A qualitative study. In M. E. Lamb & B. Sutton-Smith (Eds.), *Sibling relationships: Their nature and significance over the lifespan* (pp. 225–247). Hillsdale, NJ: Lawrence Erlbaum Associates.

Russell, G., & Russell, A. (1987). Mother–child and father–child relationships in middle childhood. *Child Development, 58,* 1573–1585.

Spanier, G. B. (1976). Measuring dyadic adjustment. *Journal of Marriage and the Family, 38,* 15–38.

Sroufe, L. A., & Fleeson, J. (1986). Attachment and the construction of relationships. In W. W. Hartup & Z. Rubin (Eds.), *Relationships and development* (pp. 51–72). Hillsdale, NJ: Lawrence Erlbaum Associates.

Stewart, R. B., Mobley, L. A., Van Tuyl, S. S., & Salvador, M. A. (1987). The firstborn's adjustment to the birth of a sibling: A longitudinal assessment. *Child Development, 58,* 341–355.

Stocker, C., Dunn, J., & Plomin, R. (1989). Sibling relationships: Links with child temperament, maternal behavior, and family structure. *Child Development, 60,* 715–727.

Tesser, A. (1980). Self-esteem maintenance in family dynamics. *Journal of Personality and Social Psychology, 39,* 77–91.

Zussman, J. U. (1980). Situational determinants of parental behavior: Effects of competing cognitive activity. *Child Development, 51,* 792–797.

6

A Comparison of Across-Family and Within-Family Parenting Predictors of Adolescent Psychopathology and Suicidal Ideation

Maria Tejerina-Allen
Columbia University School of Public Health
Murcia University, Murcia, Spain

Barry M. Wagner
Catholic University

Patricia Cohen
Columbia University
New York State Psychiatric Institute

Recent findings on both young children (Dunn & Munn, 1986) and adolescents (Daniels, Dunn, Furstenberg, & Plomin, 1985) have suggested that differences in the ways that parents relate to their different offspring (i.e., within-family variation) may be quite consequential for child development. We have found these findings to be of considerable interest, partly because they provide fresh evidence that child-rearing differences matter. This is important in light of recent work in two bodies of research in developmental psychology that has called into question the importance of child-rearing variation between families. Reviews of the socialization literature (e.g., Maccoby & Martin, 1983) have suggested that, within normal ranges, child-rearing variation between families appears to be of only modest consequence for child development.

Behavioral genetics literature has argued that whatever modest between-family effects are detected may be mostly attributable to genetic differences between children (Goldsmith, 1983). Studies of within-family effects of differences in child-rearing provide an alternative route towards identifying environmental sources of variation in child characteristics, specifically those that are not shared by siblings (Plomin & Daniels, 1987).

This study provides more direct evidence regarding the relationship of non-shared family environment with children's problems. Specifically, the questions to be answered included the following:

1. How similar is reported parenting between adolescent siblings?
2. How similar are siblings in their levels of depression, oppositional behavior, and suicidal behavior?
3. What shared aspects of parenting relate to the depression, oppositional behavior, and suicidal behavior of siblings?
4. What differences in parenting relate to differences in depression, oppositional behavior, and suicidal behavior of siblings?
5. Are within-family differences in parenting more consequential than between-family differences?
6. Are different parenting dimensions important for within-family child outcomes as compared to between-family child outcomes?

SAMPLE

The current study used 178 sibling pairs originating from a larger sample of about 800 children (the Children in the Community study sample) who have been followed longitudinally since 1975 when they were ages 1–10. The original sample, consisting of one child per family, was randomly drawn from 100 randomly selected neighborhoods in two upstate New York counties (see Kogan, Smith, & Jenkins, 1977, for a full description of the sampling procedure). In 1983 and 1985–1986, 766 of the original 976 children were successfully interviewed in one or both follow-up surveys. A new random sample of 54 children living in areas of urban poverty was added in order to replace children from these kinds of neighborhoods who had been disproportionately lost to follow-up. Children from this larger sample are referred to as *study children*.

In 1987, following the second follow-up of the study children, a sample of siblings was drawn to study suicidal behavior and attitudes in the siblings of three groups of study children: children who had reported suicide attempts or who had elevated suicidal feelings (25%), children who had not attempted suicide but who were high on risk factors for such suicidal behavior (25%), and children with neither high risk nor suicidal behavior (50%).

Sampling of families with eligible siblings was limited to those who had siblings in the 12- to 18-year age range, for whom both children lived with the biological mother, and who lived in the immediate geographical area (the latter because of financial limitations of our project). Approximately 300 families were eligible on these grounds. Of the 200 families sampled for this study, 179 (90%) were interviewed; in one of these families, only the child was successfully interviewed. In each family, we attempted to interview the sibling who was closest in age to the study child, although in some cases it was necessary to substitute a more available or willing sibling. Forty-seven (26%) of the siblings were from two-child families, 55 (31%) were from three-child families, and the remainder

(43%) were from families with more than three children. Other than the absence of only-child families, demographic characteristics of this sample were very similar to the larger sample from which it came, which in turn was representative of the counties from which the sample was originally drawn. Seventeen percent of the children lived with a divorced mother who had not remarried, and 12% lived with mother and stepfather. Fifty-three percent of the study children were males.

Measures

Mothers and children were interviewed simultaneously but separately in their homes by two trained interviewers. Interview protocols included information on parenting and parent–child relationship as reported by both mother and child, parent and child interviews regarding symptoms and diagnoses of psychopathology, and extensive information on school, neighborhood, peers, parent characteristics, child personality, and demographics.

Siblings and mothers were interviewed, on the average, about 15 months after the interviews of study child and mother were completed. The protocol for study child and sibling were the same except for the inclusion of a measure of attitudes toward suicide in the sibling protocol. Mother interviews were the same as the earlier mother interview except for the addition of the suicide attitude measures and a full family history for psychiatric symptoms and illness. Interviews generally took between 2 and 2½ hours to complete.

Eight scales from the youth interviews and 13 scales from the mother interviews measured the character and quality of mother–youth interaction. Preliminary analyses with the full sample, based on factor analyses and on family theory, reduced these scales to four summary dimensions. Two of these dimensions, mother–child bond and maternal involvement, were highly correlated in the present reduced sample ($r = .70$). Two others, discipline and maternal control, were also correlated although more modestly ($r = 0.20$). In order to avoid any problems of colinearity we have used only mother–child bond and maternal discipline in the current analyses. These dimensions were measured as follows:

Mother–child bond: A summary score from three scales: (a) maternal affection (Schaefer, 1965; e.g., She frequently shows her affection for me), (b) communication with mother (Schaefer, 1965; e.g., She is very easy to talk to), (c) maternal support (Avgar, Bronfenbrenner, & Henderson, 1977; e.g., I can count on her to help me out in all situations). Average α-based on component scale items was .65. Scales were scored separately for mothers and youth.

Discipline: A summary score from two scales: (a) maternal discipline (Avgar et al., 1977; e.g., If I do something she does not like she deprives me of some of my privileges), (b) power assertive punishment (Kogan et al., 1977; e.g., Mother has spanked the child in the past month). The second scale was asked of mothers only; average $\alpha = 0.66$.

The measure of *child oppositional behavior* was taken from the Diagnostic Interview Schedule for Children (DISC) (Costello, Edelbrock, Dulcan, & Kalas, 1984), combining mother and youth responses to the 11 items relevant to this diagnosis ($\alpha = .77$). *Depression* was measured by 39 items written by Orvaschel (1983) covering all criteria for major depressive disorder and dysthymia, pooling maternal and youth responses ($\alpha = .86$).

Suicide items include six youth-report items from the DISC:

1. Have you thought that life was hopeless and that there was nothing good for you in the future?
2. Did you sometimes think that life wasn't worth living?
3. Did you sometimes think that your family would be better off without you?
4. Did you think a lot about death and dying?
5. Have you wished that you were dead?
6. Have you thought about killing yourself in the past year? ($\alpha = .73$).

Each of these dependent and independent measures had also been used for both the second and the third wave of data collection on the longitudinal sample. Stabilities over the 2½-year interval were approximately .45 for youth reported scales, .70 for parent reported scales, and .65 for the combination.

METHOD

Examination of sibling similarity was carried out by correlational or tabular analysis, covarying linear and quadratic effects of age, gender, and the age by gender interaction as necessary. A number of different data analytic strategies present themselves with these data, as discussed in the concluding section of this chapter. We determined to attempt to contrast the effects of differences in parenting on children in different families with the differences in parenting of children in the same family.

Early analyses contrasted estimates of effects generated by analysis of each child's data in the usual "one-child-to-a-family" design with effects generated by analysis of sibling difference data. For reasons discussed here, we shifted to the sibling average scores as the best representative of the shared aspects. Ideally, we would be able to average all siblings in a family, in this study we used the best available substitute; the average score for the two siblings. Analyses of these data provided estimates of the effects of shared parenting. Thus, shared parenting in this study is equivalent to the average parenting experienced by the two siblings studied, and may be likened to the between-families effect in an analysis of variance design.

Nonshared parenting effects were estimated by within-family difference scores for sibling pairs on both dependent and independent variables. The study children whose siblings were employed in this study were on the average between 2 and 3 years older than their sibling. However, because the siblings were interviewed 15–18 months later, the average sibling age when assessed was only about 1½ years younger than for the study children. In addition, in about one third of the families, the sibling was older than the study child at the time of assessment. Because the child's age tended to be correlated with both dependent and independent variables these age differences were seen as an important methodological problem.

Two logical possibilities arose with regard to calculating difference scores for examination of the within-family effects. We could subtract the scores of the sibling from those of the study child, essentially considering study children and siblings as separate cohorts, and then use study child age and sibling age as covariates in the analyses. Alternatively, we could follow the example of most other studies using this methodology and subtract the scores of the younger child from those of the older child, and then use older child age and younger child age as covariants.

Early analyses suggested that using the first method, study child minus sibling, the age variables did not add to the regression prediction. Because both dependent and independent variables tend to be somewhat associated with age we were nevertheless aware that this source of variance remained as a proportion of the unexplained variance. We therefore determined to subtract younger from older, resulting in a cleaner analysis and more comparability with the literature on adolescence. We note that one study that did not use such older minus younger scores (Daniels et al., 1985) failed to find age and gender differences in the dependent variable where such might ordinarily have been expected.

Several independent or dependent variables for older as compared to younger children differed not only in their mean but also in their variances. As a result, the within and between family scores (the sum and the difference scores) were not entirely orthogonal as the model would suggest (see the postscript discussion). In order that the shared and nonshared estimates not be positively correlated, we carried out set correlational analyses of the effects of parenting on psychopathology, in which difference scores (as well as age and gender) were partialled from all variables representing the between family or shared components, and vice versa.

FINDINGS

How Similar is Reported Parenting Between Siblings?

Table 6.1 shows parent–child agreement in reported parenting as well as concordance in parenting as reported by siblings. The average correlation between reports of experienced parenting by siblings was only .15. This figure may be

TABLE 6.1
Correlations Between Sibling and Mother Reports
of Parenting and Psychopathology

	Correlation Between Parent and Child-Reported Parenting Study	
	Child/Mother	Sibling/Mother
Maternal closeness	.38	.30
Maternal discipline	.22	.38

	Correlation Between Siblings		
	Child Report	Mother Report	Combined
Depression			.20
Suicidality	.17		
Opposition			.27
Maternal closeness	.19	.62	.36
Maternal discipline	.11	.62	.33

compared to the average stability of .51 in a single child's report over a 2½-year period; thus the low correlation is clearly not simply attributable to unreliability or changes with age. Mother-reported parenting of the two siblings correlated .62 on the average, also lower but approaching in magnitude the stability over time in maternal report of parenting of a particular child (.72). The finding that resemblance in parenting is lower as reported by siblings than as reported by the parent may be attributed in part to the fact that one parent rates each of the two siblings while the two siblings each make their own rating (Daniels et al., 1985). The correlations between mother and study children perceptions of parenting were moderate in magnitude and were very similar to those for mother and sibling perceptions of parenting. The level of agreement for mother and child was thus higher than self-reported agreement across siblings but lower than maternal reports of the two siblings.

How Similar are Siblings on the Outcome Variables?

Correlations between siblings on the depression and opposition measures were .20 and .27, respectively. These findings are similar to those reported in other studies of nontwin siblings, with an average sibling correlation of .16 for personality traits (Ahern, Johnson, Wilson, McClearn, & Vandenberg, 1982) and similar to studies on less severe forms of psychopathology in which sibling concordance is less than 20% (Fuller & Thompson, 1978; Rosenthal, 1970). These correlations are much smaller than the stabilities over a 2½-year period in a single child, .63 and .68 respectively.

There was no concordance between siblings in suicide attempts, as attempts were reported by eight study children and eight siblings all in different families.

There was, however, significant although modest concordance in suicidal idea- tion between siblings ($r = .17$). This figure may be compared with the .24 corre- lation over a 2½-year period for this measure in the study children. Thus, suicidal ideation was noticeably less stable than was either depression or opposition. Suicide attempts in first degree relatives reported in a family history interview of the mother were elevated for children who had made attempts or had elevat- ed suicidal ideation.

What Parenting Variables Related to Depression, Suicidal, and Oppositional Behavior of Children in Different Families?

In Table 6.2 we present the analyses of the relationships of the parenting dimen- sions to the three measures of child psychopathology. As noted, each of these equations also included a series of covariants, partialling the relevant age and

TABLE 6.2
Partial Relationships of Depression and Opposition with the Parenting Variables

		Sibling Sums			Sibling Difference		
		Informant			Informant		
		Child	Mother	Both	Child	Mother	Both
Depression							
Bond	B	$-.35^1$	$-.48^1$	$-.28^*$	$-.06$	$-.51$	$-.04$
	β	$-.14$	$-.13$	$-.15$	$-.02$	$-.08$	$-.02$
Punishment	B	$.75^1$	$.62^1$	$.51^*$	$.48$	$.31$	$.34$
	β	$.14$	$.15$	$.17$	$.11$	$.05$	$.10$
R^2 parenting		$.04^*$	$.05^*$	$.06^*$	$.02$	$.01$	$.01$
Suicidal Ideation							
Bond	B	$-.08^*$	$-.07$	$-.05^*$	$-.04$	$-.06$	$-.02$
	β	$-.23$	$-.13$	$-.20$	$-.11$	$-.11$	$-.09$
Punishment	B	$.02$	$.06$	$.04$	$.14^*$	$.09$	$.08^*$
⋅	β	$.02$	$.07$	$.08$	$.20$	$.10$	$.18$
R^2 parenting		$.05^*$	$.02$	$.05^*$	$.06^*$	$.02$	$.05^*$
Opposition							
Bond	B	$-.24^*$	$-.34^*$	$-.17^*$	$-.21^*$	$-.63^*$	$-.18^*$
	β	$-.26$	$-.26$	$-.26$	$-.23$	$-.32$	$-.23$
Punishment	B	$.16$	$.41^*$	$.27^*$	$.42^*$	$.61^*$	$.35^*$
	β	$.08$	$.27$	$.25$	$.24$	$.26$	$.30$
R^2 parenting		$.08^*$	$.17^*$	$.15^*$	$.14^*$	$.20^*$	$.18^*$

$^*p < .05.$
$^1p < .10.$

gender variables, and partialling between-family variation (average scores) in the within-family analyses and within-family variation (difference scores) in the between-family analyses.

By examining the between-family analyses, we can see that both mother-child bond and maternal discipline of the children were significant predictors of both depression and oppositional behavior, although the relationships with opposition were far larger. Across families, the closer the perceived relationship with the mother, the lower the suicide ideation scores. Punishment, however, was not related to average suicide ideation scores. Reports by the individual child and mother informants were generally consistent with those of the pooled except that mother reports of punishment were more strongly related than youth reports to oppositional behavior, and youth reports of the maternal bond were more strongly related to suicidal ideation than maternal reports.

What Parenting Variables Related to Difference in Depression, Suicidal, and Oppositional Behavior of Children in the Same Family?

Table 6.2 also presents the regression of sibling differences in depression, suicidal, and oppositional behavior on the parenting dimensions. Again, analyses control for the age and gender of both siblings. No parenting effects on within-family differences in sibling depression were statistically significant. There was no within-family effect of affective bond on sibling differences in suicide ideation; however youth receiving more severe punishment than their siblings had higher suicide ideation on the average. Again, youth perceptions of the relationship were more closely linked with suicide ideation than maternal perceptions. Both parenting variables showed large and independent effects on differences between siblings in oppositional behavior.

Are Within-Family Differences in Parenting More Consequential Than Between-Family Differences?

Three different kinds of coefficients are potentially relevant to this comparison. First, the raw regression coefficients reflect the effect of a change in parenting on a change in child outcome in units that are constant across both between- and within-family analyses. A second relevant contrast is the proportion of dependent variable variance not attributable to covariates associated with parenting in each analysis (i.e., the R^2 produced by the set correlation analysis). Finally, we may also be interested in the standardized regression coefficients (β) because they are comparable within a given analysis and are in a familiar metric. Table 6.2 presents these comparisons separately for youth-, parent-, and combined report.

The answer to this question is that it depends upon the dependent variable under consideration. That is, when depression in children is the dependent variable, between-family effects are uniformly larger; indeed, as noted above, none of the within-family effects were significant. In contrast, the within-family effects of parenting differences on differences in offspring opposition are, if anything, slightly larger than the between family effects. For suicide ideation, differences between families in the affective bond are related to ideation but, within families, differences in punishment are predictive of ideation.

Are Different Parenting Dimensions Important for Within-Family Child Outcomes as Compared to Between-Family Child Outcomes?

Again, the answer depends on the dependent variable in question. We found no evidence that a specific independent variable was more important in the shared parenting context whereas the other was more important in the nonshared parenting context. The exception was with suicide ideation, where maternal bond held influence between families but punishment exacted an influence within families.

SUMMARY AND DISCUSSION

In summary, regarding parenting practices the nonshared environment did not account for more variance in sibling psychopathology than did the shared family environment. Differences in parenting were more consequential for predicting depression of children in different families. Shared and non-shared family effects of parenting were both important when suicidal ideation was the dependent variable, although the specific aspect of parenting that mattered differed in the two contexts. However, differences in parenting within families were perhaps slightly more consequential when child oppositional behavior was the dependent variable. These findings did not depend on the informant when the dependent variable was depression or oppositional behavior. For suicidal ideation, in contrast, parenting as reported by youth informant tended to be related more powerfully. This is probably because this dependent variable came from youth self-reports, whereas the depression and opposition measures pooled information from youth and parent interviews. Thus, this informant effect may be partly a function of the common method variance, or what Patterson and colleagues have termed the *glop* problem (Bank, Dishion, Skinner, & Patterson, 1990). However it may also indicate that youth perceptions of the family are a key factor with regard to their suicide ideation.

It is of interest that the aspects of the parent–child relationship that related to suicide ideation differed for the between- versus within-family analyses.

Sibling differences in punishment were influential with regard to ideation, whereas in the between-family analysis only parent–child bond had an effect on suicidal ideation of offspring. The between family findings are consistent with prior studies of suicidal adolescents that have found that youth perceptions of family communication and support are related to suicidal behavior (Dubow, Kausch, Blum, Reed, & Bush, 1989; Hawton, Osborn, O'Grady, & Cole, 1982; Rubenstein, Heeren, Housman, Rubin, & Stechler, 1989). Prior studies of youth suicide have not assessed the mothers' perceptions of the relationship; however, the present results indicate that the youths' perceptions are a more important correlate of their suicide ideation than are the mothers' perceptions. Interestingly, within-family differences in mother–child supportiveness, communication, and warmth were only marginally related to differences in suicidal ideation, indicating that the adolescent with higher suicidal ideation does not necessarily perceive his or her mother as less emotionally supportive than does the sibling with lower suicide ideation.

Prior studies have found that suicidal behavior is associated with harsh parental punishment (Jacobs, 1971) and that suicidal youth are more likely to have been exposed to family aggression (Pfeffer, 1989). The present findings extend these prior between-family results by suggesting that differences between siblings in harshness of punishment are an important correlate of differences in their suicide ideation. Youth who reported that they were treated more harshly than their brother or sister reported were likely to have higher suicide ideation than their sibling. Although we did not directly assess the degree to which youth compare their own experience of punishment with that of their sibling, it is possible that the youth with higher suicide ideation perceive that they are being singled out for more punishment than their siblings. Thus, although youth with higher suicide ideation than their siblings were not lower on maternal closeness their siblings, and although their mothers were not necessarily more severe with their children in general than mothers in other families, they reported their mothers to be more strict and severe with them than did their siblings.

Siblings in the same family experienced mostly different family environments as self-reported although mothers reported a much higher level of consistency. These experienced differences between siblings were related to differences in their psychopathology, confirming results from prior research. As yet we have little theory to provide us with specific hypotheses as to when shared-sibling parenting may be more influential, and when differences within families may be important. As is generally true in this field, the data that we have presented here are also cross-sectional, and therefore we have little basis for determining the direction of effect between what we have chosen to call the child outcomes and family environment. One may speculate that nonshared aspects of parent–child relationships and rearing are likely to be more strongly influenced by the character of the child than by the parental characteristics, since the genetics, personality, and beliefs of at least one parent are fairly fixed across the two children. Nevertheless, it takes little introspection to appreciate that parental handling of two successive offspring may also be quite responsive to changing perspectives, experiences, and environmental influences.

Postscript: A Little Light Algebra

In the analyses reported here we operated on the assumption that the relationship between the sibling differences in dependent and independent variables reflected the nonshared component of environmental effects (and perhaps nonshared genetic components for which we could not control with the present design). In implicit contrast, we initially examined the relationships between the same variables across families, via the more conventional one-child-to-a-family analysis (not reported here), in the assumption that this conveyed information about shared environment. As we proceeded we gradually appreciated that the latter analysis necessarily included both parenting effects that may be shared with siblings and those that may be unique to the child. For example, the relationship between maternal bond and child depression for a given child could theoretically be partitioned into a component that is unique for that child and one which is common to siblings in the family. Therefore we altered our strategy and opted to use as the between-family estimate the average of the scores for the two siblings on both dependent and independent variables. This strategy for estimating between- and within-family effects is directly analogous to the familiar method of partitioning between- and within-group effects in the analysis of variance. We then realized that averages and differences were not necessarily orthogonal, and therefore we examined both in simultaneous equations in order to purge each estimated parenting effect (within and between) of the potential influence of the other set of variables. In fact, as can be readily proven, the correlation between the average and difference scores reflects only the variance difference between the two variables.

Nevertheless, these analyses left us uneasy. Were these between-family effects really a conceptual equivalent to shared environmental effects? Which variables have the largest influence on these between-family analyses, and how does that differ from the within-family analyses? A little light algebra led us to additional appreciation of the effects of component covariances on these estimates based on sibling differences and sums. (Here we use sibling sums rather than averages to simplify; the difference is only a constant for all observations.) These can be readily comprehended when the correlation between sums and differences are expressed as a function of the variances and covariances, limiting the equation to a bivariate relationship for simplicity and without loss of conceptual generalization. To avoid the confounding effects of differences in variance we also assume that all variables have been standardized to a variance of 1.0.

Turning to the correlation between dependent and independent variables when all variables are either sums or differences, let y and z be the scores on a dependent variable (e.g., depression) for Siblings A and B, respectively, while x and w represent their respective independent variables (e.g., parenting). The equations representing the correlations of sibling sums as independent and dependent variables can be represented as follows:

$$r_{(x + w)(y + z)} = \frac{r_{xy} + r_{wz} + r_{yw} + r_{zx}}{2\,[(1 + r_{xw})(1 + r_{yz})]^{1/2}} \tag{1}$$

and the comparable relationships for sibling differences are:

$$r_{(x - w)(y - z)} = \frac{r_{xy} + r_{wz} - r_{yw} - r_{zx}}{2\,[(1 - r_{xw})(1 - r_{yz})]^{1/2}} \tag{2}$$

Making the reasonable assumption that $r_{xy} = r_{wz}$ and $r_{yw} = r_{zx}$, that is, that the correlation between a child's own dependent and independent variables are the same for each group of siblings, and that the correlation between a child's own dependent variable and sibling's independent variable is the same for each group of siblings:

$$r_{(x + w)(y + z)} = \frac{r_{xy} + r_{yw}}{[(1 + r_{xw})(1 + r_{yz})]^{1/2}} \tag{1a}$$

$$r_{(x - w)(y - z)} = \frac{r_{xy} - r_{yw}}{[(1 - r_{xw})(1 - r_{yz})]^{1/2}} \tag{2a}$$

Thus, there here are only four components to the correlations between dependent and independent variables based on the sibling sums or the sibling differences, namely:

r_{xy} (or r_{wz}) = the correlation between the dependent and independent variable for each sibling.

r_{xw} = the correlation between the siblings on the independent variable.

r_{yz} = the correlation between the siblings on the dependent variable.

r_{yw} (or r_{zx}) = the correlation between Sibling A's (B's) dependent variable and Sibling B's (A's) independent variable.

The correlations between siblings on dependent and independent variables can be represented by the average of the two correlations r_{xw} and r_{yz}, (r_o), so that with very little loss of accuracy we may simplify as follows:

$$r_{(x + w)(y + z)} = \frac{r_{xy} + r_{wy}}{1 + r_o} \tag{3}$$

and

$$r_{(x - w)(y - z)} = \frac{r_{xy} - r_{wy}}{1 - r_o} \tag{4}$$

Thus, the numerator of the correlation between the sum of two sibling's parenting and the sum of their problem behavior is the correlation between parenting and problems for each child plus the correlation of each child's problems with the parenting received by the other child. The denominator of this equation reduces to 1 plus the average between-sibling correlation for the dependent and independent variables.

The numerator of the correlation between the difference between two siblings' parenting and the difference between their problem behavior is the correlation between each child's dependent and independent variables minus the correlation between each child's problems and the sibling's parenting (the cross-sibling effect).

These algebraic manipulations make very clear that the essential term in these two equations is the cross-sibling effect. In order to understand this effect we turned to a path diagram.

First, suppose that there is no direct effect on a child's dependent variable of the sibling's parenting as shown in Fig. 6.1. By standard path analytic rules, the correlation between y and w would be equal to $r_{xy}r_{xw} + r_{zw}r_{yz}$, and since $r_{xy} = r_{zw}$:

$$r_{wy} = r_{xy} (r_{xw} + r_{yz})$$

Therefore, substituting for r_{wy} in Equations 3 and 4:

$$r_{(x + w)(y + z)} = \frac{r_{xy} (1 + 2r_o)}{1 + r_o} \tag{5}$$

$$r_{(x - w)(y - z)} = \frac{r_{xy} (1 - 2r_o)}{1 - r_o} \tag{6}$$

Using these formulas, a higher correlation between siblings (r_o) produces a larger shared than nonshared estimate. This is a reasonable result. It is also consistent with the well-known psychometric advantage, whereby the correlation between two variables is enhanced if each is represented by a greater number of positively correlated variables (in this case 2) rather than fewer (e.g., 1) and their correlation is high rather than low. If siblings are not correlated (x with w, y with z), $r_o = 0$ and the correlations of sums and differences are

FIG. 6.1.   The association between sibling variables when there are no cross-sibling effects.

equal and also equivalent to the standard one-child-to-a-family correlation. If one assumes the correlations between siblings (r_{xw} and r_{yz}) come from the reliable portion of these variables, correlating the differences will result in an inflated error proportion, and thus a lower correlation. This, too, is consistent with the known lesser reliability of difference scores.

Equations 5 and 6, however, are posited on the absence of any direct cross-sibling effect. Should the causal paths include effects of x on z and of w on y in Fig. 6.1, the relative estimates of "between" and "within" or "shared" and "nonshared" effects will depend on both the size and the sign of these cross-sibling effects.

All of these manipulations tend to focus attention on this cross-sibling effect. In contrast, our theories tend to be weak in this very area. Only the family systems theorists have provided a serious discussion of the effect of a particular member's role in the family on other family members (translated here as a cross-sibling effect). In this literature and on reflection it becomes immediately clear that these effects need not even be in the same direction as the effect of Sibling A's experienced parenting on Sibling A's outcome variable. For example, it may be that harsh punishment received by a sibling has an entirely different effect on a child than would the same punishment personally experienced. Similarly, a very close mother–child relationship may not have the same beneficial effects on other offspring that it does for the child experiencing it.

In our view, therefore, the attention focused on the problem of nonshared family environment has been very helpful, but has revealed a need for a new body of empirical and theoretical work. Empirically it has been helpful by revealing how little of the parenting experience is shared by siblings, at least by separate self-reports. Theoretically it has led us to an appreciation of the need to understand and model the effects on a child of the parenting received by a sibling.

The methodological aspects of this comparison are not yet completely solved. For example, we carried out a series of analyses of the absolute differences in independent and dependent without producing significant or revealing findings. Perhaps we need to try again, focusing on a specific sibling. Both our theorizing and our empirical tests may benefit from a move from an analysis of difference scores to the direct consideration of effects on the characteristics of a child of parenting, parenting of siblings, and possibly the interaction of the two. An alternative model would examine the effect of shared parenting (the sibling average) and nonshared parenting (the difference between a given child and the sibling average). Full models may also require consideration of the ages and gender of the siblings as well as other siblings beyond the target pair. Such models would also allow consideration of the interactions among different aspects of parenting, effects which we found to be essentially untestable in the current design (Tejerina-Allen, 1990). Finally, they would facilitate the simultaneous consideration of the relationships between or among the siblings.

ACKNOWLEDGMENTS

This research was supported by National Institute of Mental Health Grant No. MH36971, by the W. T. Grant Foundation (Patricia Cohen, P.I.), and by the New York State Office of Mental Health.

REFERENCES

Ahern, F. M., Johnson, R. C., Wilson, J. R., McClearn, G. E., & Vandenberg, S. G. (1982). Family resemblances in personality. *Behavior Genetics, 12,* 261–280.

Avgar, A., Bronfenbrenner, J., & Henderson, C. R., Jr. (1977). Socialization practices of parents, teachers, and peers in Israel: Kibbutz, Moshav, and city. *Child Development, 48,* 1219–1227.

Bank, L., Dishion, T., Skinner, M., & Patterson, G. R. (1990). Method variance in structural equation modeling: Living with "glop." In G. R. Patterson (Ed.), *Depression and aggression in family interaction* (pp. 247–279). Hillsdale, NJ: Lawrence Erlbaum Associates.

Costello, A. J., Edelbrock, C. S., Dulcan, M. K., & Kalas, R. (1984). *Testing of the NIMH Diagnostic Interview Schedule for Children (DISC) in a clinical population* (Contract No. RFP-DB-81-0027). Rockville, MD: National Institute of Mental Health, Center for Epidemiological Studies.

Daniels, D., Dunn, J., Furstenberg, F. F., Jr., & Plomin, R. (1985). Environmental differences within the family and adjustment differences within pairs of adolescent siblings. *Child Development, 56,* 764–774.

Dubow, E. F., Kausch, D. F., Blum, M. C., Reed, J., & Bush, E. (1989). Correlates of suicidal ideation and attempts in a community sample of junior high and high school students. *Journal of Clinical Child Psychology, 18,* 158–166.

Dunn, J., & Munn, P. (1986). Sibling quarrels and maternal intervention: Individual differences in understanding and aggression. *Journal of Child Psychology and Psychiatry and Allied Disciplines, 27,* 583–595.

Fuller, F. L., & Thompson, W. R. (1978). *Foundations of behavioral genetics.* New York: Mosby.

Goldsmith, H. H. (1983). Genetic influences on personality from infancy to adulthood. *Child Development, 54,* 331–355.

Hawton, K., Osborn, M., O'Grady, J., & Cole, D. (1982). Classification of adolescents who take overdoses. *British Journal of Psychiatry, 140,* 124–131.

Jacobs, J. (1971). *Adolescent suicide.* New York: Wiley.

Kogan, L. S., Smith, J., & Jenkins, S. (1977). Ecological validity of indicator data as predictors of survey findings. *Journal of Social Services Research, 1,* 117–32.

Maccoby, E. E., & Martin, J. A. (1983). Socialization in the context of the family: Parent–child interaction. In P. H. Mussen (Series Ed.), E. M. Hetherington (Vol. Ed.), *Handbook of child psychology, Vol. 4. Socialization, personality, and social development* (4th ed., pp. 1–102). New York: Wiley.

Pfeffer, C. R. (1989). Life stress and family risk factors for youth fatal and nonfatal suicidal behavior. In C. R. Pfeffer (Ed.), *Suicide among youth: Perspectives on risk and prevention* (pp. 143–164). Washington, DC: American Psychiatric Press.

Plomin, R., & Daniels, D. (1987). Why are children in the same family so different from one another? *Behavioral and Brain Sciences, 10,* 1–60.

Rosenthal, D. (1970). *Genetic theory and abnormal behavior.* New York: McGraw-Hill.

Rubenstein, J. L., Heeren, T., Housman, D., Rubin, C., & Stechler, G. (1989). Suicidal behavior in "normal" adolescents: Risk and protective factors. *American Journal of Orthopsychiatry, 59,* 59–71.

Schaefer, E. S. (1965). Children's report of parental behavior. An inventory. *Child Development,*
   36, 413–424.
Tejerina-Allen, M. (1990). *Within-family parenting predictors of differential psychopathology in children.* Unpublished master's thesis. New York: Columbia University, School of Public Health.

7

Peers and Friends as Nonshared Environmental Influences

David C. Rowe
E. Jeanne Woulbroun
Bill L. Gulley
University of Arizona

Biological siblings, despite sharing many common experiences, can be very different in personality and in intellectual traits. This difference may result partly from the socializing influence of siblings' friendship cliques and close friends. In this chapter, we review the evidence that peers and friends operate as "nonshared environmental influences" on siblings' behavioral differences. Siblings belonging to different peer groups possessed personality differences that match with their peers' characteristics. However, we report data indicating that siblings often share the same friends, so that within family differences in peer exposure should be empirically assessed rather than merely assumed. We reviewed studies of the causes of friends' resemblance and concluded that selection ("birds of a feather flock together") is often more powerful than peer influence. Thus, because selection is at work, peers can serve to reinforce preexisting (and sometimes genetic) differences between siblings. Nevertheless, because some peer influence exists, peers can also be regarded as a nonshared environmental influence.

We know that siblings raised in the same family can be very different. One sibling may be schizophrenic, another normal. Similarly, tremendous variation occurs among siblings in personality and intellectual traits. This chapter is concerned with the role of peer groups in producing such sibling differences in personality and behavior. Our goal is determining whether peer groups are a source of nonshared environmental influence (NSE) on personality development.

The background to this chapter is a fundamental result of behavioral genetic studies—that environmental influences on personality development are mainly nonshared influences (Plomin & Daniels, 1987; Rowe & Plomin, 1981), as explained by Plomin et al. (this volume). The term *nonshared* refers to influences that operate differently on each child in a family. If the results of behavioral genetic research are correct, then we should pay a great deal of attention to influences that might cause siblings to differ from one another in personality. Peer groups are a logical candidate for nonshared influence because siblings may have different friends and may belong to different social cliques. Hence, the influence of friends and cliques may cause differences in siblings' traits. Despite the potential importance of peers as a source of nonshared environment, this topic has not been systematically reviewed previously, largely because initial work on nonshared environment has focused on differential experiences within the family.

Our task, however, is not an easy one. First, we must deal with a number of subtle concepts. We must be clear about the definition of types of influences and about what we consider as evidence of NSE as opposed to some other kind of influence. Second, the empirical evidence is limited. Only a few studies have been done looking directly at peer groups as a source of NSE. To augment this evidence, however, we can search the general literature on peer group effects. We want to show that peer groups influence individuals; if so, such peer influences are probably differential experiences within the family.

Ideally, we would seek a general answer—that is, across most traits, do peer groups contribute to nonshared environment? However, existing research has not distinguished among categories of traits clearly. In general, we would expect that the more heritable a trait, the weaker the possibility of peer influence. For instance, highly heritable physical traits would be unlikely to show peer group nonshared environmental effects, because normal environmental variation produces little change in them. (Note that a highly heritable trait may also be a malleable trait, but by environmental influences new to an ecological and social context, e.g., eye glasses and heritable visual acuity.) As personality traits are generally less heritable than intelligent quotient, we would expect greater peer influence on them than on IQ. Mental illnesses such as schizophrenia have strong genetic components. Because of the lack of systematic study of different types of traits, and because of the dearth of data on the influence of peers on mental illness, we cannot provide a general answer to the peer influence question. In this chapter, we mainly consider normal personality traits (e.g., sociability, emotionality, self-esteem), various deviant behaviors (e.g., drinking, smoking, and sexual intercourse in young adolescents; delinquency), and achievement orientation, for the reason that most studies have dealt with these traits and behaviors.

DEFINITION OF THE PEER GROUP

How do we define the peer group? Various definitions would focus on different sized units of analysis. *Friendships* are often defined in terms of relationships that are reported to be close and intimate and in which the friendship choices are independently reciprocated by both individuals. By this definition, the typical child has only a few friends at any one time, as fourth and eighth graders typically named an average of one to two close friends (Berndt & Hoyle, 1985). A more liberal definition of friendship can reveal larger networks (e.g., using a definition of a high degree of mutual liking, Berndt and Hoyle's fourth and eighth graders named an average of three to four friends). *Cliques* may be defined as small groups with many mutual friendship choices. Although cliques of a few persons may be identified, not all individuals belong to one. Cohen (1977) identified friendship cliques averaging 5.2 persons; but only 9% of the boys and 40% of the girls in the school belonged to any clique strictly defined. In adolescence, cliques themselves are embedded in larger structures such as crowds, often named groups of different social orientations. Athletes and academically oriented youths form different crowds, and may associate more often with one another than with outsiders. The multilayer nature of adolescent friendships imposes ambiguity on any definition of the peer group. For our purpose, we focus on the close friendship/clique level of analysis because this is the apparent peer unit in the behavioral genetic studies reviewed next.

RECOGNIZING NONSHARED
PEER GROUP EFFECTS

How can we recognize nonshared peer group influences? Clearly, at a minimum, we would expect siblings to occupy different peer groups. Data from the Arizona sibling study bear on this question. The Arizona sibling study is a representative survey of children 10–16 years old in a Southwestern city. Two siblings per family were sampled, with the restriction that the siblings be adjacent in birth order. Of these siblings, 135 were brother pairs; 142 were sister pairs; and 141 were opposite-gender pairs.

Table 7.1 gives siblings' responses to two items: (a) the number of siblings' mutual friends, and (b) the frequency of contact with the mutual friends.

Our expectations were not completely fulfilled: While the modal response of mixed-gender siblings was no mutual friends (35.8%), it was two to three friends in brothers (34.4%) and in sisters (28.9%). About the same proportion of siblings who reported zero mutual friends also reported never having had contact with mutual friends. Summing the "mutual contact" categories of "some-

TABLE 7.1
The Number of Mutual Friends and Frequency of Contact With Friends
By Siblings 10–16 Years Old

Number of Mutual Friends	Brothers	Sisters	Mixed-Gender
None	23.7%	26.1%	35.8%
1	12.2	14.4	13.1
2–3	34.4	28.9	28.7
4–6	19.6	16.5	12.4
7 or more	10.0	14.1	9.9
Contact With Mutual Friend			
Never	17.8	24.3	31.2
Rarely	34.8	41.2	44.0
Sometimes	27.4	21.8	17.0
Often	16.7	10.2	7.1
Always	3.3	2.5	.7

times," "often," and "always" revealed that contact with mutual friends was fairly common for sibling pairs, and somewhat greater for same- than for mixed-gender pairs (brothers, 47.4%; sisters, 34.5%; and mixed-gender, 24.8%). Although siblings separated in birth order may have fewer mutual friends than siblings in neighboring birth orders, it is clear that same-gender siblings often have overlapping peer group networks. We conclude that, in studies of non-shared effects of siblings' peer groups, an attempt should be made to assess directly both mutual and nonmutual friends. The frequency of contact with mutual friends, as well as the friends' qualities, might be important moderating variables for analyses of within-family peer group influences that have not been exploited in previous research.

The demonstration of a nonshared friend influence is difficult. This requires that we show a statistical association between quantity and frequency of mutual friends and outcome traits. If such a statistical association is found, we must investigate whether NSE is responsible for the association. Friends' statistical association is important for the argument of NSE because it suggests that friends might effect each other. However, another possibility looms large in explaining this phenomenon: the similarity of friends could be due to selection of similar friends–assortative friendship in the sense of assortative mating in behavioral genetics.

Supporting possible influence, friends are similar to one another on a wide range of characteristics (Kandel, 1978b). Similarity is greatest for sociodemographic traits, next strongest for deviant behaviors and school activities, and weakest for selected social attitudes and for relationships with parents.

Such possible friendship effects become NSE influence when siblings are differentially influenced by their friends. For example, Daniels, Dunn, Furstenberg, and Plomin (1985) investigated differential peer experience of siblings. Their sample had the advantage of national representativeness and large size, including data from two siblings 11 to 17 years of age in 348 families. Parents, and each child, reported separately on perceptions of family environment and on adjustment (e.g., delinquency, emotional distress). Most measures were short scales of just a few items. Differential peer group experience was associated with adolescent personality and behavior. For instance, differential peer friendliness correlated with emotional distress, delinquency, and disobedience. This study is valuable because it shows that sibling trait differences correspond to peer group experiential correlates.

In general, we can identify NSE influences through a number of research designs. Differences between siblings' phenotypic traits can be compared with differences in measurements of their peer associates. That is, as in Daniels et al. (1985), the signed difference score on a phenotypic trait, Sibling A–Sibling B, may be correlated with the signed difference on the personality or social qualities of Sibling A's friends–Sibling B's friends. In monozygotic twins, such an association would be unambiguous evidence for nonshared environmental influences (because any genetic effects would be removed in the subtraction).

The desire to attribute any friend or peer group effect to socialization, however, must be tempered by an alternative process: friend selection. Individuals may select their friends; drop and add friends; have more than a single friend at any one time; and associate with close friends and acquaintances. Any statistical similarity between friends' and "ego's" traits may have resulted from the initial selection of friends who were already similar. And because traits may be intercorrelated, selection on one trait will impose noncausal similarity on the related ones as well.

The power of selection is clearly demonstrable for nonmalleable traits, where a causal direction may be inferred from similarity. For example, friends' racial identity (Black vs. White) correlates .757 in 6th grade and .886 in 12th grade (Epstein, 1983, p. 46). Friends' biological gender correlates .902 in 6th grade and .690 in 12th grade—a decline reflecting increased heterosexuality. In adulthood, friends resemble one another in social class, religion, and political ideology (Verbrugge, 1977). Although more ambiguous than gender or race, one infers that most resemblance in adult friendships is due to selection, rather than socialization. Nonetheless, the opposite inference pervades the literature on childhood and adolescent peer groups—the belief that socialization in the peer group greatly exceeds the effects of selection (Hallinan, 1983).

The positive assortment of friends could be due to genetic influence on the selection of environmental context. For instance, if genetically more social people associated with more extraverted individuals, then the correlation between "ego's" sociability and her friends' extroversion would be mediated genetically.

Of course, people select one another on their phenotypes, not on their geno-types. Because traits are not totally heritable, perfect assortment on the pheno-type would not imply that friends are identical genetically in their genotypes. Nevertheless, insofar as phenotypes and genotypes are correlated, assortment for the former will induce some correlation on the latter. Moreover, difference correlations between peer experiences and trait outcomes computed for first degree relatives can contain this genetic component—because first degree rela-tives differ at about one half their genes (other than genes fixed in the population).

In summary, in a behavior genetic study, evidence of a NSE peer influence may be obtained directly from MZ twins. A different approach is to conduct studies of peer groups that separate the selection and socialization components of peer assortment. The presence of peer socialization implies that peer groups might exert a nonshared environmental influence on traits. The presence of selec-tion effects in the case of heritable traits implies genetic mediation and a lack of peer influence on traits (except insofar as the peer context is required for the full expression and maintenance of particular traits). Possibly, both influence pathways may affect as single trait.

BEHAVIORAL GENETIC STUDIES
OF NONSHARED ENVIRONMENT

In this section, we consider a small set of studies that investigated genetic in-fluence on (a) measures of nonshared environment, and (b) the association of NSE measures and outcome traits. The notion that an environmental assess-ment may be imbued with genetic influence, although relatively unfamiliar to social scientists, is understood in behavioral genetics. This confounding can oc-cur because most assessments of environment actually assess someone's be-havior, or the degree of exposure to someone's behavior. As noted earlier, if the latter is a choice itself partly dependent on inherited traits, then the "en-vironmental" assessment may contain genetic variation.

Daniels and her colleagues present data relevant to genetic variation in a new measure of nonshared environment, the Sibling Inventory of Differential Ex-perience (SIDE). The inventory covers parental treatment, sibling interaction, peer characteristics, and events specific to the individual (Daniels & Plomin, 1985). Three qualities of peer groups were assessed: orientation toward col-lege, delinquency, and popularity. The items were rated on 5-point scales with the midpoint "3" representing both siblings' friends have the same characteris-tics; with "1" representing my sibling's friends have more of the characteris-tics; and with "5" representing my friends have more of the characteristic. The SIDE may be scored in two ways. In absolute scoring, the alternatives were recoded on a 3-point scale: 3 as 0 = no difference, 2 and 4 as 1 = a bit of difference, and 1 and 5 as 2 = much difference. In relative scoring, the items retain their original response scale.

Daniels and Plomin's (1985) sample consisted of 171 adoptees and 255 biological siblings (12 to 28 years of age). Differential peer experience was greater than differential experience in other domains. For instance, 9% reported "much difference" in parental treatments and 18.7% reported "much difference" in sibling interaction versus 20.3% reporting much difference in the peer domain. Daniels and Plomin compared the mean absolute scores for the adoptive and biological siblings. The SIDE's three scales, peer college orientation, peer delinquency, and peer popularity all evidenced genetic mediation. Adoptive siblings reported belonging to more dissimilar peer groups than did biological siblings. Scale means of adoptive siblings ranged from .84–.96; but they ranged from .72–.80 for biological siblings.

Subsequently, Baker and Daniels (1990) extended analyses of the SIDE to include identical and fraternal twins recruited through newspaper and radio advertisements in Los Angeles. Twenty-nine DZ twin and 75 MZ twin pairs responded to the survey. The twins were adults (mean age = 35 years), so their reports on the SIDE were retrospective of their environments when growing up. The twin study confirmed genetic mediation of differential peer group experience. MZ twins reported lower means on the peer scales (.31–.43) than DZ twins (.64–.77). Together with the first study, the peer SIDE scales nicely rank order from most to least similar: MZ twins, DZ twins or nontwin siblings, and adoptive siblings. For peer delinquency, there was an indication of a twinship effect: DZ twins were more alike than nontwin siblings. Neither study, however, can reveal the exact mechanism of peer group selection. Presumably, traits with some genetic determination partly determine social association with peers who have particular traits because of the general positive assortment of friendship choice.

Other studies have investigated possible genetic mediation of NSE-outcome trait associations. Daniels (1986) compared the regression of SIDE peer scores on trait differences for 50 biological and 98 adoptive sibling pairs. Her expectation was that genetic mediation of the association would be revealed if the associations were stronger in the adoptive siblings than in the biological siblings. This reasoning may appear to be opposite of the usual genetic study where genetically more alike relatives are more alike phenotypically. Recognize, however, that the NSE-trait outcome correlations are based on within-family differences. In this comparison, unrelated adoptive siblings are more unlike than ordinary siblings genetically, so that the genetic component should induce a stronger within-family correlation in the former than in the later groups.

Contrary to the genetic mediation hypothesis, these within-family correlations were no greater for adoptive than biological siblings. Daniels' result is puzzling because it contradicts the apparent genetic mediation of the absolute scoring of the SIDE scales on this same sample (Daniels & Plomin, 1985). Why does the difference score analysis fail to find genetic mediation, if more genetically dissimilar individuals choose more dissimilar peer groups? One possibility is that the dimensions of peer selection are different from those measured by peer college orientation, peer delinquency, and peer popularity. However, this hypothesis is unlikely to be correct because these dimensions are involved in positive friendship assortment (Kandel, 1978b).

A second possibility is that a difference score correlation analysis is not a good statistical test of genetic mediation. The reason for this is subtle. A difference correlation is standardized in relation to the variation of difference scores rather than in relation to the total variation. For example, an MZ twin NSE-outcome correlation could be 1.0; but the NSE influence may explain only a small part of total trait variation. The average difference between MZ twin pairs might be one point on a behavioral scale where the range of differences was 10 points. The one point difference would be entirely explained by the NSE influence, but other influences would account for another component of the trait variation (i.e., the difference between high and low scoring MZ twin pairs). Explicit genetic model-fitting, which was not undertaken by Daniels and Plomin, is needed to test alternative hypotheses.

Baker and Daniels (1990), however, provided more direct evidence of purely environmental NSE influences. They relied on differences within pairs of MZ twins. Among their findings were: The MZ twin in the more popular peer group while growing up was more extraverted ($r = .41$) and had a higher level of positive mood than the cotwin ($r = .28$). SIDE peer college orientation and delinquency failed to find associations with personality outcomes, but the set of dependent variables did not include variables conceptually related to college orientation (such as academic achievement or IQ). These associations naturally do not constitute proof of causality between differential peer experiences and twin differences within a family. However, if peer group influence could be independently demonstrated on extraversion, a strong case would be made for a nonshared peer effect. Although both MZ and a small number of DZ twins were included in their study, Baker and Daniels did not report an analysis in which MZ and DZ twins are compared on the NSE-outcome relations.

Rowe and Osgood (1984) performed this kind of analysis for the relationship of twins' within-family delinquency differences with their differential friends' delinquency. The latter can be regarded as a possible measure of NSE influences. Adolescent MZ ($N = 168$ pairs) and DZ ($N = 97$ pairs) twins completed a standard self-report delinquency inventory and reported on their friends' contacts with the police. Self-delinquency and friends' delinquency were moderately correlated (rs about .60—a result with many replications in the delinquency literature). The pattern of twin correlations, however, suggested that this association was genetically mediated. The correlation of twin pair differences, for example, was weaker for MZ twins (.08 males, .11 females) than for DZ twins (.31 males, .31 females). This relationship may be interpreted in terms of friendship selection instead of friendship influence: The nonidentical genotypes of DZ twins should reinforce different preferences and choices, thus the forming of friendships with peers who differ in their rates of delinquent behavior.

In summary, our review supports both influence and selection processes. Studies of the absolute scoring of the SIDE supported genetic mediation—DZ twins and nontwin siblings had more dissimilar peer groups than MZ twins; adoptive siblings, more dissimilar peer groups than DZ twins or biological siblings. Genetic mediation was more difficult to establish for the personality differences among siblings. Rowe and Osgood (1984) reported it; but Daniels (1986) did not. One study indicated associations of peer characteristics with differences within pairs of MZ twins, indicating a nonshared environmental effect directly. We now turn to a different approach to the same issue—studies directed at the issue of peer selection versus peer influence.

FRIENDSHIPS AND CLIQUES: SELECTION OR INFLUENCE?

A selection process is unavoidable because, although most individuals are embedded in friendship networks, the particular individuals who serve as close friends, clique members, and casual acquaintances change over time. For example, in Berndt and Hoyle's (1985) study of two grade levels, about 30%–50% of friendships were unstable within one academic year. If friendships dissolve independently, then a child with three close friends may have only a .125 chance of retaining all three during a school year. Naturally, the odds of retaining friends would decrease further over a long period and during school transitions, such as moving from geographically separated elementary schools to a single high school. Cohen (1977) defined a stable clique as one that retained half the same membership over the academic year. By this definition, about 74% of cliques were stable over a school year (but note that this "stability" permitted change in half of the membership). Although these data show that friendships are far from ephemeral, they also indicate that most children have many opportunities to make new friendships.

As each of these opportunities permits a selection process to operate— whereby initially similar individuals select one another as friends—selection as a cause of friendship likeness cannot be ignored. A similar process of "assortative mating" appears to determine spousal similarity for many traits (Buss, 1985; Mascie-Taylor & Vandenberg, 1988; Vandenberg, 1972). How can we estimate the relative magnitudes of selection versus influence? The ideal research study is one that measures the characteristics of target children and their friends independently. Relying on the target child to report on the characteristics of friends introduces the possibility of projection bias, whereby "ego" inaccurately attributes personal traits to the friends (Bauman & Fisher, 1986; Urberg, Shyu,

& Liang, 1990; Wilcox & Udry, 1986). Second, the study should follow the friendships longitudinally, so that the characteristics of the friends can be assessed
prior to their entry into the friendship and after some duration of the friendship.
Initial similarity is a measure of selection; convergence or conditional probabilities of change are measures of influence. Although it is possible friends might
influence one another to be different, such a process has not been postulated
because of the universal tendency toward alikeness within friendships.

REVIEW OF SELECTION
VERSUS INFLUENCE STUDIES

Several studies are worth special attention because they possess these methodological strengths. In a classic study, 957 friendship pairs were identified either
at the beginning or end of an academic year; 70% of the friendships were stable
over the year (Kandel, 1978a). Table 7.2 shows Kandel's data on the similarity
of stable friends at Time 1 and Time 2. Convergence, the degree the friends
are more alike at Time 2 than at Time 1, indicates peer influence. As a percent
of the Time 2 similarity of the close friends, convergence effects ranged from
8.7% for educational aspirations to 19.0% for political orientation.

   The data permitted several methods of assessing friendship selection, but
a conservative approach is to compare the similarity of friends-to-be at Time
1 who became friends later at Time 2 with the similarity of stable friendships
at Time 2. By this analysis, a mean of 71.4% of friendship similarity is due to
selection. This represents the average similarity of friends-to-be at Time 1 divided by the average similarity of stable friends at Time 2. The average influence
effect was estimated as 12.3%. This represents the average increase in friends'
similarity over Times 1 and 2 divided by their similarity at Time 2. (Note that
the two components do not sum to the total friendship resemblance, because
the friends-to-be at Time 1 were not the same individuals as the stable friends
at Times 1 and 2.) Kandel, using these same data but a different analytic approach, concluded that about half of friendship similarity was due to influence
and half was due to selection.

   Using a methodology that focused on small friendship cliques of about five
individuals rather than on pairs of friends, Cohen (1977) compared the relative
importance of influence and selection in producing homogeneity from fall to spring
of the high school year. Clique homogeneity was examined over a range of behaviors and attitudes, including domains such as minor deviance (e.g., smoking
and drinking), value on achievement, and desire for popularity and recognition.
Clique members were more alike than nonclique members. Influence was assessed as the average change in group homogeneity from fall to spring for fall
clique members. Ostracism was assessed as the loss from fall to spring of group
members who were extreme relative to a clique on a behavioral dimension.

TABLE 7.2
Presentation of Kandel's Data on Friends' Alikeness in Attitudes and Behaviors

	Frequency Current Marijuana Use	Educational Aspirations	Political Orientation	Minor Delinquency	M
Stable Friends Time 1	.451	.349	.201	.255	.314
Stable Friends Time 2	.505	.382	.248	.286	.355
INFLUENCE	10.7%	8.7%	19.0%	10.8%	12.3%
Friends-to-Be at Time 1	.327	.348	.107	.248	.258
SELECTION	64.8%	91.1%	43.1%	86.7%	71.4%
Unexplained	24.5%	.4%	37.9%	2.5%	16.3%

Note. Coefficient of similarity, Kandel's τ-b. Data from rows 2, 4, and 5 of Kandel's (1978a) Table 1.

Selection was assessed as the initial similarity of new clique members in the fall, prior to the formation of a clique in the spring.

Cohen (1977) concluded that selection was the dominant process in producing homogeneity of attitudes and behaviors in friendship cliques. Selection also appeared to be a more potent force for new cliques in the spring, when students knew each other better, than for cliques at the start of the school year. Contrary to beliefs about group conformity, groups did not expel deviant members at greater rates than other members; selection operated only initially in clique formation, and less powerfully, in the addition of new members to an already existing clique.

Selection and influence processes on sexual intercourse were investigated by Billy and Udry (1985) for data collected on students in Grades 7–9 and then in a follow-up 2 years later. Their analysis of selection and influence depended on conditional probabilities. If the adolescents who had same-gender nonvirgin friends became nonvirgin at Time 2 more often than those with virgin friends, then the change was attributed to influence. If an adolescent who remained stable in behavior from Time 1 to Time 2 was more likely to acquire a similar friend at Time 2 than a dissimilar friend (e.g., virgin if the respondent was nonvirgin at both times), then the effect was attributed to selection. A third process was also examined: deselection, whereby individuals dropped friends who were dissimilar to themselves between times. Blacks were also included in the study, but Black friends were not homogeneous for sexual behavior. The sexual behavior of same-gender White friends was correlated. Billy and Udry found that deselection did not operate in any group; that White males and females acquired friends who were similar to themselves; and that only White females were influenced by their same-gender friends' sexuality.

Fisher and Bauman (1988) used longitudinal data collected on adolescents twice, 1 year apart, to separate selection and influence on smoking and drinking behavior. As with Billy and Udry's study, negligible support was found for a deselection process. For smoking, respondents were likely to acquire a new friend similar to themselves than dissimilar to themselves. This selection process was considerably stronger than influence, the tendency of respondents to change in the direction of their friends. For drinking, the two processes were about equally strong when the friends' own report of drinking behavior was used; selection was the stronger process when the respondents' report of the friends behavior was used to assess friends' drinking. Overall, Fisher and Bauman believe that selection accounted for more of the resemblance of friends than influence.

Epstein (1983) tested for friends' influence on adolescents' academic achievement. Selection was readily evident because of the association of friends' achievement levels at Time 1 of the two-round study. An issue was whether influence created additional similarity for initially mismatched friends—a low achieving individual paired with a high achieving friend and vice versa. Epstein concluded that such an influence process was operating. We view her conclusion as weakened by her failure to test the statistical significance of changes, that is, whether mismatched friends changed more than matched friends between the two data collection rounds. Examination of Epstein's figures (p. 195) also suggest that, if the changes are regarded as influence, they are much less in magnitude than selection effects—the changes fail to close the large gap between friends matched on achievement (low with low, or high with high). On the other hand, influence effects may be underestimated because there is no way to assess prior influence effects in the similarity of the friends at the start of the school year.

Two studies included independent data on friends in structural equation models of adolescent deviant behaviors (Kandel & Andrews, 1987; Urberg et al., 1990). In the Kandel study, best friends' marijuana use had a direct influence on "ego's" marijuana use; a weaker effect on frequency of alcohol use; and surprisingly, no direct effect on the initiation of alcohol use. In the Urberg study, friends' actual smoking had a direct and large effect on "ego's" smoking. However, the data were cross-sectional, somewhat weakening the argument for causality.

The aforementioned studies dealt with the influence versus selection issue using adolescents as subjects. Unfortunately, the research design of following friendship dyads or cliques over time, and obtaining independent reports from "self" and "friend," has not been used with younger children. Nonetheless, one elegant experiment using elementary school children indirectly addresses our concerns.

Coie and Kupersmidt (1983) first identified popular, rejected, neglected, and average fourth-grade children from different schools and brought them together in groups of four unacquainted children: one drawn from the popular classification, one from the rejected, one from the neglected, and one from the average. After interacting with one another, children were asked to make sociometric nominations of their group members. These new nominations were highly correlated with the children's original sociometric statuses, and classification in the new groups was based on behavioral differences such as the rejected children's greater aggressiveness and the popular children's greater social skills and physical attractiveness.

In most school contexts, friendships are more likely between popular children and between rejected children than across these classifications (e.g., Cairns, Cairns, Neckerman, Gest, & Gariepy, 1988). Neglected children are marked by an absence of friendship ties.

Coie and Kupersmidt's (1983) experimental manipulation indicates that it is the characteristics of children that contribute to these different statuses rather than peer reputation or peer influence. These results are consistent with a selection process in friendship similarities, although they do not directly prove it. That is, if individuals display consistent traits across peer groups, then the matching of friends on these traits is probably the result of prior selection. Coie and Kupersmidt's innovative design might have tested this latter possibility by including several popular and rejected children in an experimental group and then determining whether mutual friendship choices developed among rejected and popular children, but not across categories.

In summary, the foregoing studies support notions of both selection and influence, but selection tends to be the stronger of the two processes. Ostracism of nonconforming members from a group, and abandoning an already existing friendship because a friend was different in behavior, received no support.

IMPLICATIONS AND CONCLUSIONS

This chapter opened by posing the question, "Are peer groups a nonshared environmental influence?" The answer to this question is certainly affirmative. In the section on behavioral genetic studies, even MZ twins belonging to different peer groups were demonstrably different in the expected ways. And in the review of selection versus influence, most studies revealed some degree of influence of friends.

Nonetheless, massive peer influence effects read by lay person and expert alike into friendship homophily were absent. To find the true influence of friends, effects of prior selection must be first subtracted from friendship homophily. As selection was usually the stronger of the two processes, the remainder would be necessarily small. Yet it is from this remainder that any nonshared effects of the peer group must emerge.

Perhaps a part of the problem is the idea that an influence can operate independently of the characteristics of the individual who is the target of the influence. In the smoking literature, peers were once seen as the major determinant of smoking habits. Now, the notion of peer pressure is viewed with some skepticism because we know that adolescents often enter group situations with a plan to try cigarettes, and that most adolescents perceive little pressure to smoke (Friedman, Lichtenstein, & Biglan, 1985). Our review reinforces this conclusion: Little evidence was found for the ostracism or rejection of friends who were different. Rowe, Chassin, Presson, Edwards, and Sherman (1992) suggested that peers provide the initial opportunity to smoke, but that the transition to regular smoking may depend on the addicting and pleasure giving properties of nicotine itself. The notion that behaviors are maintained for their functional values, whether cast in an economic, behavioristic (Herrnstein, 1990), or sociobiological sense (Wilson, 1975), offers a powerful alternative to viewing the maintenance of human behavior patterns in terms of simple exposure to peer pressures, however defined. Thus, we conclude that the peer group is a nonshared environmental influence on siblings, but that its most important influence is not this, but is instead the reinforcement of existing genotypes through the functional consequences of behavior for the individual.

ACKNOWLEDGMENT

This chapter was partly supported by National Institute of Drug Abuse grant DA06287-01.

REFERENCES

Baker, L. A., & Daniels, D. (1990). Nonshared environmental influences and personality differences in adult twins. *Journal of Personality and Social Psychology, 58*, 103–110.

Bauman, K. E., & Fisher, L. A. (1986). On the measurement of friend behavior in research on friend influence and selection: Findings from longitudinal studies of adolescent smoking and drinking. *Journal of Youth and Adolescence, 15*, 345–353.

Berndt, T. J., & Hoyle, S. G. (1985). Stability and change in childhood and adolescent friendships. *Developmental Psychology, 21*, 1007–1015.

Billy, J. O. G., & Udry, J. R. (1985). Patterns of adolescent friendship and effects on sexual behavior. *Social Psychology Quarterly, 48*, 27–41.

Buss, D. M. (1985). Human mate selection. *American Scientist, 73*, 47–51.

Cairns, R. B., Cairns, B. D., Neckerman, H. J., Gest, S. D., & Gariepy, J. (1988). Social networks and aggressive behavior: Peer support or peer rejection? *Developmental Psychology, 24*, 815–823.

Cohen, J. M. (1977). Sources of peer group homogeneity. *Sociology of Education, 50*, 227–241.

Coie, J. D., & Kupersmidt, J. B. (1983). A behavioral analysis of emerging social status in boys' groups. *Child Development, 54*, 1400–1416.

Daniels, D. (1986). Differential experiences of siblings in the same family as predictors of adolescent sibling personality differences. *Journal of Personality and Social Psychology, 51*, 339–346.

Daniels, D., Dunn, J., Furstenberg, F. F., & Plomin, R. (1985). Environmental differences within the family and adjustment differences within pairs of adolescent siblings. *Child Development, 56*, 764–774.

Daniels, D., & Plomin, R. (1985). Differential experience of siblings in the same family. *Developmental Psychology, 21*, 747–760.

Epstein, J. L. (1983). Examining theories of adolescent friendship. In J. L. Epstein & N. Karweit (Eds.), *Friends in school: Patterns of selection and influence in secondary schools* (pp. 39–61). New York: Academic Press.

Fisher, L. A., & Bauman, K. E. (1988). Influence and selection in the friend-adolescent relationship: Findings from studies of adolescent smoking and drinking. *Journal of Applied Social Psychology, 18*, 289–314.

Friedman, L., Lichtenstein, E., & Biglan, A. (1985). Smoking onset among teens: An empirical analysis of initial situations. *Addictive Behaviors, 10*, 1–13.

Hallinan, M. T. (1983). Commentary: New directions for research on peer influence. In J. L. Epstein & N. Karweit (Eds.), *Friends in school: Patterns of selection and influence in secondary schools* (pp. 219–231). New York: Academic Press.

Herrnstein, R. J. (1990). Rational choice theory: Necessary but not sufficient. *American Psychologist, 45*, 356–367.

Kandel, D. B. (1978a). Homophily, selection, and socialization in adolescent friendships. *American Journal of Sociology, 84*, 427–436.

Kandel, D. B. (1978b). Similarity in real-life adolescent friendship pairs. *Journal of Personality and Social Psychology, 36*, 306–312.

Kandel, D. B., & Andrews, K. (1987). Process of adolescent socialization by parents and peers. *International Journal of the Addictions, 22*, 319–342.

Mascie-Taylor, C. G. N., & Vandenberg, S. G. (1988). Assortative mating for IQ and personality due to propinquity and personal preference. *Behavior Genetics, 18*, 339–345.

Plomin, R., & Daniels, D. (1987). Why are children in the same family so different from one another? *Behavioral and Brain Sciences, 10*, 1–60.

Rowe, D. C., Chassin, L., Presson, C. C., Edwards, D., & Sherman, S. J. (1992). An "epidemic" model of adolescent cigarette smoking. *Journal of Applied Social Psychology, 22*, 261–285.

Rowe, D. C., & Osgood, D. W. (1984). Heredity and sociological theories of delinquency: A reconsideration. *American Sociological Review, 49*, 526–540.

Rowe, D. C., & Plomin, R. (1981). The importance of nonshared (E_1) environmental influences in behavioral development. *Developmental Psychology, 17*, 517–531.

Urberg, K. A., Shyu, S., & Liang, J. (1990). Peer influence in adolescent cigarette smoking. *Addictive Behavior, 15*, 247–255.

Vandenberg, S. G. (1972). Assortative mating, or who marries whom? *Behavior Genetics, 2*, 127–157.

Verbrugge, L. M. (1977). The structure of adult friendship choices. *Social Forces, 56*, 576–597.

Wilcox, S., & Udry, J. R. (1986). Autism and accuracy in adolescent perceptions of friends' sexual attitudes and behavior. *Journal of Applied Sociology, 16*, 361–374.

Wilson, E. O. (1975). *Sociobiology: The new synthesis*. Cambridge: Harvard University Press.

8

Nonshared Environments and Heart
Disease Risk: Concepts and Data
for a Model of Coronary-Prone Behavior

Craig K. Ewart
Johns Hopkins University

This chapter presents a model for investigating environmental and genetic origins of coronary-prone behavior and emotion. Chronic antagonistic hostility has been identified as an independent risk factor for coronary heart disease, the leading cause of death in the United States and in other developed nations (Booth-Kewley & Friedman, 1987; Matthews & Haynes, 1986). Initial precursors of heart disease appear in childhood, and point to the possibility that learning environments conducive to hostile emotion might accelerate the early progression of atherogenesis, hypertension, and related disorders. Yet, although many studies link hostile affect to increased risk, research in this field has been dominated by an atheoretical epidemiology devoid of a guiding conceptual framework. This lack makes it difficult to interpret conflicting findings or to identify promising avenues of investigation. Moreover, behavioral researchers have devoted far more energy to measuring coronary-prone traits than to devising theoretical models that might explain how problematic behavioral dispositions could originate and how and why they are expressed. The present model strives to correct this imbalance by providing a causal explanatory framework grounded in contemporary social cognitive theory and behavioral genetics.

The chapter's central thesis is that coronary-prone behavior is usefully described in terms of goals, expectations, strategies, and capabilities arising from genetically based predispositions and from social experiences that affect siblings in the same family differently. Certain types of nonshared experience may foster problematic strivings and skill deficits that increase personal vulnerability to cardiac illness. From recent developments in social cognitive theory, social competence constructs now make it possible to bridge the gap between genes and social learning on the one hand, and situational stress reactions, emotional expression, behavioral coping, and eventual illness on the other.

Research on genetic origins of personality points increasingly to nonshared environments as sources of significant individual variation in the coping patterns and health habits that contribute to heart disease risk. The concept of nonshared environmental influences, coupled with the behavioral model described here, offers a powerful new tool for clarifying how nature and nurture may affect health. Longitudinal study of siblings who differ in genetic relatedness, driven by a theory specifying how nonshared social experiences might increase risk, could greatly advance our understanding of how heart disease develops over the life span. This chapter lays the foundation for such research by identifying sources of nonshared experience that might explain individual differences in coronary-prone behavior, by relating these experiences to the acquisition of protective competencies, and by presenting data linking social competence deficits to early indices of cardiovascular risk.

The chapter is divided into three major sections. The first summarizes evidence for genetic and environmental origins of coronary heart disease, describes its early pathogenesis, and considers the role of antagonistic hostility as contributing risk factor with identifiable genetic and nonshared environmental origins. Next a social competence analysis of the emergence and maintenance of chronically hostile emotion and behavior is presented. This model identifies critical components of competence and organizes them within a broader "social action" framework that clarifies their potential contribution to coronary-prone behavior. The last part of the chapter illustrates the application of social competence constructs to the study of coronary-prone response patterns in adolescents by presenting data from a study examining the influence of coping goals and skills on blood pressure during a stressful social encounter. These findings suggest directions for further investigation.

ORIGINS AND EARLY ANTECEDENTS
OF CORONARY HEART DISEASE

Genes play an important role in determining vulnerability to coronary heart disease. Early heart disease in a parent increases one's risk, and genetic influences have been demonstrated in major risk factors including elevated blood cholesterol, high blood pressure, obesity, and increased insulin resistance. In the case of blood cholesterol, population studies have revealed strong correlations between parents, offspring, and siblings for plasma levels of total cholesterol, low density lipoprotein (LDL) and high density lipoprotein (HDL) cholesterol (Kwiterovich,

1986). Path analytic investigations have demonstrated significant genetic and cultural influences on plasma levels of lipids and lipoproteins; for example, Rao et al. (1982) found that genetic heritability for LDL cholesterol was 0.62, whereas cultural heritability was 0.072.

Genetic transmission of hypertension risk has been established by family-twin and adoption studies conducted in diverse populations over the past several decades (Rose, 1986). Blood pressure levels tend to aggregate within families (Feinleib et al., 1977). Intraclass correlations of casual blood pressures within monozygotic and dizygotic twin pairs reliably differ and yield heritability estimates, h^2, in the range of 0.50 to 0.60, indicating that about half of the blood pressure variation can be attributed to an additive genetic effect. Research on twins in cultures with dissimilar lifestyles yield estimates of h^2 that are quite consistent, although the assumption of additive genetic influence implicit in these studies may be overly simplistic in not considering that genetic influences often vary with age and development. Obesity and increased insulin resistance contribute to higher blood pressure and heart disease risk; these conditions aggregate in families and appear to be influenced by genes and environment (Reaven & Hoffman, 1987; Stunkard et al., 1986).

Although genes clearly affect risk, the finding that genetic models leave large portions of risk factor variance unexplained suggests that genes act in concert with environmental influences. Moreover, the potential importance of the environment is indicated by controlled trials of family-oriented behavioral intervention to alter diet and exercise patterns in children (Epstein, 1986; Klesges et al., 1983). Behavior changes effected by these interventions have been shown to reduce obesity, insulin levels, and blood pressure (Epstein, Wing, Koeske, & Valoski, 1984; Rocchini, Katch, Schork, & Kelch, 1987), thereby lowering heart disease risk. Behavioral and social-environmental factors appear capable of inhibiting or accelerating the expression of genetically determined vulnerabilities.

Pathogenesis in Childhood

Heart disease is known to begin early in life (Berenson et al., 1983). Fatty streaks that represent the initial stages of atherosclerosis are detectable in the aortas of 3-year-olds and are believed to become grossly visible in the proximal portion of the left anterior descending coronary artery after the age of 10 (McGill, 1984). Gross fibrous plaques and frequent, microscopically detectable areas of necrosis appear by the age of 20. Epidemiologic studies suggest that blood cholesterol and blood pressure in childhood and adolescence may accelerate the progression of atherogenesis: Systolic blood pressure levels and lipoproteins are correlated with the early stages of plaque formation in adolescents (Newman et al., 1986), and a blood pressure that repeatedly is found to be in the upper range of normal pressure for this age predicts later hypertension (Lauer,

Clarke, & Beaglehole, 1984; Shear, Burke, Freedman, & Berenson, 1986).

Studying the early pathogenesis of heart disease could yield enormous benefits in the form of more effective preventive intervention. For some risk factors, causal relationships may be more evident early in life than in maturity; for example, correlations between exercise habits and blood pressure tend to be stronger in children than in adults (Strazzullo et al., 1988). Also, pathways via which risk factors affect pathogenesis may vary. In adolescence, chronic anger or hostility might affect the cardiovascular system via increased autonomic reactivity, while contributing simultaneously to the adoption of health-damaging habits such as tobacco, alcohol, or drug use (Kellam, Brown, Rubin, & Ensminger, 1983).

Hostility Risk Factor

Epidemiologic research consistently has shown that all known risk factors combined (e.g., smoking, obesity, elevated blood cholesterol, high blood pressure), account for no more than half of the variation in disease outcomes (Keys et al., 1972). Moreover, studies in developing countries have shown that the rise in heart disease that accompanies increasing urbanization cannot be explained by changes in diet (e.g., Garcia-Palmieri et al., 1978). These findings have led many to suspect that emotional stress may play an important yet little understood role in pathogenesis. From the 1960s through the early 1980s, the notion of Type A behavior—a heterogeneous cluster of tendencies involving excessive time-urgency, impatience, and competitiveness—dominated efforts to unravel the connection between emotion, behavior, and cardiovascular disease (Friedman & Rosenman, 1959). In the past decade, however, epidemiologic investigation has suggested that perhaps only one or a very few subcomponents of the global Type A behavior pattern actually increase heart disease risk. Attention increasingly has focused on *potential for hostility*, defined as "a stable predisposition to respond to a broad range of frustrating circumstances with varying degrees of anger, irritation, disgust, contempt, resentment, and the like, which may or may not be associated with overt behavior directed against the source of the frustration" (Dembroski, MacDougall, Williams, Haney, & Blumenthal, 1985, p. 230). Evidence from early Type A research and from more recent prospective and retrospective studies implicates hostility in the pathogenesis of coronary heart disease (Dembroski, MacDougall, Costa, & Grandits, 1989; Matthews & Haynes, 1986; McCann & Matthews, 1988).

Potential for hostility represents a specific form of hostile expression involving a tendency to become openly antagonistic, irritable, and generally disagreeable when challenged or frustrated by an interviewer. This antagonistic interpersonal stance is modestly correlated with attitudes of hostile cynicism and mistrust as measured by the Cook and Medley subscale of the MMPI (Cook

& Medley, 1954) but the two forms of hostility appear to have somewhat different health correlates. Potential for hostility has been linked specifically to death from heart disease, whereas Cook–Medley cynicism has been related to death from cardiovascular illnesses, cancer, and all other causes (Shekelle, Gale, Ostfeld, & Paul, 1983). As an enduring predisposition, potential for hostility also differs from anger, which is an emotional state often associated with increased autonomic nervous system arousal. It is likely, however, that people who tend to become obnoxious when frustrated will often provoke anger-arousing reactions from others. Angry interpersonal exchanges are known to elevate blood pressure (Ewart, Taylor, Kraemer, & Agras, 1984, 1991), and may provide a mechanism through which potential for hostility increases cardiovascular risk.[1]

Origins of Antagonistic Hostility

Research on subcomponents of Type A behavior has suggested that loudness of speech, competition for control of the interview, and hostility directed at an interviewer are heritable (Matthews, Rosenman, Dembroski, MacDougall, & Harris, 1984). Other studies have disclosed modest familial aggregation on measures of trait anger (Ditto, France, & Miller, 1989) and "quarrelsomeness" (Buss, 1984), and a recent analysis of data from the Swedish Adoption/Twin Study of Aging indicates that up to 20% of the variance in self-reported trait hostility can be ascribed to genetic sources (Pedersen et al., 1989). On the other hand, an analysis of Cook–Medley hostility scale (Cook & Medley, 1954) responses in adult male twins has suggested that genetic variation may contribute less to differences in this measure of trait hostility than to variance in other measures, and that early learning environments may contribute substantially to the development of cynical hostility and mistrust (Carmelli, Rosenman, & Swan, 1988). Considering that antagonistic hostility is probably modulated by temperamental factors involving reactive irritability or sociability (Goldsmith et al., 1987), and appears to be related to the basic personality dimension of "agreeableness" (Costa,

---

[1]The connection between openly antagonistic behavior and cardiovascular disease appears inconsistent with a frequently-reported finding that persons with high blood pressure tend to suppress the expression of anger and other unpleasant emotions (Shapiro & Miller, 1987). Yet there is evidence that anger suppression may be a consequence rather than a cause of the elevated blood pressure: A recent study comparing self-reported anger in hypertensives who were aware of their diagnosis with anger in hypertensives who had been diagnosed but not informed of their condition found evidence for diminished anger expression only in the informed hypertensives (Irvine, Garner, Olmsted, & Logan, 1989). The unaware hypertensives did not differ from a normotensive comparison group with respect to self-reported anger. People who have been told they have high blood pressure or heart disease may try to dampen emotions associated with rapid heart rate, flushing, and other symptoms of arousal (Dembroski & Czjakowski, 1989). Anger suppression also is a predictable response to situations where voicing one's anger could threaten a relationship, get one fired, or have other undesired consequences. Frequent anger suppression may simply reflect prolonged exposure to anger-provoking conditions that cannot be rectified (Averill, 1982).

McCrae, & Dembroski, 1989), genetic influences on temperament and personality undoubtedly contribute to antagonistic affect and behavior.

Several considerations suggest that genetic influences are not overwhelming, however. First, although relevant genetic studies are few, the small size of the heritability coefficients reported thus far leave ample room for environmental influences. Second, field research shows that anger is usually occasioned by the actions of others in one's social milieu; the frequency and intensity of hostile emotion is significantly affected by the environment (Averill, 1982). The challenge is to discover how genetically influenced preferences, tempos, or capabilities lead people to select or create anger arousing situations that, in turn, predispose them to further anger provocation and arousal.

Nonshared Environmental Contributions
to Hostility and Chronic Anger

Research on genetic and environmental origins of personality suggests that environments foster individual variation via processes that affect siblings in the same family differently; personality owes more to nonshared than to shared social influences (Plomin & Daniels, 1987). In adulthood, studies of interspousal resemblance with respect to blood pressure level and reactivity indicate that spouses do not come to resemble each other more as they live together longer, implying that sharing the same family environment has little cardiovascular effect (Ditto & France, 1990). On the other hand, occasional reports of spousal resemblance on blood pressure are consistent with the view that people may select spouses who mirror their goals, capabilities, or interactive strategies; this "assortative mating" can be ascribed to the genetic predispositions and social learning experiences of the individual spouses. For example, longitudinal data from the Framingham heart disease study indicate that people tend to marry individuals whose dietary habits, level of obesity, and smoking and alcohol consumption patterns resemble their own (Sackett, Anderson, Milner, Feinleib, & Kannel, 1975).

Personality characteristics that may lead people to create coronary-prone lifestyles and environments can be traced to early social experiences that children in the same family do not necessarily share. In a pioneering attempt to find systematic relationships between differences in sibling behaviors and nonshared family experiences, Daniels and her colleagues found that mothers perceived their children to experience the family differently, and that the siblings themselves perceived even larger differences in the family environment than did their mothers. Both parental and sibling reports of the family environment agreed in indicating that the better adjusted sibling experienced more maternal closeness, more sibling friendship, more peer friendliness, more say in family decision making, and more domestic chore responsibilities in comparison with the other sibling (Daniels, Dunn, Furstenberg, & Plomin, 1985).

What might cause these differences in experience? Apart from genetic influences—which I consider later—a review of existing research literature suggests that potential nonshared environmental influences capable of shaping social competence could result from family structure, differential parental treatment related to chronic marital conflict, and sibling or peer relationships characterized by coercion and dominance.

Family Structure

Birth order is an important structural source of nonshared experiences within the same family; for example, a firstborn child is not exposed to the social modeling influences of older siblings, and later born children may benefit from being raised by "more experienced" parents. Hence, the simple fact of birth order may differentially affect sibling interaction, competition, and socialization. Effects of birth order reported in personality studies include the finding that compared to their later born siblings, firstborn children conform more to authority, attain higher levels of education, and exhibit higher occupational achievement (Adams, 1972). Firstborns also have been found to score higher than later borns on measures of intelligence, pride, self-esteem, and social status (Zajonc, Markus, & Markus, 1979). Moreover, firstborns display more dominance when interacting with later born siblings (Sutton-Smith & Rosenberg, 1970). Yet there appear to be advantages in having an older sibling. Compared to firstborns, later borns have been found to be less anxious, less neurotic, less likely to punish in a Buss teacher–learner paradigm, and to manifest higher levels of social skill (Ickes & Turner, 1983). It is true that the effects of birth order on major personality traits often appear small, and have been inconsistent across studies, yet conventional trait measures usually are not designed to tap mid-level competence constructs envisioned in the present social-contextual model. The latter (narrower) constructs would be expected to be more sensitive to family structure than would broader personality traits.

For example, the effects of birth order and gender on dimensions of social competence have been demonstrated in a study reported by Ickes and Turner (1983). Mixed-gender dyads were observed unobtrusively while they waited for a psychology experiment to begin. Subjects selected for the study had an opposite gender, nontwin sibling. The factorial design crossed birth order (subject is an older or a younger sibling) and gender to create four dyad types: firstborn female with firstborn male; firstborn female with later born male; later born female with firstborn male; later born female with later born male. Social behaviors during the waiting interval were rated from videotapes made without the subjects' awareness. After being debriefed, subjects rated their partner on adjective scales.

Effects of birth order were evident in both genders but were most pronounced in males. Compared to firstborn men, later born men talked longer, asked more questions, evoked more gaze from their female partner, and were rated by their partners as more "likeable," "assertive," and "exciting." Compared to first-born women, later born women initiated interaction more often, smiled more, were less confrontive and less reserved, and were rated as more "likeable" by their male partners. Thus, birth order—a nonshared environmental dimension—may influence the development and expression of social goals and capabilities, especially in males. Perhaps later borns must work harder to get attention and must master social engagement skills in order to achieve this. Through exposure to an older sibling's peers, later born children may have more opportunities to learn social skills from influential models. Family size and density might moderate the birth order effect, with larger families providing more learning opportunities. To the extent that hostility and its health-damaging consequences are affected by social competence, birth order could be expected to influence the acquisition of coronary prone patterns. Birth order has been related to Type A competitiveness (Strube & Ota, 1982); future investigation should examine its possible association with potential for hostility.

Marital Conflict and Distress

Marriage therapists have noted that marital conflict often fosters the development of destructive parent–child alliances as children are drawn into the interspousal conflict. A child who becomes allied with one parent experiences the family conflict differently than siblings not allied with that parent; marital tensions therefore may constitute an important and ubiquitous source of nonshared environmental influences. The best evidence for this is provided by observational data reported by Gilbert, Christensen, and Margolin (1984) who recorded problem-solving interactions of nondistressed and multiproblem families. They characterized family interactions in terms of *alliance behavior* and *alliance strength*: The alliance behaviors were specific communications exchanged by parent to parent, parent to child, and child to child pairs during a family discussion task, while alliance strength was the ratio of positive to negative comments a given pair exchanged during the task. Results indicated that parent-to-parent alliances were weaker in distressed families than in the nondistressed families. Moreover, mother-to-child interactions were more negative in the distressed families, and children in these families reported that their parents treated them less similarly than did the children in nondistressed families.

Other investigators have linked marital conflict with child deviance (Grych & Fincham, 1990); marital tensions presumably foster hostile and competitive behavior in offspring by modeling aggression, by creating unstable alliances, and by engendering coercion cycles within the family (Patterson, 1982). Each of these processes has the potential to affect children in the same family differently, thus leading to pronounced individual differences in susceptibility to hostile feelings and aggressive behavior. Hostile confrontations within families have been shown to elevate blood pressure (Ewart, Burnett, & Taylor, 1983; Ewart et al., 1984, 1991).

There is some evidence that the effects of marital conflict on child behavior may be moderated by gender. For example, Schwartz and Getter (1980) found that indices of emotional distress and alienation in adolescents were explained by a *triple* interaction of parental marital conflict, dominance, and gender. The most distressed and alienated children were males exposed to parental conflict in which the mother dominated the marital relationship (e.g., in decision making). In females, distress and alienation were associated with exposure to marital conflict and a dominant father. Curiously, in families without marital conflict, having a dominant opposite-gender parent was associated with the lowest levels of distress and alienation.

It is interesting to note that research relating Type A behavior in children with parental Type A tendencies also suggests an interaction between gender, family dynamics, and emotion. Links between parent and offspring Type A behavior have been more evident in boys than in girls (Matthews, Stoney, Rakaczky, & Jamison, 1986); boys in families rated lower on positive affiliation and supportiveness exhibit increased hostility and display larger cardiovascular responses to laboratory challenges than do girls from similar families (Woodall & Matthews, 1989).

Interactions with Siblings and Peers

Marital distress is believed to stimulate conflict between siblings and to render children more susceptible to peer influences. Daniels has reported important evidence that sibling personality differences can be explained by siblings' past interactions with one another. In one study (Daniels, 1986), pairs of biological (50% genetically related) and adoptive (genetically unrelated) adolescent siblings completed questionnaires measuring personality traits, reported their anticipated educational and occupational attainments, and completed a new measure of non-shared environment: The Sibling Inventory of Differential Experiences (SIDE). The SIDE made it possible to compare siblings' perceptions of their interactions with each other, as well as their perceptions of their own and each other's peer groups. They rated their relationship on SIDE scales that describe sibling antagonism, caretaking, jealousy, and closeness, and rated differences in their peer groups on the dimensions of differential college orientation, popularity, and delinquency. The personality measure was a temperament inventory that assessed traits of emotionality (anger, fear, distress), activity, sociability, and shyness; this questionnaire also asked subjects to rate their expected educational and occupational attainments.

Multiple regression analyses revealed that differential sibling interaction explained from 6% to 11% of the variance in sibling personality differences. For example, the sibling who reported more angry emotionality as compared with his or her sibling had experienced more antagonism and jealousy from the other sibling. The sibling who reported more sociability had experienced more closeness from the other. Differential peer characteristics explained from 6% to 26% of the personality variance. For example, the sibling who reported more emotionality-anger as compared to his or her sibling also experienced a less college-oriented peer group. The more sociable sibling belonged to a more popular peer group than did the less sociable sibling. Effects of family structure also were detected; the later born sibling in each pair tended to report more sociability.

Genetic influences might create differences in child temperament that could, in turn, elicit differential treatment by siblings or peers. Regression analyses for the whole sample, the biological siblings, and the adopted siblings, failed to support this possibility, however. Regression results (R, R^2, and adjusted R^2) did not differ for biological and adoptive siblings, indicating that the relationships were environmentally mediated. Although differences in personality may cause adolescents to seek different peer groups or elicit differential treatment from their siblings, Daniels' findings support the view that nonshared environments help create personality differences.

A subsequent study provided an even more stringent test of environmental influences by including data from monozygotic and dizygotic twins (Baker & Daniels, 1990). Monozygotic twins reported more similar environments than did dizygotic twins, suggesting that genes do influence exposure to social environments (the SIDE thus should not be viewed as a "pure" measure of siblings' environments but partly reflects inherent personality differences between siblings). However, correlations between differences in monozygotic twins' experiences and differences in their personalities showed that their social environments did affect their development. The sibling who was more antagonistic and more often acted as caretaker while growing up scored higher on a measure of "masculinity" (e.g., greater aggressiveness and leadership) administered in adulthood. Hence, differences in childhood experience fostered greater dominance in adulthood independently of genetic influences. Comparison of various sources of nonshared experience revealed that sibling interactions in childhood contributed the most to adult personality differences, whereas differential treatment by parents contributed least to adult personality.

To summarize, nonshared environmental influences capable of fostering potential for hostility via their effects on social competence can be shown to operate systematically, appear fairly specific in their effects, and are probably capable of explaining at least a modest portion of the observed sibling variance in personality measures. On the other hand, a developmental model of coronary-prone behavior need not account for all of personality. Nonshared environments may influence the acquisition of specific behavior patterns sufficiently to increase hostile emotion and elevate long-term risk.

We have seen how nonshared environments might differently predispose children in the same family to manifest coronary-prone hostility. How do we determine if the development of social competence and emergence of hostility are related to the early pathogenesis of cardiovascular disease? The feasibility of research on this question is supported by evidence that blood pressure and heart rate responses to emotional stressors are stable over time in adolescents (Ewart & Kolodner, 1991a) and across developmental transitions in childhood (Matthews, Rakaczky, Stoney, & Manuck, 1987). Comparable stability has been demonstrated in components of coronary-prone behavior assessed by Type A interview (Steinberg, 1986; Visintainer & Matthews, 1987). A greater barrier to progress in this area, however, is the lack of a guiding theoretical framework. Without such a structure, findings often are ambiguous and inconsistencies may be difficult to interpret. The next section presents a social cognitive model designed to guide future efforts.

A SOCIAL COMPETENCE MODEL
OF CORONARY-PRONE BEHAVIOR

The social-contextual model proposed here provides an alternative to conceptual approaches that have dominated past research on personality and heart disease. Foremost among these is a tendency to view angry emotions as simple components of biologically based stress response syndromes. This tendency is evident in the influential work of Walter Cannon (1932) and Hans Selye (1950) who borrowed the term *stress* from physics to describe the orchestrated defense, or "general adaptation syndrome," mounted by physiologic systems to protect the body against environmental challenges. In like fashion, the Type A behavior pattern was first described as an "action-emotion complex" (Friedman & Rosenman, 1959) comprised of physiologic and behavioral changes evoked by challenging social encounters. An extreme form of this view holds that Type A behaviors and correlated physiologic changes are merely co-effects of heightened autonomic nervous system activity (Krantz, Arabian, Davia, & Parker, 1982).

The problem with this notion is that human emotional and physiologic responses to stressors are not uniform, but vary as a function of social context, personality differences, or subjective appraisals. This makes it difficult for biologic response-based definitions of emotion or stress to account for individual variation in stress responsivity (Hobfoll, 1989), or to explain situations in which people experience anger subjectively without exhibiting the expected physiologic responses (Averill, 1982). Thus, some investigators have proposed that physiologic responsivity to situations is moderated by stable personality traits (Spielberger, 1972). For example, the tendency of Type A individuals to exhibit greater autonomic arousal than Type B's during competitive games but not in noncompetitive situations has been attributed to the formers' enduring need for control (Glass, 1977) or for achievement (Matthews & Siegel, 1983).

Yet even these conceptions tend to ignore the role people play in shaping their own social environments, and fail to consider that the resulting social experiences may gradually alter or intensify dispositional tendencies (Smith & Anderson, 1986). Hostile people tend to create aversive social situations and, as a consequence, may become even more hostile.

The social-contextual alternative proposed here envisages a reciprocal relationship between persons and situations (Bandura, 1986), and thus provides a conceptual framework for examining the interplay of personal and situational influences. A fundamental concern is to discover how people become "both architects and victims" of situations shaped in part by their own actions (Patterson, 1982). Mechanistic interactionism is avoided by treating hostile traits as patterns of *hostility engendering* thought and behavior.

In a social-contextual view, dispositions such as hostility are expressed in terms of a person's goals, expectancies, strategies, and capabilities. In the language of personality theory, these constructs represent "mid-level" units of analysis describing the intentional structure of personality in specific contexts (Cantor, 1990; Little, 1989). They are not intended to provide a comprehensive account of personality, nor do they preclude the influence of broader trait or temperament dimensions including, for example, the major traits of neuroticism, extraversion, openness to experience, agreeableness, and conscientiousness that comprise the so-called "Big Five" dimensions of personality (McCrae, 1989).

A framework for organizing social-cognitive processes contributing to social competence is depicted in Fig. 8.1. In this framework, hostile acts or utterances ("interpersonal actions") represent strategies a person uses to influence

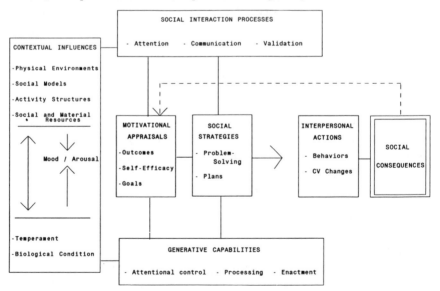

FIG. 8.1.   Social action model of coronary-prone hostility and behavior.

others in specific situations; hostile strategies are shaped by expectations about how other people are likely to act ("outcome expectancies"), appraisals of one's social capabilities ("self-efficacy"), and judgments concerning one's goals or strivings in the situation. Motivational appraisals and strategy choices both are determined by an individual's generative capabilities (e.g., how one attends to and processes social information), and by the social-interactive capabilities of the relationship systems of which the individual is a part. These interactive capabilities include the ability of relationship members to be aware of each other's goals, to communicate, problem solve, and identify mutual strivings. Midlevel self-regulatory processes are facilitated or constrained by broader contextual factors such as one's biologic condition, temperament, and mood, as well as by the larger physical and social environment.

This conceptual framework performs several useful tasks. First, the model provides a way to link hostile traits to hostile motives, and to translate both into observable hostile acts, thus bridging the gap between what personality is and what personality does. Chronically hostile behavior can be explained in terms of its hierarchical structure, its intentional nature, and its contextual embeddedness (Little, 1989). Second, evidence for a behavior–disease link is found at different levels of analysis (e.g., physiologic, cognitive, social) and in widely varying domains (e.g., family, school, or work environment). A social-contextual view of hostile actions integrates these diverse phenomena. Third, the present scheme is theoretically fruitful in that it suggests a competence-based approach to chronic hostility: The notion of goal-directed action focuses our attention on the character and adequacy of personal goals, expectancies, strategies, and capabilities, thus encouraging us to ask which competencies a person would have to possess—and lack—in order to be chronically hostile. Finally, this conceptual structure is of practical value in that it forces us to frame our hypotheses in terms of cognitive, social, and affective processes that can be targeted by known intervention techniques.

The social-contextual framework suggests how a predisposition to antagonistic hostility could arise and be maintained. Recall that the problem is to explain an increased susceptibility to chronic, repeated angry arousal, rather than to explain anger in all its varied manifestations. Unlike mechanistic theories that assume hostile tendencies lie dormant until activated by situations, the present model holds that people partly create the stressful environments of which they are also victims. How do they do this?

Consider first the motivational component. Research by personality theorists suggests that people can be described in terms of their commitments to personal goals and goal structures variously labelled "personal strivings" (Emmons, 1986), "projects" (Little, 1989), or "life tasks" (Cantor, 1990). At the goal level (Fig. 8.1), a person who is committed to projects that involve dominating, influencing, or controlling other people (as in projects that involve managing or leading others) is likely to encounter frustrating and potentially anger-provoking situations more often than will a person who is committed to socially affiliative or intimacy-enhancing goals (as in developing friendships), or to self-focused projects (as in improving one's skills or knowledge). The latter projects will less often provoke opposition than will efforts at interpersonal control, and hence are less apt to evoke situations in which the actor finds that others are trying to block a valued goal.

Goal-blockage does not invariably give rise to anger (Bandura, 1973). The likelihood of hostile emotion and behavior is increased, however, if the one who is blocked believes that angry displays and coercive acts are justified and will produce favorable results (positive outcome expectancy), lacks confidence in his or her ability to win others' support through less hostile means (low self-efficacy for friendly persuasion), and is confident that he or she can behave coercively (high self-efficacy for aggressive dominance). This combination of goals and expectations should increase the likelihood of pursuing coercive social strategies, thereby generating hostile acts ("interpersonal actions," Fig. 8.1) that provoke predictable counterresponses from others. The latter responses may, in turn, reinforce the actor's expectations so as to increase the probability of further anger.

The likelihood that an actor will form hostile goals, appraisals, or strategies is strongly affected by declarative and procedural knowledge schemas, or "generative capabilities." Declarative schemas encode factual knowledge of the social world and others' motives; procedural schemas represent "how to" skills and routines for applying declarative knowledge. Hostile affect and behavior are more likely in persons with well-developed dominance schemas, or who lack the schematic knowledge or skills that are needed in reading social cues, and in selecting, evaluating, and enacting socially effective behaviors (Cantor, 1990). Moreover, the problem does not reside solely within the individual. People whose intimate personal relationships are characterized by frequent coercive exchanges and infrequent opportunities for problem solving and corrective feedback would seem more likely to pursue hostile strategies in their dealings with others (Patterson, 1982). Persisting mood states possibly related to one's biologic condition, temperament, or aversive physical environment also would be expected to affect the ways people process social information and identify strategies.

Note that the social action framework makes specific predictions about pathways via which genes and environment might influence the development of chronic hostility. Genetic and environmental factors that affect basic generative capabilities and microsocial interaction processes can influence an individual's personal goals or projects, appraisals of personal efficacy, and outcome expectations. Goals and expectations, in turn, influence hostility by causing people to pursue poorly conceived or misguided social strategies.

Note also that deficits in one component of this model may be offset by strengths in others: If a person who wants to dominate others has the necessary social skills and a supportive environment, he or she might not experience chronic anger or elevated disease risk. On the other hand, while the individual contribution of any one component might be small (making replications of single-component studies more difficult), their aggregated impact could be large, a possibility supported by research on social information processing and aggressive behavior in children (cf. Dodge & Crick, 1990).

Social Competence Deficit in Chronic Hostility

Research on hostility and adult coronary risk is a newly developing area of investigation; in children and adolescents, very few studies have been undertaken (Thoresen & Pattillo, 1988). Yet the potential value of the present approach is suggested by existing research on social-cognitive processes in the different but related behavioral domain of childhood aggression. Much of this work has focussed on the operation of cognitive schemas, prototypes, or scripts; the generative capabilities (Fig. 8.1) of aggressive and nonaggressive youngers (Dodge & Crick, 1990; Dodge & Frame, 1982). Aggressive children have difficulty reading social cues; they infer other children's intentions impulsively (Sancillo, Plumert, & Hartup, 1989), rely on the most recently presented cue even when prior information suggests a different interpretation (Dodge & Tomlin, 1987), and display inaccuracies in interpreting the benign intentions of their peers (Dodge, Pettit, McClaskey, & Brown, 1986). They also have difficulty accessing nonaggressive and competent social responses (Dodge & Crick, 1990).

At the level of motivational appraisal, aggressive children report higher confidence that they can enact physically and verbally aggressive behaviors in conflict and peer group entry situations, and lack confidence in their ability to withdraw from threatening situations or to inhibit an aggressive response if provoked (Dodge & Crick, 1990). Aggressive children also expect more favorable outcomes to result from aggressive acts and less favorable outcomes to occur as a consequence of prosocial or submissive behaviors (Perry, Perry, & Rasmussen, 1986). They evaluate aggressive behavior more favorably on dimensions such as friendliness, goodness, assertiveness, and kindness than do less aggressive children, and judge competent social behavior less favorably on these dimensions than do their less deviant peers (Asarnow & Callan, 1985).

Little is known about the social goals and projects of chronically aggressive or hostile children. Research on Type A behavior in children has examined self-evaluative processes and goal-setting in achievement situations but these have not been related to chronic hostility (Matthews & Siegel, 1983). A content analysis of items on the widely used Cook–Medley hostility scale of the MMPI suggests that high responders would be likely to report goals or strivings that involve trying to dominate, defeat, frustrate, or control threatening others; the commitment to superior achievement demonstrated in Type A children does not necessarily imply an investment in hostile strivings.

IDENTIFYING NONSHARED ENVIRONMENTAL
ORIGINS OF CHRONIC HOSTILITY

The present social competence model, combined with the notion of nonshared environmental origins of behavior, suggests an explicit agenda for research on the development of coronary-prone emotion and behavior. Further progress will entail four major investigative tasks. First among these is the task of identifying social goals, expectancies, strategies, and generative capabilities—or combinations thereof—that typify chronically hostile children who are at increased cardiovascular risk due to tracking on blood pressure, blood cholesterol, insulin, or other indices. Studies of these children and others in their immediate social environment should focus on the number, type, or structure of personal goals or projects (Emmons & King, 1985; Little, 1983), interpersonal strategies (Cantor, 1990), and social skills assessed by behavioral observation (e.g., interviewer, teacher, parent, peer), story completion techniques (Ewart, Taylor, Kraemer, & Agras, 1991; Ford, 1982; Kendall & Fischler, 1984), and self-report. Research examining the physiologic consequences of manipulating hostility-related cognitive or social processes can help determine which behavioral variables are most likely to affect pathogenesis and thus deserve more intensive study.

The second task is to link these "higher risk" social-cognitive processes to children's family and peer environments, with specific attention to ways in which microsocial processes may foster nonshared experiences among children in the same family. It will be necessary to include other members of a child's social environment in the analysis, and to examine the hostile child's exchanges with siblings and peers as well as with parents (Daniels, 1986).

Demonstrating covariation between nonshared experiences, antagonistic hostility, and indices of cardiovascular risk sets the stage for a third task—the longitudinal descriptive investigation. A high risk child, and at least one sibling, must be followed over time to determine if differences in their social experiences are stable, and are consistently related to differences in tracking on cardiovascular risk indices. For example, evidence that a consistent pattern of sibling dominance by one child is related to more frequent anger and a higher age-gender adjusted blood pressure, would be compatible with the notion that nonshared family environments may increase cardiovascular risk by fostering chronic hostility.

Longitudinal correlations do not establish environmental causation, however. This can only be accomplished by twin and adoption studies that can ascertain the extent to which the observed behavioral and cardiovascular patterns are mediated genetically. Thus the fourth task is to determine if hypothesized relationships between nonshared environments, chronic hostility, and cardiovascular risk indices vary with degree of genetic relationship in analyses of identical twins, fraternal twins, genetically related nontwin siblings, and adopted siblings. Yet although these designs are potentially quite powerful, their usefulness at present is constrained by our limited ability to specify the precise nature of the hostility risk factor or its presumed nonshared environmental origins. This brings us back to Question 1: Are differences in social goals and skills related to differences in cardiovascular risk?

EFFECT OF SOCIAL COMPETENCE
ON BLOOD PRESSURE REACTIVITY

The relevance of a social competence approach to cardiovascular risk is suggested by data collected in a continuing a longitudinal study of high blood pressure tracking and heart growth in urban adolescents. This project is designed to determine if blood pressure reactions to emotional stress predict long-term blood pressure tracking and heart growth in adolescents at increased risk for essential hypertension. Additional questions include the role of social competence in determining cardiovascular responses to social challenges, and the extent to which competence constructs mediate relationships between trait hostility, trait anger expression, and blood pressure.

In this research, "higher risk" adolescents are identified via schoolwide blood pressure screenings of ninth-grade students in public high schools, a program involving approximately 1,200 individuals. From this population, a sample of 250 adolescents in the upper deciles of normal blood pressure was selected. Their blood pressure was measured under various conditions in the laboratory (quiet rest, exercise, cognitive and perceptual-motor tasks, social interview) and over the course of a typical 6-hour school day using an ambulatory monitoring device to obtain recordings at 10-minute intervals. Their resting blood pressures and echocardiographic dimensions were also assessed longitudinally over a 2-year interval. Measures of social competence were obtained. The final panel consists of 220 students and is balanced with respect to race and gender.

Social competence variables measured in the study include personal goals or strivings, expectancies (e.g., self-efficacy), social skills and strategies, interpersonal behavior, and affect. These are assessed by means of interviews, story completion tasks, self-report instruments, teacher ratings, and parent ratings. The findings described here address relationships between personal goals, self-expectancies, and blood pressure reactivity in a pilot group of 32 subjects. Hypertension risk in adolescents and young adults has been related to the magnitude of cardiovascular responses to laboratory stress tasks such as mental arithmetic, video games, and tracing an image reflected in a mirror (McCann & Matthews, 1988). Adolescents' blood pressure responses were compared to mental arithmetic, video game, and mirror drawing stress to blood pressure responses during a personal interview that simultaneously assessed key dimensions of social competence. The analysis attempted to determine if increases in blood pressure during the interview were related to the adolescent's social goals and strategies.

Study Design and Hypotheses

Subjects completed a stress interview (Ewart & Kolodner, 1991a) and the battery of cognitive and perceptual-motor tasks in our school-based laboratory during their physical education period. The order in which subjects completed the interview and the battery of cognitive/perceptual-motor tasks was counterbalanced across subjects to control for cardiovascular changes due to novelty or accommodation. Measures of blood pressure reactivity to the interview, video game, mirror drawing, and mental arithmetic were obtained by subtracting the mean of the pretask and posttask readings from the mean of the readings recorded during the task.

We tested two hypotheses suggested by the competence model. First, as strivings for social dominance are presumed to evoke more opposition than social-affiliative or nonsocial (self-development) goals, subjects whose strivings in a problem situation are directed at changing a relationship or at influencing another person should exhibit larger cardiovascular responses when recalling the problem than should subjects whose strivings are directed toward changing some aspect of their own behavior, personality, or life circumstances. Secondly, the model proposes that cardiovascular stress results from an inability to enact effective goal-attainment strategies; accordingly, subjects' self-rated ability to execute their preferred strategies (self-efficacy) should be inversely related to blood pressure changes occurring when the subject re-experiences the problem situation.

Social Competence Interview

The Social Competence Interview (Ewart & Kolodner, 1991a) is designed to elicit feelings, perceptions, and cardiovascular changes related to a stressful situation in which an important self-goal or personal striving was blocked or hindered. Changes in heart rate and blood pressure are measured at 90-second intervals before, during, and after the interview. The interview is divided into an 8-minute "experiential" phase followed by a 6-minute "self-appraisal" phase. In the experiential phase, the interviewer helps the subject re-experience thoughts and feelings evoked by the problem situation via guided imagery and reflective listening techniques; in the appraisal phase, the interviewer poses a series of questions designed to elicit the subject's personal goals, expectations, skills, and strategies for coping with similar problems should they occur in the future.

We have shown that the Social Competence Interview increases adolescent blood pressure to levels that exceed responses to conventional laboratory stress tasks such as mental arithmetic, mirror drawing, or video games. Moreover, these responses are stable over a 6-month interval, even when the interview is administered by different interviewers (further description of the interview and its correlates is provided by Ewart & Kolodner, 1991b; Ewart, Sonnega,

& Kolodner, 1990). Regression analyses using blood pressure responses to the interview and other laboratory tasks to predict ambulatory blood pressure during school reveal that the interview contributes to prediction more consistently than do the more conventional stress tasks, and suggest the interview technique may have greater ecological validity (Ewart & Kolodner, 1991b).

Self Goals and Expectancies

The Social Competence Interview elicits an adolescent's goals and expectations related to a problematic situation that has been a source of recurring frustration, thus identifying potential limitations in his or her ability to formulate attainable goals, anticipate possible outcomes, appraise personal capabilities, or execute effective strategies. After selecting a problem to talk about (examples are provided in a "stress deck" of cards to serve as prompts) subjects are encouraged to recall and describe in vivid detail a situation when they experienced the problem, including internal dialogue and verbal interchanges with others. They are asked to describe other peoples' words, expressions, and gestures, and if the problem involved a social encounter, to say things they would like to have said but did not. In the appraisal phase of the interview they are invited to provide an "ideal ending" for the problem, suggest ways this ending could be achieved, and rate their confidence that they could enact their preferred strategy (self-efficacy) on a scale ranging from "1" ("completely uncertain") to "10" ("completely certain"). The subjects' comments yield insights into their goals and strivings vis-à-vis the recurring problem, as well as their self-estimated ability to cope successfully in the future.

Audiotape recordings of the interview are coded by trained observers to yield ratings of subjects' goals, expectations, skills, and strategies. To characterize subjects' goals, we developed a taxonomy of typical strivings by examining well-known taxonomies of values and social motives (e.g., Rokeach Value Survey; Leary Interpersonal Circumplex). We derived categories relevant to the social competence model that were capable of describing strivings typically mentioned by adolescents. In this system, goals are characterized as reflecting either "social" or "self"-strivings, depending on whether the goal entails trying to influence the actions of another person or affect a relationship (*inter*personal goal), versus trying to change some aspect of one's own behavior or situation (personal goal). Social goals are then subdivided further into those involving "dominance" strivings, ranging from prosocial dominance (leading, advising) to more hostile dominance (attacking, getting revenge), and those involving affiliative/intimacy-oriented social goals, ranging from submissive affiliation ("placating") to more assertive intimacy ("become closer to someone"). Typical examples of strivings in each major category and respective subcategories are shown in Fig. 8.2.

```
┌─────────────────────────────────────────────────────────────────┐
│                                                                   │
│        INTERPERSONAL GOALS: "Social Dominance / Control"          │
│  ─────────────────────────────────────────────────────────────   │
│                                                                   │
│   "Trying to persuade parent to stop interfering or nagging"      │
│                                                                   │
│   "Want sibling to respect my feelings"                           │
│                                                                   │
│   "Want teacher to be more fair"                                  │
│                                                                   │
│   "Trying to avoid a difficult or annoying individual"            │
│                                                                   │
│   "Want to 'set the record straight' about untrue rumors"         │
│                                                                   │
│   "Trying to stop someone from 'spreading lies' about me"         │
│                                                                   │
│   "Want something bad to happen to another person"                │
│                                                                   │
│  ─────────────────────────────────────────────────────────────   │
│        INTERPERSONAL GOALS:  "Affiliation / Intimacy"             │
│  ─────────────────────────────────────────────────────────────   │
│                                                                   │
│     "Want to be a 'good' son/daughter"                            │
│                                                                   │
│     "Trying to live up to parents' expectations"                  │
│                                                                   │
│     "Want to be able to talk things over"                         │
│                                                                   │
│     "Want to have a boy/girlfriend"                               │
│                                                                   │
│     "Wish to be more intimate with someone"                       │
│                                                                   │
│     "Want to be 'part of the group'"                              │
│                                                                   │
│     "Want to be accepted by stepfamily"                           │
│                                                                   │
│  ─────────────────────────────────────────────────────────────   │
│        PERSONAL GOALS:  "SELF-CONTROL"                            │
│  ─────────────────────────────────────────────────────────────   │
│                                                                   │
│       "Want to improve failing grade"                             │
│                                                                   │
│       "Trying to make the team"                                   │
│                                                                   │
│       "Trying to find an after-school job"                        │
│                                                                   │
│       "Want nicer clothes or jewelry"                             │
│                                                                   │
│       "Want to make own decisions"                                │
│                                                                   │
└─────────────────────────────────────────────────────────────────┘
```

FIG. 8.2. Typical social and personal goals threatened by situations described as chronically stressful (from the Social Competence Interview).

Results

The pilot sample was comprised of 32 subjects (equal numbers of males and females, Blacks and Whites) selected from an initial subsample of 60 individuals on the basis of goal ratings made from the audiotapes. Sixteen of the subjects expressed strivings for social dominance, whereas the other 16 were selected because they expressed strivings for self-change. Frequently mentioned social dominance strivings (Change Other) were defending oneself against unfair treatment by parents or friends; typical self-directed strivings (Change Self) included efforts to improve academic or athletic performances in the wake of distressing failures. Analysis of the blood pressure levels revealed that the two groups did not differ significantly during the pretask and posttask baselines. Mean baseline blood pressure for the total sample was 118.9 mm Hg (SD = 9.6 mm Hg) systolic, and 62.1 mm Hg (SD = 6.4 mm Hg) diastolic.

The hypothesized effect of interview-assessed goal focus on systolic and diastolic blood pressure reactivity (Hypothesis 1) was evaluated by performing planned comparisons among the blood pressure reactivity scores (Task minus Baseline) shown in Fig. 8.3. This was accomplished by an analysis of covariance with goal focus (Self vs. Other) and task type (Interview vs. Cognitive-Motor) as the independent variables, blood pressure reactivity (Task mean minus Baseline mean) as the dependent variable, and the Baseline mean as a covariate (details of the analysis are presented in Ewart et al., 1990). The two ANCOVA's disclosed a significant interaction between goal focus and task type; while the two groups had virtually identical diastolic responses to the cognitive-motor tasks, their responses to the interview differed significantly. Subjects whose goal entailed trying to change someone else's behavior exhibited a larger blood pressure increase when discussing their problem than did subjects whose goal involved trying to change themselves. Moreover, the Change Other subjects' diastolic pressure was higher during the interview than during the other tasks, while the Change Self subjects pressure responses to the interview were equivalent or lower than those recorded during the task battery.

Self and Other subjects' blood pressure responses to the cognitive-motor tasks were identical, however, indicating that individuals who wanted to change someone else's behavior were not inherently more reactive. Thus the nature of the adolescent's personal strivings in the face of a recurring problem appears to be related to degree of cardiovascular arousal in this sample of higher risk individuals.

Self-Efficacy

Our second hypothesis was that blood pressure responses to problem discussion would be related to the subject's perceived ability to execute actions needed to resolve the problem or attain a desired goal, that is, their "self-efficacy"

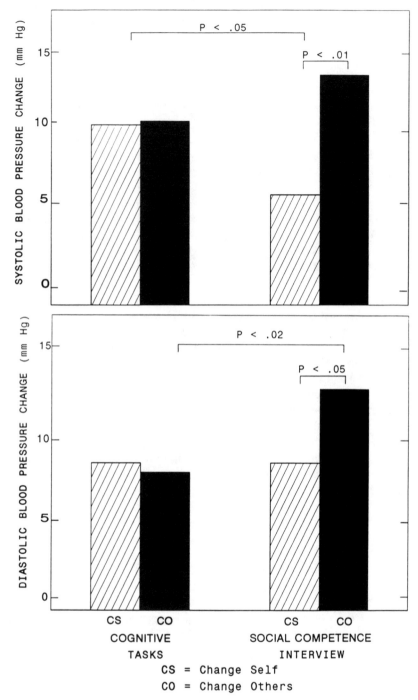

FIG. 8.3. Systolic and diastolic blood pressure changes (Task minus Baseline) during the Cognitive-Motor Task battery and the Social Competence Interview in a group of adolescents whose primary stress-coping goal (Interview) involved trying to change another person (CO), and a group whose stress-coping goal involved efforts at self-change (CS).

for goal attainment. Yet cardiovascular arousal might also be a function of the degree of anger or anxiety provoked by talking about the problem situation. We therefore examined subjects' reports of their emotions during the interview and reactivity tasks. These ratings had been made immediately after the interview and immediately after the task battery. We correlated the ratings of Anger, Nervous Tension, and Self-Efficacy with the blood pressure changes recorded during the interview and the cognitive tasks.

Pearson correlation coefficients presented in Table 8.1 indicate that self-efficacy ratings for enacting one's preferred coping strategy and blood pressure changes during the interview were inversely correlated with self-perceived ability to take effective coping action. Self-efficacy for social coping assessed during the interview was not correlated with blood pressure during the cognitive-motor task battery, however. Moreover, subjects' ratings of anger and tension were not correlated with their blood pressure responses to either the task battery or the Social Competence Interview.

Construct Validity of Goal and Efficacy Measures

Having found that interview goal and self-efficacy measures correlate with blood pressure responses to social stress, one might ask if they are measuring the components specified in the social competence model, and if they are related to trait indices of hostility and anger. This question has been examined in very preliminary way, using a different group of 30 randomly selected subjects. We computed correlations between the goal and self-efficacy measures, and: (a) subjects' verbal responses to a Means–Ends Problem Solving (MEPS) interview (Platt & Spivack, 1975); (b) self-reported anger and hostility assessed by the Multidimensional Anger Inventory (Siegel, 1986); (c) an index of self-perceived social support (Blumenthal et al., 1987); and (d) self-reported depression as measured by the Children's Depression Inventory (Kovacs, 1985). The Means–Ends Problem Solving task was administered on a different occasion than

TABLE 8.1
Pearson Correlations of Post-Interview Self-Efficacy, Anger, and
Tension Ratings with Systolic and Diastolic Blood Pressure Changes During the
Cognitive-Motor Task Battery (CT) and the Social Competence Interview (SCI)

Rating	Systolic Change		Diastolic Change	
	CT	SCI	CT	SCI
Self-efficacy	−.10	−.41**	−.29	−.38*
Anger	−.18	.16	.10	.14
Tension	−.02	.11	.05	.01

$*p < .05.$ $**p < .02.$

the Social Competence Interview by different interviewers, and transcribed responses were scored by raters who were unfamiliar with the interview scoring. The means–ends task presents imaginary situations involving typical problems and their successful outcomes; subjects are asked to tell how the ending came about. Responses indicate a respondent's ability to generate effective and appropriate interpersonal strategies; scoring procedures were those developed by Fischler and Kendall (1988).

This analysis revealed that interview goal and self-efficacy measures were significantly related to strategy selection, hostility, social support, and depression in directions predicted by the social competence model. Pearson correlations ranged from .35 to .45. Adolescents who expressed strong dominance goals in the Social Competence Interview scored higher on anger and depression. Correlations with the means–ends ratings disclosed that adolescents whose interview responses indicated investment in affiliative social goals generated means-ends strategies that demonstrated better understanding of other peoples' emotions and motives than did adolescents whose salient strivings did not indicate affiliative motives. The respondents whose goals were more ''Affiliative'' also tended to score higher on satisfaction with social support. Those who expressed high levels of confidence (self-efficacy rating) in their ability to cope with the problem discussed in the interview generated problem-solving strategies that were rated higher on dimensions of effectiveness, and active coping than did adolescents who were less confident in their ability to remove a recurring stressor. The moderate size of these correlations indicates that the interview goal and self-efficacy measures tap theoretically relevant constructs but are not redundant with MEPS or trait measures.

RESEARCH DIRECTIONS

A social-action theory of chronic hostility identifies competence components that could predispose young people to recurring anger and, by mediating the impact of social confrontations on cardiovascular arousal, might increase long-term heart disease risk. Present findings provide preliminary support for the notion that two important social action constructs, personal goals and self-expectancies, may mediate cardiovascular responses to everyday problems, and could prove to be of considerable help in explaining and altering the connection between personality traits, chronic hostile emotion, and cardiovascular disease.

A behavioral-genetic perspective complements the social action model by suggesting that the acquisition of specific competencies may be affected by genetic predispositions, and by focusing the search for environmental contributions on social processes that affect children in the same family differently. It is interesting to note that social interaction processes theoretically relevant to chronic hostility (e.g., sibling dominance, marital conflict) have been found to generate influential nonshared experiences. Moreover, sibling dominance and antagonism (nonshared experiences) are correlated with personality differences in monozygotic twins, thus indicating that the link between these experiences and behavioral differences is attributable to environmental influence.

Future research should focus on the social competencies and environments of high-risk children and adolescents with the goal of identifying units of coronary-prone cognition, personality, and behavior that might be affected by early non-shared experiences. The social-cognitive constructs proposed in the present competence model are appealing because they are implicated in hostile behavior, are correlated with cardiovascular stress responses, are "narrow" enough to be affected by specific nonshared experiences, and might be modified through preventive cognitive-behavioral intervention. Analysis at this level may help clarify at least some of the intriguing and perplexing interconnections between genes, environments, personality, and cardiovascular disease.

ACKNOWLEDGMENTS

Preparation of this chapter was supported in part by grant # RO1-HL36298 from the National Heart, Lung, and Blood Institute. I thank John R. Sonnega and Kenneth B. Kolodner for their assistance in analyzing the pilot data on social competence and blood pressure reactivity. I also thank John Dohler, Director of the Baltimore Polytechnic Institute, and Sandra Wighton, Principal of Western High School, and their respective staffs, for their assistance in implementing the longitudinal study from which these data were derived.

REFERENCES

Adams, B. N. (1972). Birthorder: A critical review. *Sociometry, 35,* 411–439.

Asarnow, J. R., & Callan, J. W. (1985). Boys with peer adjustment problems: Social cognitive processes. *Journal of Consulting and Clinical Psychology, 53,* 500–505.

Averill, J. R. (1982). *Anger and aggression: An essay on emotion.* New York: Springer-Verlag.

Baker, L. A., & Daniels, D. (1990). Nonshared environmental influences and personality differences in adult twins. *Journal of Personality and Social Psychology, 58,* 103–110.

Bandura, A. (1973). *Aggression: A social learning analysis.* Englewood Cliffs, NJ: Prentice-Hall.

Bandura, A. (1986). *Social foundations of thought and action: A social cognitive theory.* Englewood Cliffs, NJ: Prentice-Hall.

Berenson, G. S., Voors, A. W., Webber, L. S., Frank, G. C., Farris, R. R., Tobian, L., & Aristimuno, G. C. (1983). A model of intervention for prevention of early essential hypertension in the 1980s. *Hypertension, 5,* 41–54.

Blumenthal, J. A., Burg, M. M., Barefoot, J., Williams, R. B., Haney, T., & Zimet, G. (1987). Social support, Type A behavior, and coronary artery disease. *Psychosomatic Medicine, 49,* 331–340.

Booth-Kewley, S., & Friedman, H. S. (1987). Psychological predictors of heart disease: A quantitative review. *Psychological Bulletin, 101,* 343–362.

Buss, D. M. (1984). Marital assortment for personality dispositions: Assessment with three different data sources. *Behavior Genetics, 14*, 111-123.

Cannon, W. B. (1932). *The wisdom of the body* (2nd ed.). New York: Norton.

Cantor, N. (1990). From thought to behavior: "Having" and "doing" in the study of personality and cognition. *American Psychologist, 45*, 735-750.

Carmelli, D., Rosenman, R. H., & Swan, G. E. (1988). The Cook and Medley HO scale: A heritability analysis in adult male twins. *Psychosomatic Medicine, 50*, 165-174.

Cook, W. W., & Medley, D. M. (1954). Proposed hostility and pharasaic-virtue scales for the MMPI. *Journal of Applied Psychology, 8*, 343-352.

Costa, P. T., McCrae, R. R., & Dembroski, T. (1989). Agreeableness versus antagonism: Explication of a potential risk factor for CHD. In A. W. Siegman & T. M. Dembroski (Eds.), *In search of coronary-prone behavior: Beyond Type A* (pp. 41-63). Hillsdale, NJ: Lawrence Erlbaum Associates.

Daniels, D. (1986). Differential experiences of siblings in the same family as predictors of adolescent sibling personality differences. *Journal of Personality and Social Psychology, 51*, 339-346.

Daniels, D., Dunn, J., Furstenberg, F. F., Jr., & Plomin, R. (1985). Environmental differences within the family and adjustment differences within pairs of adolescent siblings. *Child Development, 56*, 764-774.

Dembroski, T. M., & Czjakowski, S. M. (1989). Historical and current developments in coronary-prone behavior. In A. W. Siegman & T. M. Dembroski (Eds.), *In search of coronary-prone behavior: Beyond Type A* (pp. 21-39). Hillsdale, NJ: Lawrence Erlbaum Associates.

Dembroski, T. M., MacDougall, J. M., Costa, P. T., & Grandits, G. A. (1989). Components of hostility as predictors of sudden death and myocardial infarction in the multiple risk factor intervention trial. *Psychosomatic Medicine, 51*, 514-522.

Dembroski, T. M., MacDougall, J. M., Williams, R. B., Haney, T. L., & Blumenthal, J. A. (1985). Components of Type A, hostility, and anger-in: Relationship to angiographic findings. *Psychosomatic Medicine, 47*, 219-233.

Ditto, B., & France, C. (1990). Similarities within young and middle-aged spouse pairs in behavioral and cardiovascular response to two experimental stressors. *Psychosomatic Medicine, 52*, 425-434.

Ditto, B., France, C., & Miller, S. (1989). Spouse and parent-offspring similarities in cardiovascular response to mental arithmetic and isometric hand-grip. *Health Psychology, 8*, 159-173.

Dodge, K. A., & Crick, N. R. (1990). Social information-processing bases of aggressive behavior in children. *Personality and Social Psychology Bulletin, 16*, 8-22.

Dodge, K. A., & Frame, C. L. (1982). Social cognitive biases and deficits in aggressive boys. *Child Development, 53*, 620-635.

Dodge, K. A., & Tomlin, A. (1987). Cue-utilization as a mechanism of attributional bias in aggressive children. *Social Cognition, 5*, 280-300.

Dodge, K. A., Pettit, G. S., McClaskey, C. L., & Brown, M. M. (1986). Social competence in children. *Monographs of the Society for Research in Child Development, 51* (2, Serial No. 213).

Emmons, R. A. (1986). Personal strivings: An approach to personality and subjective well-being. *Journal of Personality and Social Psychology, 51*, 1058-1068.

Emmons, R. A., & King, L. A. (1989). Personal striving differentiation and affective reactivity. *Journal of Personality and Social Psychology, 56*, 478-484.

Epstein, L. H. (1986). Treatment of childhood obesity. In K. D. Brownell & J. P. Foreyt (Eds.), *Handbook of eating disorders: Physiology, psychology, and treatment of obesity, anorexia, and bulimia* (pp. 159-179). New York: Basic Books.

Epstein, L. H., Wing, R. R., Koeske, R., & Valoski, A. (1984). Effects of diet plus exercise on weight change in parents and children. *Journal of Consulting and Clinical Psychology, 52*, 429-437.

Ewart, C. K., Burnett, K. F., & Taylor, C. B. (1983). Communication behaviors that affect blood pressure: An A-B-A-B analysis of Marital interaction. *Behavior Modification, 7*, 331-344.

Ewart, C. K., & Kolodner, K. B. (1991a). Social competence interview for assessing physiological reactivity in adolescents. *Psychosomatic Medicine, 53*, 289-304.

Ewart, C. K., & Kolodner, K. B. (1991b, March). *Predicting blood pressure during school: Effectiveness of social versus nonsocial reactivity tasks in Black and White adolescents.* Paper presented at the meeting of the Society for Behavioral Medicine, Washington, DC.

Ewart, C. K., Sonnega, J. R., & Kolodner, K. B. (1990, April). *Chronic stress, social competence, and adolescent blood pressure.* Paper presented at the meeting of the Society for Behavioral Medicine, Chicago, IL.

Ewart, C. K., Taylor, C. B., Kraemer, H. A., & Agras, W. S. (1984). Reducing blood pressure reactivity during interpersonal conflict: Effects of marital communication training. *Behavior Therapy, 15,* 473–485.

Ewart, C. K., Taylor, C. B., Kraemer, H. A., & Agras, W. S. (1991). High blood pressure and marital discord: Not being nasty matters more than being nice. *Health Psychology, 10,* 155–163.

Feinleib, M., Garrison, R. J., Fabsitz, R., Christian, J. C., Hrubec, Z., Borhani, N. O., Kannel, W. B., Rosenman, R., Schwartz, J. T., & Wagner, J. O. (1977). The NHLBI twin study of cardiovascular disease risk factors: Methodology and summary of results. *American Journal of Epidemiology, 106,* 284–295.

Fischler, G. L., & Kendall, P. C. (1988). Social cognitive problem solving and childhood adjustment: Qualitative and topological analyses. *Cognitive Therapy and Research, 12,* 133–153.

Ford, M. E. (1982). Social competence and social cognition in adolescence. *Developmental Psychology, 18,* 323–340.

Friedman, M., & Rosenman, R. H. (1959). Association of a specific overt behavior pattern with increases in blood cholesterol, blood clotting time, incidence of arcus senilis and clinical coronary artery disease. *Journal of the American Medical Association, 169,* 1286–1296.

Garcia-Palmieri, M. R., Costas, R., Cruz-Vidal, M., Cartes-Alicea, M., Patterne, D., Rojas-Franco, L., Sorlie, P. D., & Kannel, W. (1978). Urban-rural differences in coronary heart disease in a low incidence area. *American Journal of Epidemiology, 107,* 206–215.

Gilbert, R., Christensen, A., & Margolin, G. (1984). Patterns of alliances in nondistressed and multiproblem families. *Family Process, 23,* 75–87.

Glass, D. C. (1977). *Behavior patterns, stress, and coronary disease.* Hillsdale, NJ: Lawrence Erlbaum Associates.

Goldsmith, H. H., Buss, A. H., Plomin, R., Rothbart, M. K., Thomas, A., Chess, S., Hinde, R. A., & McCall, R. B. (1987). Roundtable: What is temperament? Four approaches. *Child Development, 58,* 505–529.

Grych, J. H., & Fincham, F. D. (1990). Marital conflict and children's adjustment: A cognitive-contextual framework. *Psychological Bulletin, 108,* 267–290.

Hobfoll, S. E. (1989). Conservation of resources: A new attempt at conceptualizing stress. *American Psychologist, 44,* 513–524.

Ickes, W., Turner, M. (1983). On the social advantages of having an older, opposite-sex sibling: Birth order influences in mixed-sex dyads. *Journal of Personality and Social Psychology, 45,* 210–222.

Irvine, M. J., Garner, D. M., Olmsted, M. P., & Logan, A. G. (1989). Personality differences between hypertensive and normtensive individuals: Influence of knowledge of hypertension status. *Psychosomatic Medicine, 51,* 537–549.

Kellam, S. G., Brown, C. H., Rubin, B. R., & Ensminger, M. E. (1983). Paths leading to teenage psychiatric symptoms and substance use: Developmental epidemiological studies in Woodlawn. In S. B. Guze, F. J. Earls, & J. E. Barret (Eds.), *Childhood psychopathology and development* (pp. 17–51). New York: Raven.

Kendall, P. C., & Fischler, G. L. (1984). Behavioral and adjustment correlates of problem solving: Validational analyses of interpersonal cognitive problem solving measures. *Child Development, 55,* 879–892.

Keys, A., Aravanis, C., Blackburn, H., Vanbuchem, F. S. P., Buzina, R., Djordjenic, B. S., Fidanza, F., Karvonen, M. J., Menotti, A., Puddu, V., & Taylor, H. L. (1972). Probability of middle-aged men developing coronary heart disease in 5 years. *Circulation, 45,* 815–828.

Klesges, R. C., Coates, T. J., Brown, G., Sturgeon-Tillisch, J., Moldenhauer-Klesges, L. W., Holzer, B., Woolfrey, J., & Vollmer, J. (1983). Parental influences on children's eating behavior and relative weight. *Journal of Applied Behavior Analysis, 16*, 371–378.

Kovacs, M. (1985). The Children's Depression Inventory (CDI). *Psychopharmacology Bulletin, 21*, 995–998.

Krantz, D. S., Arabian, J. M., Davia, J. E., & Parker, J. S. (1982). Type A behavior and coronary artery bypass surgery: Intraoperative blood pressure and perioperative complications. *Psychosomatic Medicine, 44*, 273–284.

Kwiterovich, P. O., Jr. (1986). Biochemical, clinical, epidemiological, genetic, and pathological data in the pediatric age group relevant to the cholesterol hypothesis. *Pediatrics, 78*, 349–362.

Lauer, R. M., Clarke, W. R., & Beaglehole, R. (1984). Level, trend, and variability of blood pressure during childhood: The Muscatine study. *Circulation, 69*, 242–249.

Little, B. R. (1989). Personal projects analysis: Trivial pursuits, magnificent obsessions, and the search for coherence. In D. M. Buss & N. Cantor (Eds.), *Personality psychology: Recent trends and emerging directions* (pp. 15–31). New York: Springer-Verlag.

Little, B. R. (1983). Personal projects: A rationale and method for investigation. *Environment and Behavior, 15*, 273–309.

Matthews, K. A., & Haynes, S. G. (1986). Type A behavior pattern and coronary disease risk: Update and critical evaluation. *American Journal of Epidemiology, 123*, 923–960.

Matthews, K. A., & Siegel, J. M. (1983). Type A behaviors by children, social comparison, and standards for self-evaluation. *Developmental Psychology, 19*, 135–140.

Matthews, K. A., Rakaczky, C. J., Stoney, C. M., & Manuck, S. B. (1987). Are cardiovascular responses to behavioral stressors a stable individual difference variable in childhood? *Psychophysiology, 24*, 464–473.

Matthews, K. A., Rosenman, R. H., Dembroski, T. M., MacDougall, J. M., & Harris, E. (1984). Familial resemblance in components of the Type A behavior pattern: A reanalysis of the California Type A twin study. *Psychosomatic Medicine, 46*, 512–522.

Matthews, K. A., Stoney, C. M., Rakaczky, C. J., & Jamison, W. (1986). Family characteristics and school achievements of Type A children. *Health Psychology, 5*, 453–468.

McCrae, R. R. (1989). Why I advocate the five-factor model: Joint factor analyses of the NEO-PI with other instruments. In D. M. Buss & N. Cantor (Eds.), *Personality psychology: Recent trends and emerging directions* (pp. 237–245). New York: Springer-Verlag.

McCann, B. S., & Matthews, K. A. (1988). Influences of potential for hostility, Type A behavior, and parental history of hypertension on adolescents' cardiovascular responses during stress. *Psychophysiology, 25*, 503–511.

McGill, H. C. (1984). Persistent problems in the pathogenesis of atherosclerosis. *Arteriosclerosis, 4*, 443–451.

Newman, W. P., III, Freedman, D. S., Voors, A. W., Gard, P. D., Srinvasan, S. R., Cresanta, J. L., Williamson, G. D., Webber, L. S., & Berenson, G. S. (1986). Relation of serum lipoprotein levels and systolic blood pressure to early atherosclerosis. *The New England Journal of Medicine, 314*, 138–144.

Patterson, G. R. (1982). *A social learning approach to family intervention: Coercive family processes (Vol. 3)*. Eugene, OR: Castalia.

Pedersen, N. L., Lichtenstein, B. A., Plomin, R., DeFaire, U., McClearn, G. E., & Matthews, K. A. (1989). Genetic and environmental influences for Type A-like measures and related traits: A study of twins reared apart and twins reared together. *Psychosomatic Medicine, 51*, 428–440.

Perry, D. G., Perry, L. C., & Rasmussen, P. R. (1986). Aggressive children believe that aggression is easy to perform and leads to rewards. *Child Development, 56*, 700–711.

Platt, J. J., & Spivack, G. (1975). *Manual for the Means-End Problem-Solving Procedure*. Philadelphia: Hahnemann Community Mental Health/Mental Retardation Center, Department of Mental Health Services.

Plomin, R., & Daniels, D. (1987). Why are children in the same family so different from each other? *Behavioral and Brain Sciences, 10,* 1–16.

Rao, D. C., Laskarzewski, P. M., Morrison, J. A., Khoury, P., Kelley, K., Wette, R., Russell, J., & Glueck, C. J. (1982). The Cincinnati Lipid Research Clinic Family Study: Cultural and biological determinants of lipids and lipoprotein concentrations. *American Journal of Human Genetics, 34,* 888–903.

Reaven, G. M., & Hoffman, B. B. (1987). A role for insulin in the aetiology and course of hypertension. *Lancet, 2,* 435–436.

Rocchini, A. P., Katch, V., Schork, A., & Kelch, R. P. (1987). Insulin and blood pressure during weight loss in obese adolescents. *Hypertension, 10,* 267–273.

Rose, R. J. (1986). Familial influences on cardiovascular reactivity to stress. In K. Matthews, S. Detre, T. Dembroski, B. Falkner, S. Manuck, & R. Williams (Eds.), *Handbook of stress reactivity and cardiovascular disease* (pp. 259–272). New York: Wiley.

Sackett, D. L., Anderson, G. D., Milner, R., Feinleib, M., & Kannel, W. B. (1975). Concordance for coronary risk factors among spouses. *Circulation, 52,* 589–595.

Sancilio, M. R. M., Plumert, J. M., & Hartup, W. W. (1989). Friendship and aggressiveness as determinants of conflict outcomes in middle childhood. *Developmental Psychology, 25,* 812–819.

Schwartz, J. C., Getter, H. (1980). Parental conflict and dominance in late adolescent maladjustment: A triple interaction model. *Journal of Abnormal Psychology, 89,* 573–580.

Selye, H. (1950). *The physiology and pathology of exposure to stress.* Montreal: Acta.

Shapiro, A. P., & Miller, R. E. (1987). Behavioral consequences of hypertension and their relationship to personality of patients with this disorder. In S. Julius & D. R. Bassett (Eds.), *Handbook of hypertension, Vol. 9* (pp. 246–258). Amsterdam: Elsevier.

Shear, C. L., Burke, G. L., Freedman, D. S., & Berenson, G. S. (1986). Value of childhood blood pressure measurements and family history in predicting blood pressure status: Results from 8 years of follow-up in the Bogalusa heart study. *Pediatrics, 77,* 862–869.

Shekelle, R. B., Gale, M., Ostfeld, A. M., & Paul, O. (1983). Hostility, risk of coronary disease, and mortality. *Psychosomatic Medicine, 45,* 219–228.

Siegel, J. M. (1986). The Multidimensional Anger Inventory. *Journal of Personality and Social Psychology, 51,* 191–200.

Smith, T. W., & Anderson, N. B. (1986). Models of personality and disease: An interactional approach to Type A behavior and cardiovascular risk. *Journal of Personality and Social Psychology, 50,* 1166–1173.

Spielberger, C. D. (Ed.). (1972). *Anxiety: Current trends in theory and research* (Vols. 1–2). New York: Academic Press.

Steinberg, L. (1986). Stability and instability of Type A behavior from childhood to young adulthood. *Developmental Psychology, 22,* 393–402.

Strazzullo, P., Cappuccio, F. P., Trevisan, M., De Leo, A., Krogh, V., Giorgione, N., & Mancini, M. (1988). *American Journal of Epidemiology, 127,* 726–733.

Strube, M. J., & Ota, S. (1982). Type A coronary-prone behavior pattern: Relationship to birthorder and family size. *Personality and Social Psychology Bulletin, 8,* 317–323.

Stunkard, A. J., Sorensen, T. I. A., Hanis, C., Teasdale, T. W., Chakraborty, R., Schull, W. J., & Schlesinger, F. (1986). An adoption study of human obesity. *New England Journal of Medicine, 314,* 193–198.

Sutton-Smith, B., Rosenberg, B. G. (1970). *The sibling.* New York: Holt, Rinehart, & Winston.

Thoresen, C. E., & Pattillo, J. R. (1988). Exploring the Type A behavior pattern in children and adolescents. In B. Houston & C. Snyder (Eds.), *Type A behavior pattern: Research, theory, and intervention* (pp. 98–145). New York: Wiley.

Visintainer, P. F., & Matthews, K. A. (1987). Stability of overt Type A behaviors in children: Results from a two- and five-year longitudinal study. *Child Development, 58,* 1586–1591.

Woodall, K. L., & Matthews, K. A. (1989). Familial environment associated with Type A behaviors and psychophysiological responses to stress in children. *Health Psychology, 8,* 403–426.

Zajonc, R. B., Markus, H., & Markus, G. B. (1979). The birth order puzzle. *Journal of Personality and Social Psychology, 37,* 1325–1341.

9

Sibling Similarity as an Individual Differences Variable: Within-Family Measures of Shared Environment

James E. Deal
University of Arizona

Charles F. Halverson, Jr.
University of Georgia

Karen Smith Wampler
Texas Tech University

Behavior geneticists are fond of asserting that the family environment has little or no effect on similarity among siblings, noting that full siblings raised within the family are no more alike than unrelated children raised in different families (Plomin & Daniels, 1987; Rowe, 1990). This assertion is based on evidence obtained from extensive studies of twins, full siblings, half siblings, and adopted siblings. The preponderance of evidence in these studies appears relatively clear: The degree of similarity between siblings follows along genetic lines, with monozygotic twins sharing identical genetic material and having the most similarities, and adopted siblings sharing no genetic material and having the fewest similarities.

This finding has led researchers to turn their focus within families rather than between them. As Halverson and Wampler (in press) and Plomin and Daniels (1987) have noted, developmental psychology and family studies have been built upon the study of one child (and often one parent) within the family, with the assumption that whatever developmental and environmental factors operate on that child also operate on others. If siblings bear no more than chance resemblance to one another, however, this assumption may be erroneous, and, as Dunn and Stocker (1989) noted, attention must be focused on the within-family processes that serve to make children either more or less alike.

In a summary of the recent literature, Dunn and Stocker (1989) examined parental consistency as an important variable. Parental consistency refers to similar parental treatment of siblings when they are the same age—how the first child was treated at age 4, for example, compared with how the second child was treated at age 4. Reporting on data from the Colorado Adoption Project, Dunn and Stocker reported high levels of parental consistency across children (average correlations of .70), and examined the effects of maternal personality and child temperament on this consistency. As interesting as these results were, however, they were plagued by a serious methodological problem that has been consistently found in the behavior genetics literature. This problem deals with the lack of attention to similarity as a variable characterizing actual sibling pairs.

Measurement Issues

Plomin (1989) argued that the behavioral genetic approach has as a general implication "the recognition of and respect for individual differences among children" (p. 131). He stressed the importance of studying individual differences rather than group level differences. It is somewhat surprising, then, to discover that the bulk of the strongest evidence in the behavior genetics literature—the differences in similarity among individuals of differing genetic relatedness—is based not on measures of similarity among actual sibling pairs, but rather on measures of similarity of groups of sibling pairs. In other words, for each group, monozygotic twins, dizygotic twins, full siblings, half siblings, and adopted siblings, a *single* correlation coefficient is computed that supposedly represents the degree of sibling similarity for that group.

In the same way, in most research similarity in parental treatment is actually a group assessment rather than a within-family variable. In the work of Dunn and her colleagues, for example, parental consistency across siblings is measured by a single correlation (Dunn, Plomin, & Daniels, 1986; Dunn, Plomin, & Nettles, 1985). Differences in similar treatment due to genetic relatedness are again estimated by testing for significant differences between these group-level correlations.

Aggregate Correlations. Correlation coefficients computed in this manner are aggregate correlations. Although such analyses are often interpreted as reflecting similarity at the dyadic level, they actually reflect similarity between groups (Thompson & Walker, 1982) and reveal nothing about similarity between specific individuals. A nonsignificant correlation between adopted siblings as a group, for example, does not preclude a high degree of similarity between certain individual sibling pairs; it simply means that, as a group, there is not consistency among the rank ordering of those pairs. In a similar manner, a zero correlation at the aggregate level does not mean that the average dyadic-level correlation is also zero. With an aggregate correlation of zero, for example, bisecting the scatter plot at the median for each sibling yields four cells: Those siblings who are similar on the measure and both high, those who are similar on the measure and both low, and two groups of dissimilar, mixed level siblings, one high on the measure, the other low. Behavior geneticists, then, have largely conducted group level analyses, and have inappropriately discussed them as dyadic level data. It is important to note that there is nothing "wrong" with such group analyses, so long as they are interpreted as such. They simply provide a different piece of information from true dyadic level analyses and should not be confused with them.

Difference Scores. Not all of the literature is based on these aggregate analyses, however. Some attempt has been made to use a dyadic level measure of similarity, most notably in the form of a difference score. The score of one sibling is subtracted from the score of the other sibling, with the resulting difference used as an index of sibling similarity in following analyses (cf. Daniels, Dunn, Furstenberg, & Plomin, 1985). According to Fisher, Kokes, Ransom, Phillips, and Rudd (1985), there are three problems with this type of score. The first is that it does not reflect differences in score levels—a sibling pair scoring 65 and 60 receive the same score, 5, as a pair scoring 15 and 10 despite the fact that such differences in level may be important. Second, the difference score is generally less reliable than the scores that make it up, although this is dependent upon the size of the correlation between the two scores; as this correlation goes up, the reliability of the difference score goes down, and vice versa. To the degree that the difference score is unreliable, however, its distribution will be more attenuated and have less variance, resulting in lowered power in analyses using it. Nonsignificant correlations between difference scores representing similarity of treatment and child outcome, for example, may represent a substantive finding, but may just as likely represent a statistical artifact resulting from the use of the difference score (i.e., lower power and low reliability). Finally, the difference score is limited in that it contains no information that is not contained in the relation between the two original scores and the variable under study, no information that is not "already present in the correlations between separate . . . scores and a dependent variable" (p. 218).

Dyadic-Level Similarity

One way to address the problems associated with both difference scores and aggregated correlations involves simply converting the aggregate correlation to a true dyadic score: A correlation coefficient is constructed between the test or observational items for each sibling pair for a domain. Each correlation can then be entered into a data set and analyzed as a variable representing similar treatment or similar outcome, or whatever construct is of interest. The Pearson correlation coefficient, however, is based on a linear relationship between two sets of variables that maximizes the predictability of one set from the other, not necessarily the "sameness" of the two sets (Fisher et al., 1985; Robinson, 1957; Thompson & Walker, 1982). The Pearson correlation allows differences in mean level to go undetected as long as the differences are consistent (i.e., as long as they covary). In the same way, differences in standard deviation are also understated so long as the relation between the two sets of variables remains consistent. High correlations, then, might represent agreement between responses, but might just as easily represent covariation between two sets of responses a great distance apart. It is possible to correct for this, however, by using an intraclass correlation, a technique familiar to readers of the behavior genetics literature.

As discussed by Robinson (1957), the intraclass correlation assesses, "the degree to which two observations fail to be identical, or fail to agree" (p. 19). It does this by taking into account the two factors that the Pearson correlation does not, namely differences in mean level and differences in distribution between two sets of variables. This is an adjustment of the Pearson correlation that removes any covariation based on these differences. The resulting correlation then represents how close the two sets of scores come to being the same set. Another advantage of the intraclass correlation is that its construction allows the use of multiple data points. Rather than correlating the total scores from a scale, correlations are computed across the items that go into the scale. Doing so allows a more reliable multi-item assessment of similarity on the topic under study.

PURPOSE

With these points in mind, there are two purposes for this chapter. First, an alternative manner is proposed for conceptualizing sibling similarity and similarity of parental treatment as individual differences variables, using the construction of dyadic-level intraclass correlations between siblings. Descriptive analyses of these scores are presented. Second, two alternative hypotheses regarding similar treatment of siblings are explored. The first hypothesis has a cognitive basis: Is similar treatment of siblings and, by extension, similar performance of siblings, a result of perceived similarity by parents?

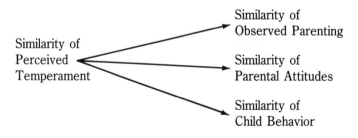

In other words, do parents cognitively appraise their children, then base the degree of similarity in their treatment of these children on the degree of similarity in personality that they perceive? The second hypothesis is somewhat more experientially based, and is termed the "prototype effect." The prototype effect is based on the view that parents are guided by results—if what they did with an earlier child worked, they will repeat it with a subsequent child.

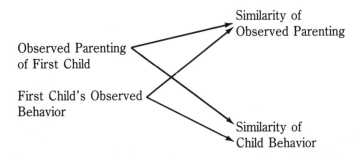

If this is the case, parental effectiveness with the target child and child behavior from the first year of the study should predict similarity of treatment between the target and the sibling as well as similarity of outcome between them.

METHODS

Participants

Participants in this report were from the first and third years of the Georgia Longitudinal Study (GLS), a 5-year study of (initially) preschool children and their families. During the first year of the study, 136 families were recruited. These families all had at least one child between the ages of 3 and 6 (the target child), no children older than 10, and no children from any previous marriage(s). In addition, the target child had to be in some kind of organized child care (preferably kindergarten or day care) from which a nonrelated adult could evaluate him or her. For each year of data collection, families participated in an evening session in an observational laboratory and completed an extensive questionnaire packet. Families were paid $25 for participation in Year 1, then $50 for each following year. Teachers were paid $5 for completing a brief (three-instrument) questionnaire. In the third year, the study was expanded to include a sibling (typically younger—84.2%) of the target child, where applicable.

The present report is based on the 71 families from the first year of the study who had also participated in the third year of the study with both the target child and with his or her sibling. To examine parental consistency, data on the target child were taken from the first year of the study, with data on the sibling taken from the third year, so that the ages of the children would be approximately the same at the time studied.

Descriptive demographic statistics were based on characteristics during the first year of the study. These families were predominantly White (91.5% of wives, 94.4% of husbands) and well educated: 49.3% of the husbands and 36.6% of the wives had completed a graduate degree; only 7% of the husbands and 4.2% of the wives had not gone beyond a high school degree. The majority of the husbands (85.9%) were employed full time, while 1.4% were employed part time, and 12.7% were full-time graduate students. Of the wives, 19.7% were employed full time, 22.5% were employed part time, and 42.3% were full-time homemakers. The remainder of the wives were either full-time students (5.6% each, undergraduate and graduate) or were part-time students, unemployed, or described themselves in some "other" category (1.4% each). The target child was a firstborn in 73.2% of the cases, and a secondborn in the remaining 26.8%; 54.9% were males, 45.1% were females. Of the siblings, 53.5% were males and 46.5% were females. Of the 71 sibling pairs, 32% were male–male, 24% were female–female, 44% were mixed gender. During the first year of the study, the mean age of the target child was 4.51 years (sd = .93); during the third year, the mean age of the sibling was 4.96 years (sd = 2.16); not a significant difference.

Instruments

Parental Attitudes. Self-reported parental attitudes were assessed with the Block Childrearing Practices Report (CRPR) (Block, 1965), a 91-item Q-sort of childrearing attitudes and behaviors. During the first 2 years of the study, each parent separately sorted the 91 items into a quasi-normal nine-step distribution. During Years 3, 4, and 5 of the study, in response to parental complaints and time constraints, the 91-item Q-sort was reduced to a 55-item Likert scale instrument.

Observed Parenting. Parenting was assessed observationally through use of the 38-item Parent Strategy Q-sort (PSQ), a modification of the Teacher Strategy Q-sort developed by Block and Block (1971). Two coders separately watched a mother–child and father–child session where each parent and child performed three tasks of increasing difficulty. Parallel forms of each task were used for mother and father, and parent order was counterbalanced across the families. Coders completed the coding of all the first parents before coding the second parents. Four cluster scores were created from the intercorrelations of the Q-items: Parental Affection, Parental Control, Parental Task Orientation, and Parental Teaching.

Child Temperament. Child temperament, as perceived by the mother and father, was assessed by the Temperament Assessment Battery (TAB) (Martin, 1984) and the Preschool Rating Scale (PRS) (Victor, Halverson, & Montague, 1985). Internal consistencies of the TAB are good, averaging .79, with acceptable 1-year test–retest reliabilities averaging .68. The PRS has reported interrater reliabilities averaging .83 and 1-year test–retest reliabilities ranging from .87 to .94.

Child Behavior. The child's behavior in the experimental settings was assessed using the Child Q-Set (CQS), a modification of the Block California Q-Set (Block & Block, 1969) and the Baumrind Preschool Q-Sort (Baumrind, 1971). Items used in this modification reflect those characteristic of competence in preschoolers as assessed by Waters, Garber, Gornal, and Vaughn (1983). Observers watched videotapes of each child in interaction tasks with each parent and with both parents together, then described the interaction using the Q-sort. Interrater Pearson product–moment correlations averaged .70 over the first 2 years of the study. Six cluster scores were obtained through principle components analysis of the items: active/energetic; confident versus anxious; direct/persistent; reflective versus impetuous; and manageable and demonstrated adult valued competence. Two summary scores, internalizing and externalizing, were created from the CQS through use of factor analysis. Internal consistencies were good: .82 for Internalizing and .72 for Externalizing.

Construction of Similarity Scores

For each measure, a target–sibling similarity score was created by computing an intraclass correlation between the target's items for that measure, from the first year of the study, with the sibling's items for that measure, from the third year of the study. The double-entry method was used in this computation (see Robinson, 1957). The resulting correlations, similarity of parental attitudes, similarity of observed parenting, similarity of child behavior, and similarity of perceived child temperament were re-entered into the data set and used as the measures of similarity (for parental perceptions of temperament, the correlation was created across the combined PRS and TAB items). It is important to note that these similarity scores are mathematically independent from any subscale scores created from these instruments. Knowing that two mothers are consistent in how each treats her child, for example, tells us nothing about the substantive nature of that treatment. One mother might consistently treat her children in an authoritative manner, while the other consistently treats her children in an authoritarian manner. The degree of consistency in behavior, then, might be the same across mothers; the substance of the behavior, however, would be very different.

RESULTS

Degree of Similarity in Sibling Pairs

The first goal investigated was to examine the degree of similarity between siblings and parental treatment of siblings using the new individual differences scores. Descriptive statistics for these variables are presented in the first column of Table 9.1. Mean levels of similarity are relatively high for similarity of observed parenting, similarity of child behavior, and similarity of parental attitudes. Levels are lower, but still moderate, for similarity of perceived temperament. Comparison of these means to zero, however, assumes that the level of similarity among unrelated individuals is zero, an assumption that may not be appropriate. Instead, it is necessary to determine the actual level of similarity among unrelated individuals and then compare the level of similarity among siblings to this figure, determining whether or not the sample of related individuals could have been drawn from the larger population of unrelated individuals. To do this, a population of pseudosibling pairs was created for each variable by pairing target children from one family with siblings from other families. Intraclass correlations were then computed for these new, pseudosibling pairs. Descriptive statistics for these populations are presented in the second column of Table 9.1. The means for the true sibling sample were then tested against the means for the corresponding pseudosibling population to determine if the true sample could have been drawn from that population using the z-test formula provided by Henkel (1976).

Significant z values were obtained for all variables, with the exception of similarity of observed parenting for fathers, which was borderline significant at the $p < .06$ level. In treatment of siblings, perceptions of their temperament,

TABLE 9.1
Means and Standard Deviations of Agreement Scores for
True and Pseudosibling Groups

Variable	True Siblings	Pseudosiblings
Similarity of Child Behavior	.71 (.19)	.66 (.16)*
Similarity of Observed Parenting		
Mother	.68 (.17)	.65 (.15)*
Father	.71 (.11)	.69 (.11)
Similarity of Perceived Temperament		
Mother	.47 (.23)	.38 (.17)*
Father	.44 (.21)	.35 (.14)*
Similarity of Parental Attitudes		
Mother	.72 (.06)	.64 (.12)*
Father	.68 (.07)	.58 (.13)*

* = Difference between true and pseudo groups significant at $p < .05$ or higher.

self-reported parental attitudes, and in sibling behavior in a laboratory setting, then, true sibling pairs were significantly more similar than would be expected by chance. It must be noted that there was a surprisingly high degree of similarity among pseudosibling pairs for different families, being described by and interacting with different parents. In addition, the differences in mean level between the two groups, while significant, were not that large.

This may be attributed to two things. First, as Cronbach (1955) noted some years ago, there is likely to be a high amount of stereotype accuracy in our measures. This is based on the fact that many of the traits or behaviors that social scientists are interested in are quite prominent in the populations that are studied (see Kenrick & Funder, 1988, for a discussion of this in the context of the person–situation debate; see Deal, Halverson, & Wampler, 1989, for a discussion of it in the context of agreement between spouses on childrearing orientations). Second, it appears that the laboratory setting may be exerting some effect on the behaviors exhibited in it. Part of the relatively high pseudosibling correlations for both child and parenting variables reflects in part the fact that parents and children were actually quite constrained by task demands (e.g., copying designs on an Etch-A-Sketch, naming objects, etc.). Along with the built-in constraints of a 43-item coding system, such limited behavioral sampling led to similar profiles for randomly paired children and parents and the real need to test whether there was any real increment in similarity among real sibling pairs.

Predictors of Similarity

The Cognitive Hypothesis.   To test the cognitive hypothesis that similarity of perceived temperament would predict similar observed parenting of siblings as well as similar behavior of siblings, zero-order correlations were computed between similarity of perceived temperament and similarity of child behavior, similarity of observed parenting, and similarity of parental attitudes. For fathers, similarity of perceived temperament was significantly related to similarity of observed parenting ($r = .22, p < .04$) and to similarity of parental attitudes ($r = .38, p < .001$). No relation was found between similarity of perceived temperament and similarity of child behavior. For mothers, similarity of perceived temperament was related only to similarity of parental attitudes ($r = .44, p < .000$), with no significant relations with similarity of observed parenting or of child behavior. In general, then, the cognitive theory was not strongly supported.

The Prototype Hypothesis.   To examine the possibility of a prototype effect operating, zero-order correlations were computed between measures of parental treatment and observed behavior of the target child in year one of the study and the target-sibling similarity scores. Obtaining a significant positive correlation from this comparison would indicate that the more competent the parent was with the target in the first year of the study, or the more competent the child's behavior was in Year 1, the greater the degree of similarity between the target child in Year 1 and the sibling in Year 3 (these analyses were done only for those sibling pairs in which the target was older than the sibling). Results examining the effects of parental interaction with the target child are presented in Table 9.2. All correlations were computed within parental gender (i.e., father's treatment scores were correlated with father's similarity scores, mother's treatment scores were correlated with mother's similarity scores). The only exception to this was the observed competency score which was computed across mothers and fathers.

For fathers, similarity of child behavior was related to two of the four observed parenting clusters, Control and Teaching: When fathers used less control and were more effective teachers with the target child, the target and the sibling were observed to behave more similarly. Similar results were found for mothers, with the Task Orientation and Teaching clusters significant: When mothers were more effective teachers and were less task oriented with the target in Year 1, target and sibling behaved more alike.

High positive correlations were found between similarity of observed parenting and quality of observed parenting with the target child. Parents who were more affectionate, less controlling, more on-task, and better teachers with the target child in Year 1 treated the sibling in a very similar manner 2 years later. It must be noted here that the similarity scores and the cluster scores were computed in such a way that they are mathematically independent: High similarity scores can occur at all levels of the distribution of cluster scores. Any relationship

TABLE 9.2
Correlations Between Sibling Similarity Scores and
Observed Parenting of Target Child in Year One

Observed Parenting	1	2
Fathers Observed Parenting		
With Target Child (Year 1)		
Affection	ns	.33
Control	− .21	− .23
Task Orientation	ns	.34
Teaching	.29	.31
Mothers Observed Parenting		
With Target Child (Year 1)		
Affection	ns	.47
Control	ns	− .37
Task Orientation	− .22	.49
Teaching	.31	.61

Note. All correlations listed are significant at the .05 level or higher.
1 = Similarity of Child Behavior (Year 1 and Year 3)
2 = Similarity of Observed Parenting (Year 1 and Year 3)

TABLE 9.3
Correlations Between Observed Behavior of Target Child in
Year One and Sibling Similarity

Target Child's Behavior, Year 1	1	2	3
Active/energetic	ns	ns	ns
Confident/anxious	.32	.30	ns
Direct/persistent	ns	ns	ns
Reflective/impetuous	.45	ns	.33
Manageable	.42	ns	.30
Adult-valued competence	.59	.36	.30
Externalizing	− .43	ns	− .32
Internalizing	− .29	− .48	ns

Note. All correlations listed are significant at the .01 level, or higher.
1 = Similarity of Child Behavior (Year 1 and Year 3)
2 = Similarity of Observed Parenting, Fathers (Year 1 and Year 3)
3 = Similarity of Observed Parenting, Mothers (Year 1 and Year 3)

between these scores, then, cannot be attributed to methodological artifacts, but must be interpreted substantively.

Relationships between the similarity scores and the observed child behavior scores are presented in Table 9.3. Similarity of child behavior was consistently predicted by the target child's behavior in the first year of the study: Children who exhibited more appropriate behaviors had siblings who behaved similarly in the third year (again, remember that these scores are independent of one another). Less consistent but still moderate relations were found between similarity of observed parenting and child behavior; again, the more appropriately behaved children had parents who treated them and their siblings in a more similar fashion.

DISCUSSION

The current effort outlined here is a beginning step toward the analysis of sibling data using an *individual difference* measure of sibling similarity instead of a group difference measure as has often been done in other studies of sibling similarity and shared environment. When the issue was moved to one of within pair similarity, it was discovered that, unlike the group difference data where very low (approaching zero) correlations have been obtained between the sibling one and sibling two groups, it was found instead that some sibling pairs are similar on temperament, behavioral, and parental treatment variables while others are less similar. Further, this individual difference measure revealed for both parenting and temperament domains that siblings, as a group, showed more similarities than unrelated pairs.

The individual difference measure of sibling similarity also allows a more direct inquiry of the correlates (and possible causes) of individual differences in sibling similarity at the pair level. With such an index one can easily ask questions of why some pairs are so much alike while others are so dissimilar. This question is not possible using the more traditional group comparisons. As outlined earlier, a correlation of zero between, say, first and second born groups on trait X obscures the fact that about half the sibling pairs would be very much alike (high–high's and low–low's), while half would be unlike. All, however, would be distributed along a dimension of similarity that is amenable to the kinds of analyses presented in this chapter.

Problematic aspects of the intraclass correlation should also be noted. The high degree of chance similarity among individuals makes an estimate of effect size difficult, a problem not encountered with group level analyses. In addition, the use of item level data in the computation of the dyadic similarity scores makes it even more critical that these items have high degrees of reliability and validity. Finally, the use of Q-sort data in this chapter demonstrates the potentially spurious effects that can accompany the forced distributional characteristics of such measures. Mean levels of similarity in both true and pseudosamples were lower when a Likert format was used.

When using the dyadic-level strategy, it was discovered that positive characteristics of the first child, coded in the first year of the study, were strongly associated with both sibling similarity on child outcome and parental treatment. This "prototype" agreement has been tentatively interpreted as consistent with the hypothesis that when the first child is "competent" and a "good" child, the parent will repeat "successful" parenting strategies (i.e., treat the two children more alike). "If it worked the first time, do it again" is one interpretation of the underlying theme predicting the similarity in observed parenting. Basically, competent children had parents who treated them and their siblings in similar ways.

The cognitive model, however, did not fare as well. Similarity in temperament did not predict either child behavior or observed parenting well. Despite the appeal of the notion that if you perceive children to be very similar in personality you would treat them similarly, this preliminary look does not support this reasonable contention.

It is important to note that the use of the intraclass correlation as the individual difference measure makes these data at times difficult to follow. The fact that there is considerable correlation among sibling pseudopairs seems troublesome, but merely reflects restrictions in the Q-sets and settings of possible behaviors sampled. All children behave somewhat similarly in the parent–child interaction sessions reported here. The important issue is whether siblings behave *more* similarly, and they did in these analyses. One might also be concerned that the variance shared by all unrelated children somehow was linked to the longitudinal relations between the target child's performance in Year 1 with the sibling performance 2 years later. That is, would a link be found between competence in Year 1 and similarity scores for unrelated sibling pairs that was significant and of the same magnitude as that for related pairs? These checks were performed using true-pair similarity as the set of outcome measures, predicting them from an unrelated sibling in Year 1. None of the relations replicated; these two independent data sets are correlated in true sibling pairs in a fashion that supports the prototype notion: Similarity stems mainly from characteristics of the child and parent–child interaction of the first child. Similarity in parental treatment may stem from actual similarity of competence. Clearly, the issue of why similarly competent sibling pairs share environmental variance and nonsimilar ones do not has not been resolved. The issue of direction of effects is not clearly solved either, even when this longitudinal data is based on Sibling 1 studied at Year 1 and Sibling 2 studied in Year 3, when both are at a comparable age. We prefer the notion that Sibling 1 competence leads to similarity in treatment and outcome because it is first in our time series, but this is only one plausible interpretation and certainly not the only one.

We show that it is possible to recast sibling data into an individual difference, pair format that reveals: (a) siblings are more alike than unrelated pairs on temperament, behavior, and parental treatment, (b) there are important characteristics of the older siblings that predict similarity of temperament and treatment by parents, and (c) parental perceptions of similarity do not predict anticipated similarity in treatment of siblings observed at the same age.

We hope other investigators will attend to the importance of using a true individual difference measure of sibling similarity. With such a measure, we can begin to untangle the complexities of why some siblings "share" environmental variance (i.e., similar personality and similar parenting) and others do not.

ACKNOWLEDGMENTS

This research was supported by National Institute of Mental Health Grant No. MH39899. The authors thank David Reiss for his thoughtful comments, the families for their participation, and the able assistants who have collected the data and coded the videotapes, especially Karen Shetterly, Carol Watson, John Moore, Dominique Gore, Leah Wampler, Jerry Tieman, Cathy Stawarski, Mike Williamson, Tommy Claxton, and Angela Pesce.

REFERENCES

Baumrind, D. (1971). Current patterns of parental authority. *Developmental Psychology Monographs*, *4* (1, Pt. 2).

Block, J. (1965). *The childrearing practices report.* Berkeley: Institute of Human Development.

Block, J. H., & Block, J. (1969). *The California Child Q-Set*. Unpublished manuscript, University of California, Berkeley, Department of Psychology.

Block, J. H., & Block, J. (1971). *The teacher strategy q-sort*. Available from J. Block, University of California at Berkeley.

Cronbach, L. (1955). Processes affecting scores on "understanding of others" and "assumed similarity." *Psychological Bulletin, 52*, 177–193.

Daniels, D., Dunn, J., Furstenberg, F., & Plomin, R. (1985). Environmental differences within the family and adjustment differences within pairs of adolescent siblings. *Child Development, 56*, 764–774.

Deal, J., Halverson, C., & Wampler, K. (1989). Parental agreement on child-rearing orientations: Relations to parental, marital, family, and child characteristics. *Child Development, 60*, 1025–1034.

Dunn, J., Plomin, R., & Daniels, D. (1986). Consistency and change in mothers' behavior toward young siblings. *Child Development, 57*, 348–356.

Dunn, J., Plomin, R., & Nettles, M. (1985). Consistency of mothers' behavior toward infant siblings. *Developmental Psychology, 21*, 1188–1195.

Dunn, J., & Stocker, C. (1989). The significance of differences in siblings' experiences within the family. In K. Kreppner & R. Lerner (Eds.), *Family systems and life-span development* (pp. 289–301). Hillsdale, NJ: Lawrence Erlbaum Associates.

Fisher, L., Kokes, R., Ransom, D., Phillips, S., & Rudd, P. (1985). Alternative strategies for creating "relational" family data. *Family Process, 24*, 213–224.

Halverson, C., & Wampler, K. (in press). Family influences on personality development. In S. Briggs, R. Hogan, & W. Jones (Eds.), *Handbook of personality psychology*. San Diego: Academic Press.

Henkel, R. (1976). *Tests of Significance* (Sage University Paper series on Quantitative Applications in the Social Sciences, series no. 07-001). Beverly Hills and London: Sage.

Kenrick, D., & Funder, D. (1988). Profiting from controversy: Lessons from the person–situation debate. *American Psychologist, 43*, 23–34.

Martin, R. (1984). *The temperament assessment battery*. Athens, GA: Developmental Metrics.

Plomin, R. (1989). Nature and nurture in the family. In K. Kreppner & R. Lerner (Eds.), *Family systems and life-span development* (pp. 129–148). Hillsdale, NJ: Lawrence Erlbaum Associates.

Plomin, R., & Daniels, D. (1987). Why are children in the same family so different from each other? *Behavioral and Brain Sciences, 10*, 1–16.

Robinson, W. (1957). The statistical measurement of agreement. *American Sociological Review, 22*, 17–25.

Rowe, D. (1990). As the twig is bent? The myth of child rearing influences on personality development. *Journal of Counseling and Development, 68*, 606–616.

Thompson, L., & Walker, A. (1982). The dyad as the unit of analysis: Conceptual and methodological issues. *Journal of Marriage and the Family, 44*, 889–900.

Victor, J., Halverson, C., & Montague, R. (1985). The relations between reflections impulsivity and behavioral impulsivity in preschool children. *Developmental Psychology, 21*, 141–148.

Waters, E., Garber, J., Gornal, M., & Vaughn, B. (1983). Q-sort correlates of visual regard among preschool peers: Validation of a behavioral index of social competence. *Developmental Psychology, 19*, 550–560.

Author Index

Subject Index

A

Academic performance, 23, 80, 170
Adjustment, 125, 129
Adoption studies, 1, 3, 5, 9, 14, 16, 18,
   21–22
Affective disorders, 17
Age, 9
Aggression, 189
Alcoholism, 16
Alcohol use, 170
Anorexia nervosa, 84
Anxiety, 13, 19, 124
  disorders of, 19
Assortative mating, 4, 10, 180
Autism, 14
Autonomy, 77–78

B

Behavior, 3, 13, 15, 21, 124, 131–133, 163,
   182
  antisocial, 15, 124, 131
  delinquent, 13, 15, 124
   drinking in adolescents, 170
  development of, 21

  deviant, 182
  oppositional, 150
  problems, 13
Blood pressure reactivity, 191–192
Birth order, 181–182
  effects of, 181
  gender differences found in, 181–182

C

Child rearing issues, 143, 147, 150, 153
  between-family effects, 143, 150, 153
  within-family effects, 143, 147, 150, 153
Cliques, 161, 167–169
Coercion, 79, *see also* Conflict
Cognitive abilities, 1–2, 6, 22–24, 199
Common factor model, 34
Competence, 64, 67, 73, 76–79, 176
  in adolescents, 64
  cognitive agency, 76–77, 79
  social, 76–77, 79, 181–182, 184–199
   agency, 76–77, 79
   birth-order effects on, 181
   gender effects on, 181
   model of, 185–199